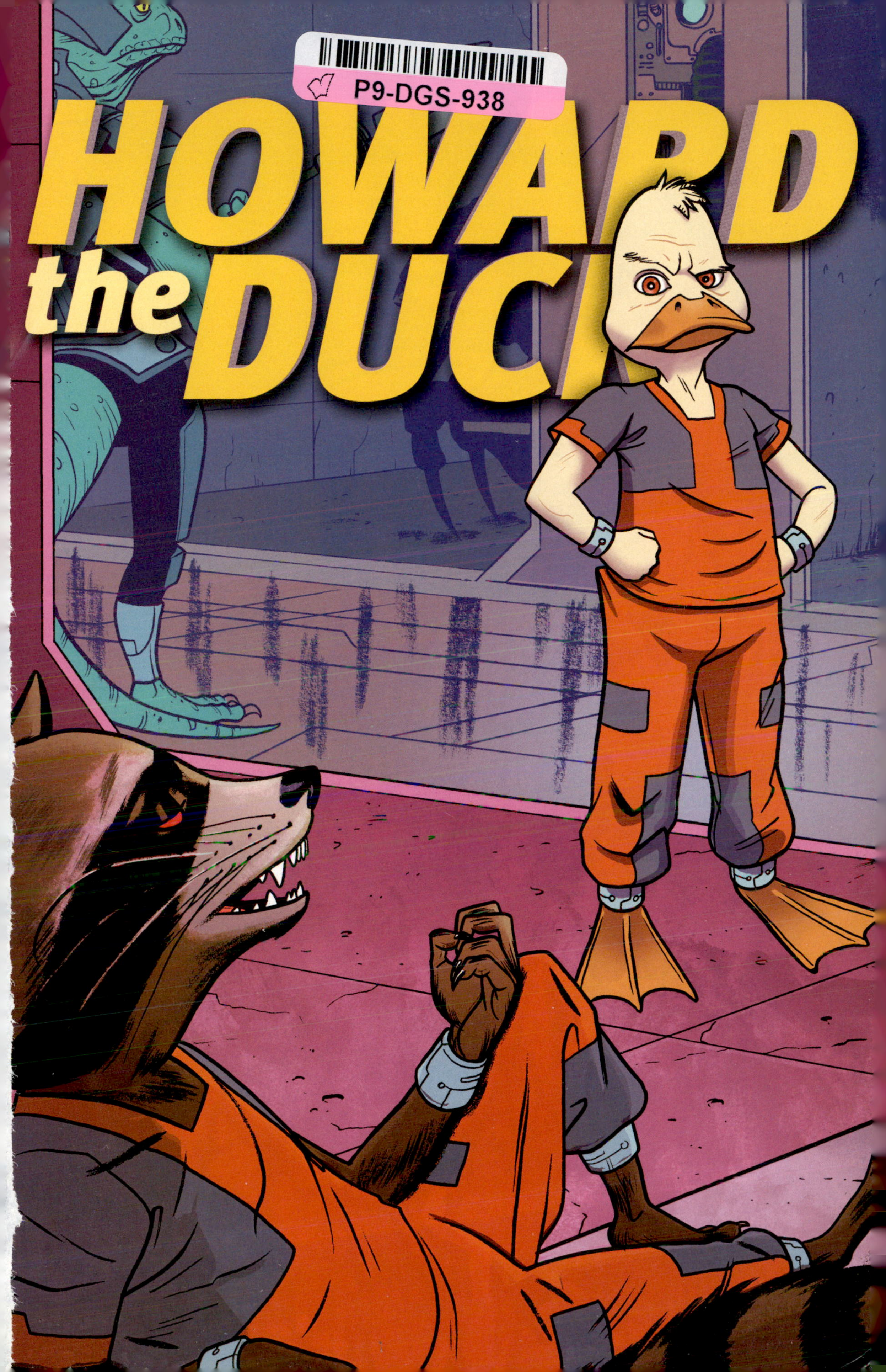
HOWARD
the DUC

HOWARD IS A DUCK, AS YOU NO DOUBT PIECED TOGETHER FROM THE TITLE OF THE BOOK AND THE COVER IMAGE. BUT! HE'S NOT **JUST** A DUCK! HE'S A DUCK WHO **TALKS!** AND DISPLAYS A REMARKABLE AMOUNT OF **COMMON SENSE** IN A **WORLD GONE MAD!**

BROUGHT HERE THROUGH **THE NEXUS OF ALL REALITIES** SEVERAL YEARS AGO, HOWARD HAS STRUGGLED TO FIND A PLACE FOR HIMSELF IN THIS WORLD OF HAIRLESS APES. HE'S BEEN A RENT-A-NINJA, A PRESIDENTIAL CANDIDATE, EVEN A GEORGE LUCAS MOVIE SUBJECT, BUT NO MATTER WHERE LIFE TAKES HIM, HE'S STILL JUST TRAPPED IN A WORLD HE NEVER MADE.

COLLECTION EDITOR: JENNIFER GRÖNWALD
ASSISTANT EDITOR: SARAH BRUNSTAD
ASSOCIATE MANAGING EDITOR: ALEX STARBUCK
EDITOR, SPECIAL PROJECTS: MARK D. BEAZLEY
SENIOR EDITOR, SPECIAL PROJECTS: JEFF YOUNGQUIST
SVP PRINT, SALES & MARKETING: DAVID GABRIEL
BOOK DESIGNER: JAY BOWEN

EDITOR IN CHIEF: AXEL ALONSO
CHIEF CREATIVE OFFICER: JOE QUESADA
PUBLISHER: DAN BUCKLEY
EXECUTIVE PRODUCER: ALAN FINE

HOWARD THE DUCK VOL. 0: WHAT THE DUCK. Contains material originally published in magazine form as HOWARD THE DUCK #1-5. First printing 2015. ISBN# 978-0-7851-9772-0. Published by MARVEL WORLDWIDE, INC., a subsidiary of MARVEL ENTERTAINMENT, LLC. OFFICE OF PUBLICATION: 135 West 50th Street, New York, NY 10020. Copyright © 2015 MARVEL No similarity between any of the names, characters, persons, and/or institutions in this magazine with those of any living or dead person or institution is intended, and any such similarity which may exist is purely coincidental. **Printed in Canada.** ALAN FINE, President, Marvel Entertainment; DAN BUCKLEY, President, TV, Publishing and Brand Management; JOE QUESADA, Chief Creative Officer; TOM BREVOORT, SVP of Publishing; DAVID BOGART, SVP of Operations & Procurement, Publishing; C.B. CEBULSKI, VP of International Development & Brand Management; DAVID GABRIEL, SVP Print, Sales & Marketing; JIM O'KEEFE, VP of Operations & Logistics; DAN CARR, Executive Director of Publishing Technology; SUSAN CRESPI, Editorial Operations Manager; ALEX MORALES, Publishing Operations Manager; STAN LEE, Chairman Emeritus. For information regarding advertising in Marvel Comics or on Marvel.com, please contact Jonathan Rheingold, VP of Custom Solutions & Ad Sales, at jrheingold@marvel.com. For Marvel subscription inquiries, please call 800-217-9158. **Manufactured between 7/31/2015 and 9/7/2015 by SOLISCO PRINTERS, SCOTT, QC, CANADA.**

10 9 8 7 6 5 4 3 2 1

HOWARD the DUCK

WHAT THE DUCK?

WRITER
CHIP ZDARSKY

PENCILER
JOE QUINONES

INKERS
JOE QUINONES (#1 & #3-4) & **JOE RIVERA** (#2-5)
WITH PAOLO RIVERA (#5)

COLOR ARTISTS
RICO RENZI
WITH RACHELLE ROSENBERG (#4)

BACK-UP STORY ARTISTS
ROB GUILLORY (#2), **JASON LATOUR** (#3)
AND **KATIE COOK** & **HEATHER BRECKEL** (#4)

LETTERER
VC'S TRAVIS LANHAM

COVER ART
JOE QUINONES
WITH RICO RENZI (#3)

EDITOR
WIL MOSS

EXECUTIVE EDITOR
TOM BREVOORT

SPECIAL THANKS LISSA PATTILLO & CASSIE KELLY
HOWARD THE DUCK CREATED BY STEVE GERBER & VAL MAYERIK

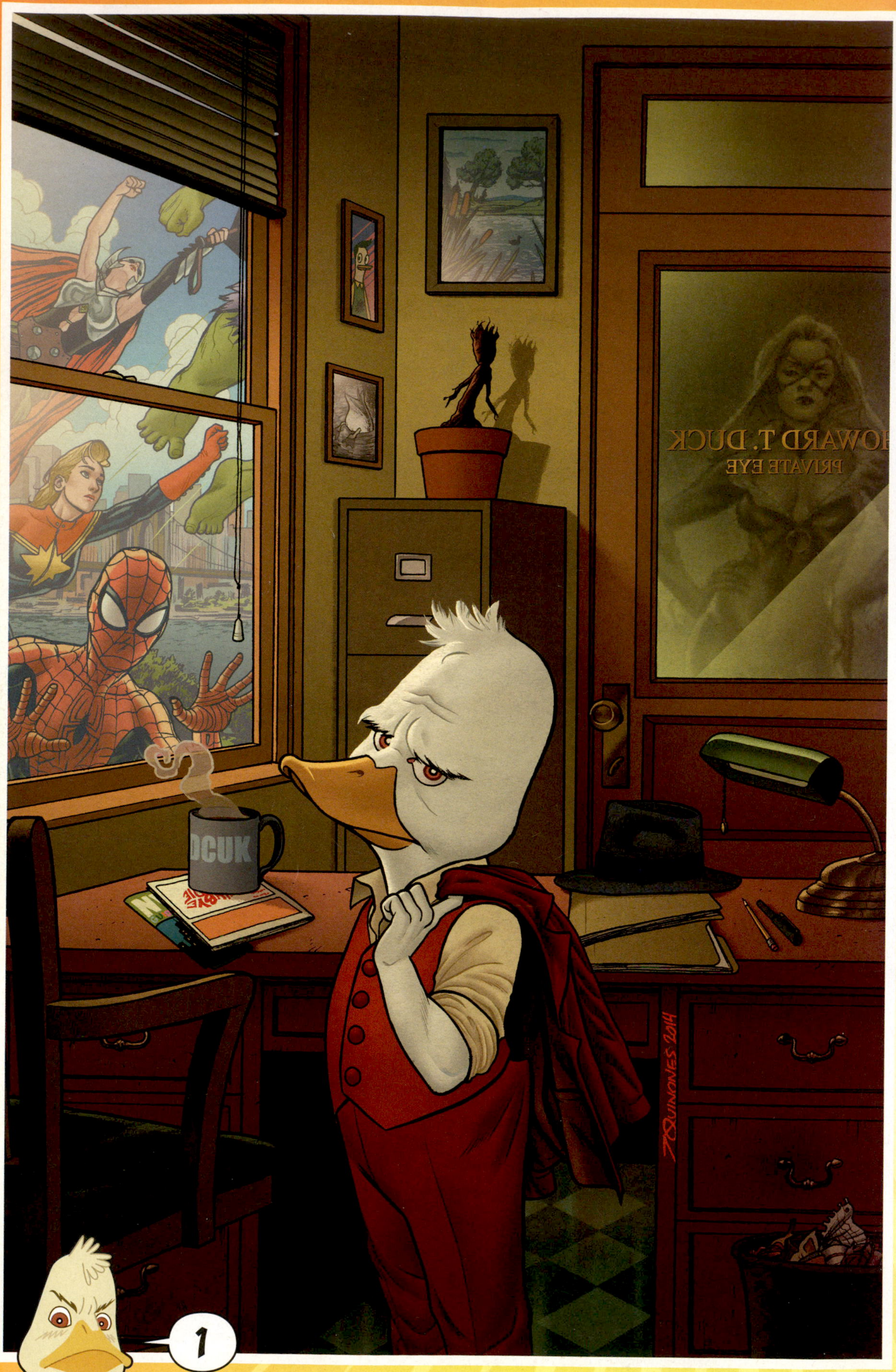
HOWARD T. DUCK
PRIVATE EYE
DCUK

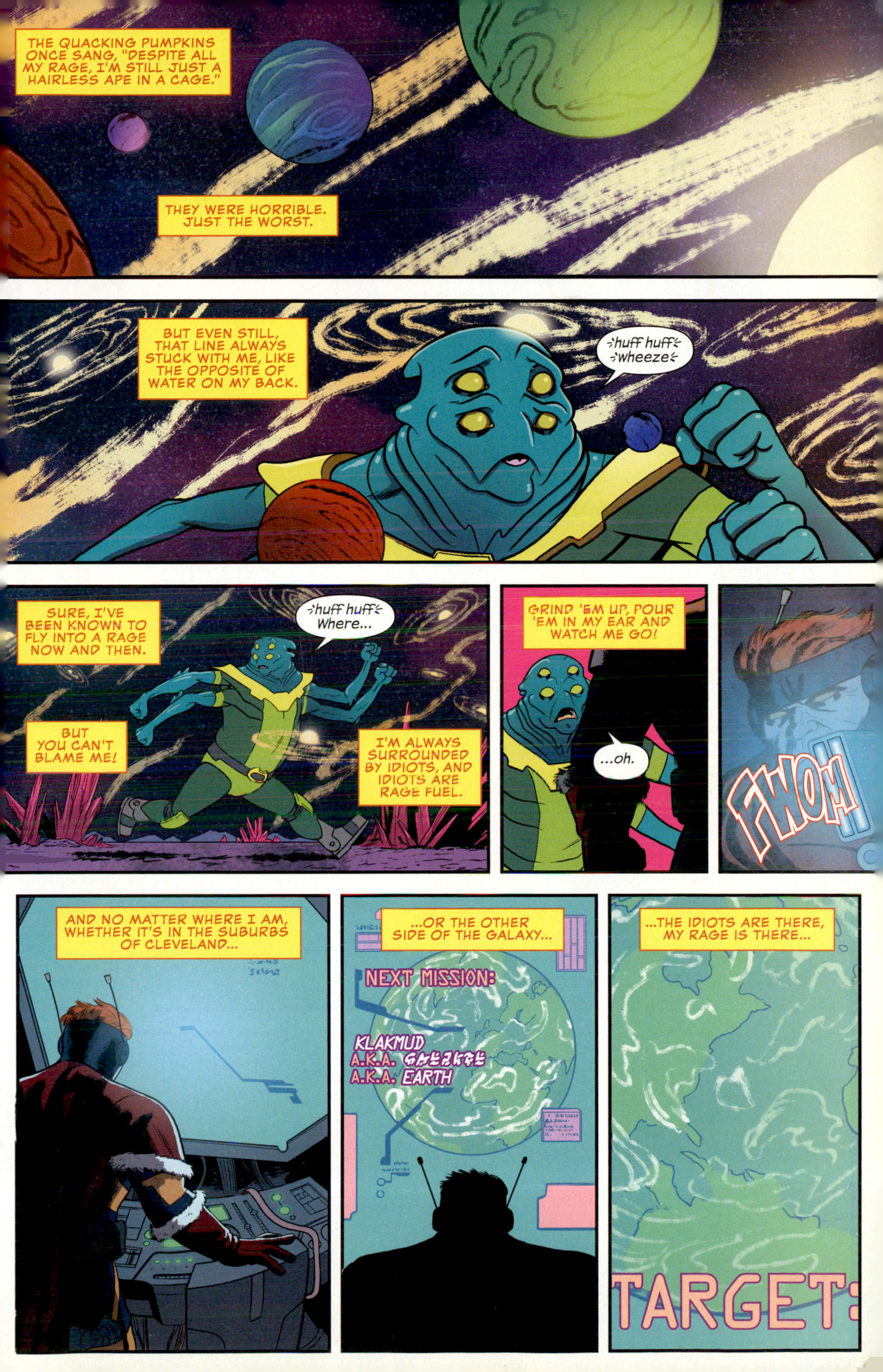
THE QUACKING PUMPKINS ONCE SANG, "DESPITE ALL MY RAGE, I'M STILL JUST A HAIRLESS APE IN A CAGE."
THEY WERE HORRIBLE. JUST THE WORST.
BUT EVEN STILL, THAT LINE ALWAYS STUCK WITH ME, LIKE THE OPPOSITE OF WATER ON MY BACK.
huff huff wheeze
SURE, I'VE BEEN KNOWN TO FLY INTO A RAGE NOW AND THEN.
huff huff Where...
BUT YOU CAN'T BLAME ME!
I'M ALWAYS SURROUNDED BY IDIOTS, AND IDIOTS ARE RAGE FUEL.
GRIND 'EM UP, POUR 'EM IN MY EAR AND WATCH ME GO!
...oh.
FWOM
AND NO MATTER WHERE I AM, WHETHER IT'S IN THE SUBURBS OF CLEVELAND...
...OR THE OTHER SIDE OF THE GALAXY...
NEXT MISSION:
KLAKMUD
A.K.A.
A.K.A. EARTH
...THE IDIOTS ARE THERE, MY RAGE IS THERE...
TARGET:

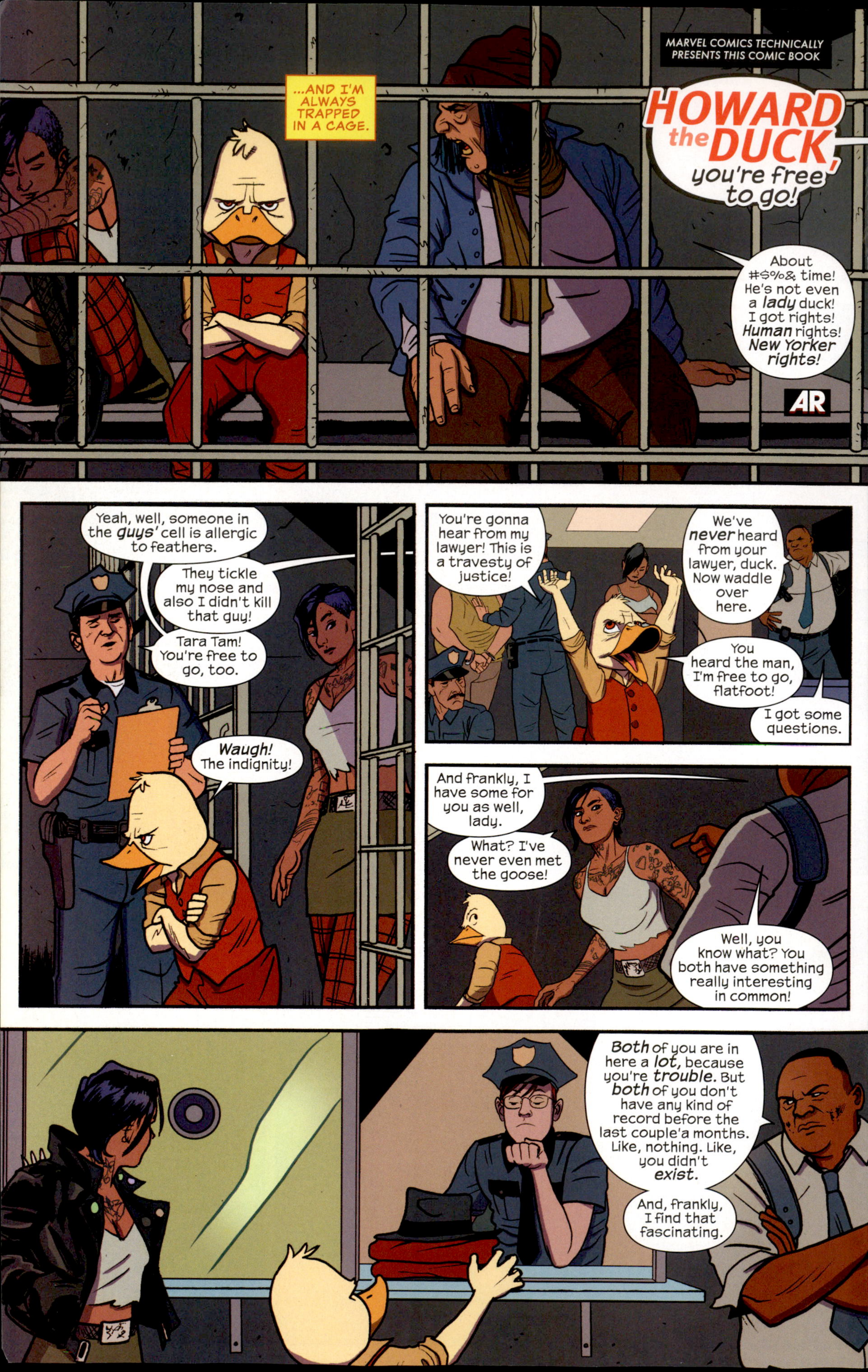
MARVEL COMICS TECHNICALLY PRESENTS THIS COMIC BOOK
...AND I'M ALWAYS TRAPPED IN A CAGE.
HOWARD the DUCK, you're free to go!
About #$%& time! He's not even a lady duck! I got rights! Human rights! New Yorker rights!
AR
Yeah, well, someone in the guys' cell is allergic to feathers.
They tickle my nose and also I didn't kill that guy!
Tara Tam! You're free to go, too.
Waugh! The indignity!
You're gonna hear from my lawyer! This is a travesty of justice!
We've never heard from your lawyer, duck. Now waddle over here.
You heard the man, I'm free to go, flatfoot!
I got some questions.
And frankly, I have some for you as well, lady.
What? I've never even met the goose!
Well, you know what? You both have something really interesting in common!
Both of you are in here a lot, because you're trouble. But both of you don't have any kind of record before the last couple'a months. Like, nothing. Like, you didn't exist.
And, frankly, I find that fascinating.

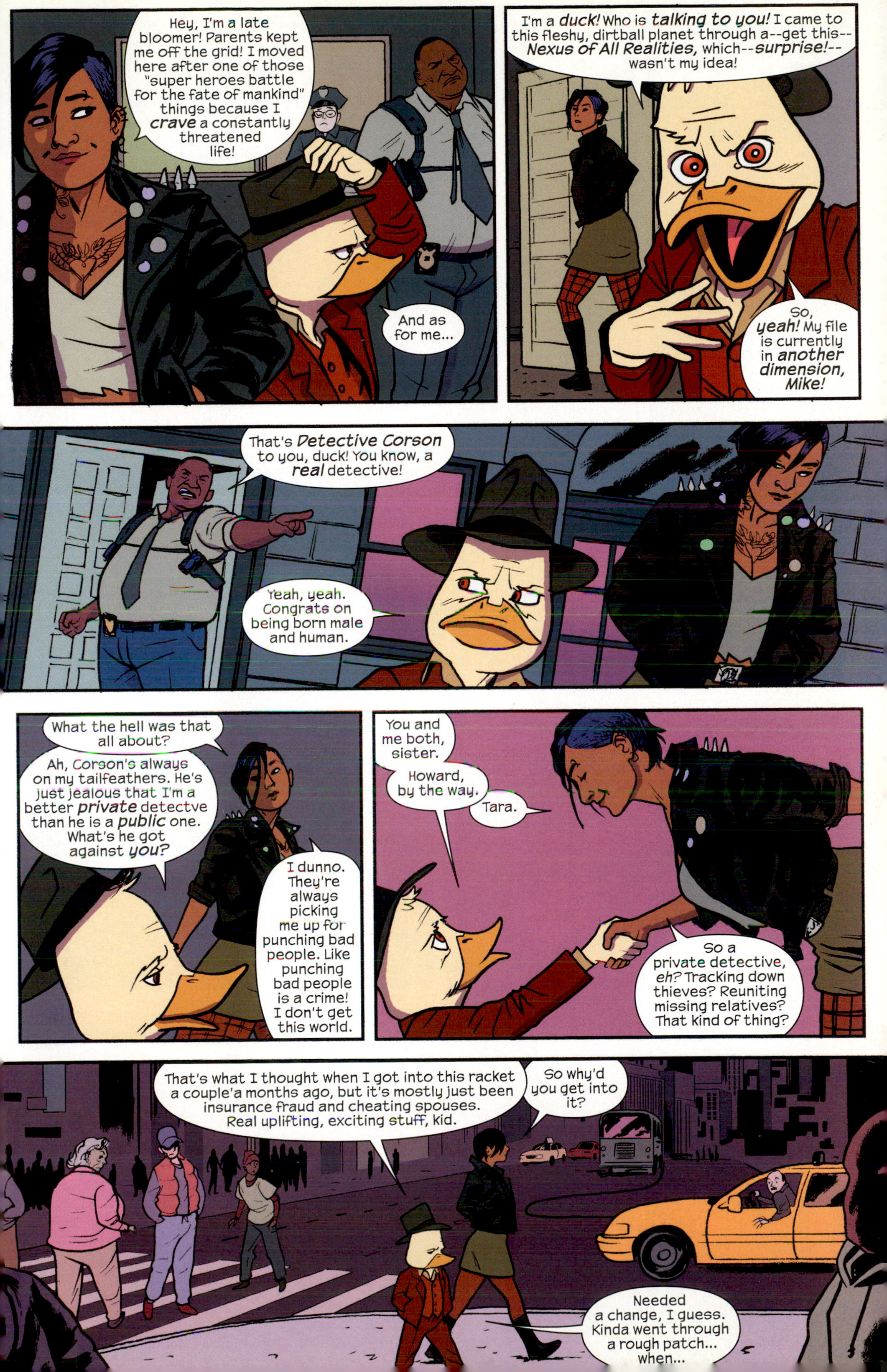
Hey, I'm a late bloomer! Parents kept me off the grid! I moved here after one of those "super heroes battle for the fate of mankind" things because I crave a constantly threatened life!
And as for me...
I'm a duck! Who is talking to you! I came to this fleshy, dirtball planet through a--get this--Nexus of All Realities, which--surprise!--wasn't my idea!
So, yeah! My file is currently in another dimension, Mike!
That's Detective Corson to you, duck! You know, a real detective!
Yeah, yeah. Congrats on being born male and human.
What the hell was that all about?
Ah, Corson's always on my tailfeathers. He's just jealous that I'm a better private detectve than he is a public one. What's he got against you?
I dunno. They're always picking me up for punching bad people. Like punching bad people is a crime! I don't get this world.
You and me both, sister.
Howard, by the way.
Tara.
So a private detective, eh? Tracking down thieves? Reuniting missing relatives? That kind of thing?
That's what I thought when I got into this racket a couple'a months ago, but it's mostly just been insurance fraud and cheating spouses. Real uplifting, exciting stuff, kid.
So why'd you get into it?
Needed a change, I guess. Kinda went through a rough patch... when...

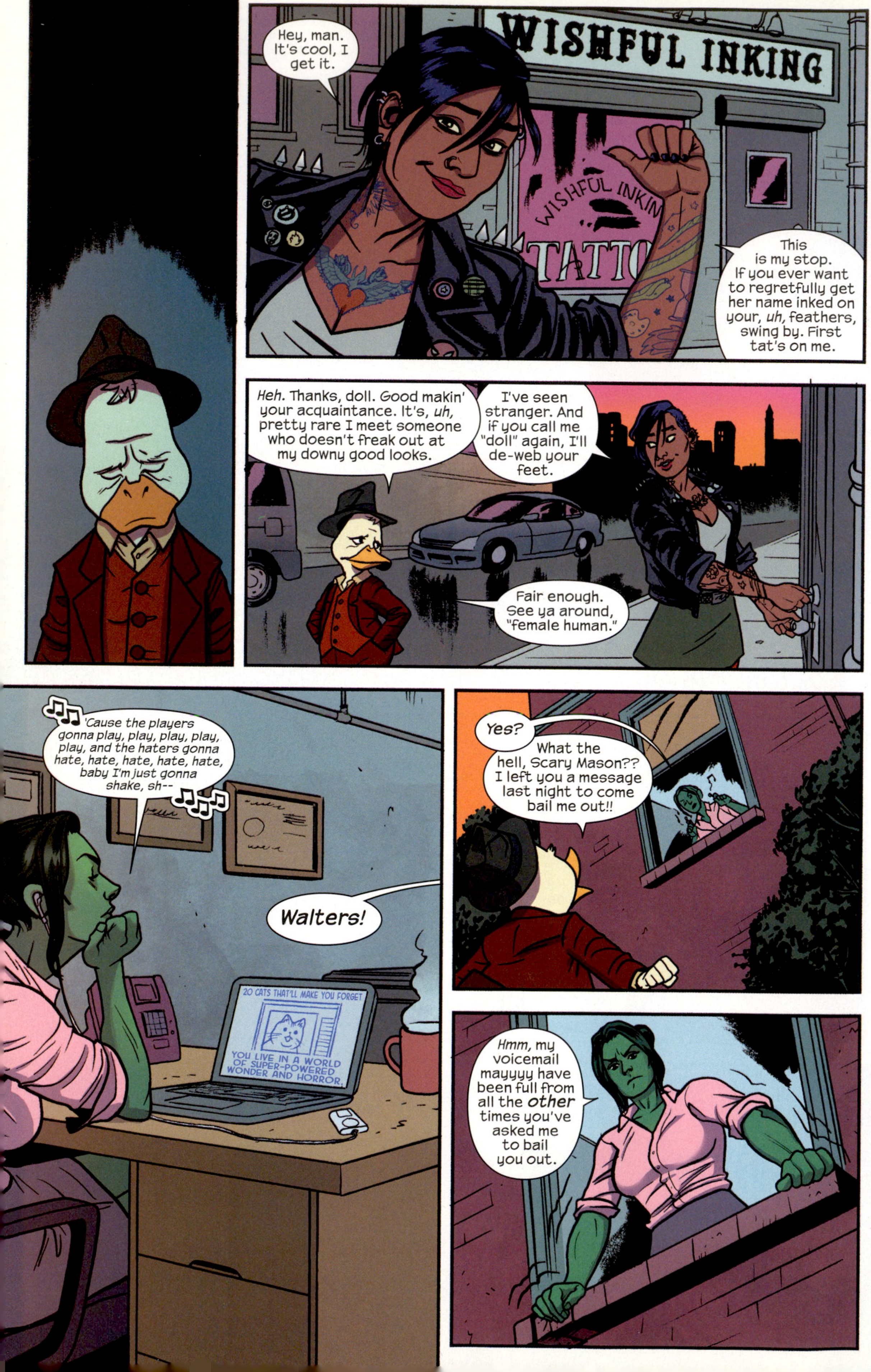
WISHFUL INKING
Hey, man. It's cool, I get it.
WISHFUL INKING TATTO
This is my stop. If you ever want to regretfully get her name inked on your, uh, feathers, swing by. First tat's on me.
Heh. Thanks, doll. Good makin' your acquaintance. It's, uh, pretty rare I meet someone who doesn't freak out at my downy good looks.
I've seen stranger. And if you call me "doll" again, I'll de-web your feet.
Fair enough. See ya around, "female human."
'Cause the players gonna play, play, play, play, play, and the haters gonna hate, hate, hate, hate, hate, baby I'm just gonna shake, sh--
Walters!
20 CATS THAT'LL MAKE YOU FORGET YOU LIVE IN A WORLD OF SUPER-POWERED WONDER AND HORROR.
Yes?
What the hell, Scary Mason?? I left you a message last night to come bail me out!!
Hmm, my voicemail mayyyy have been full from all the other times you've asked me to bail you out.

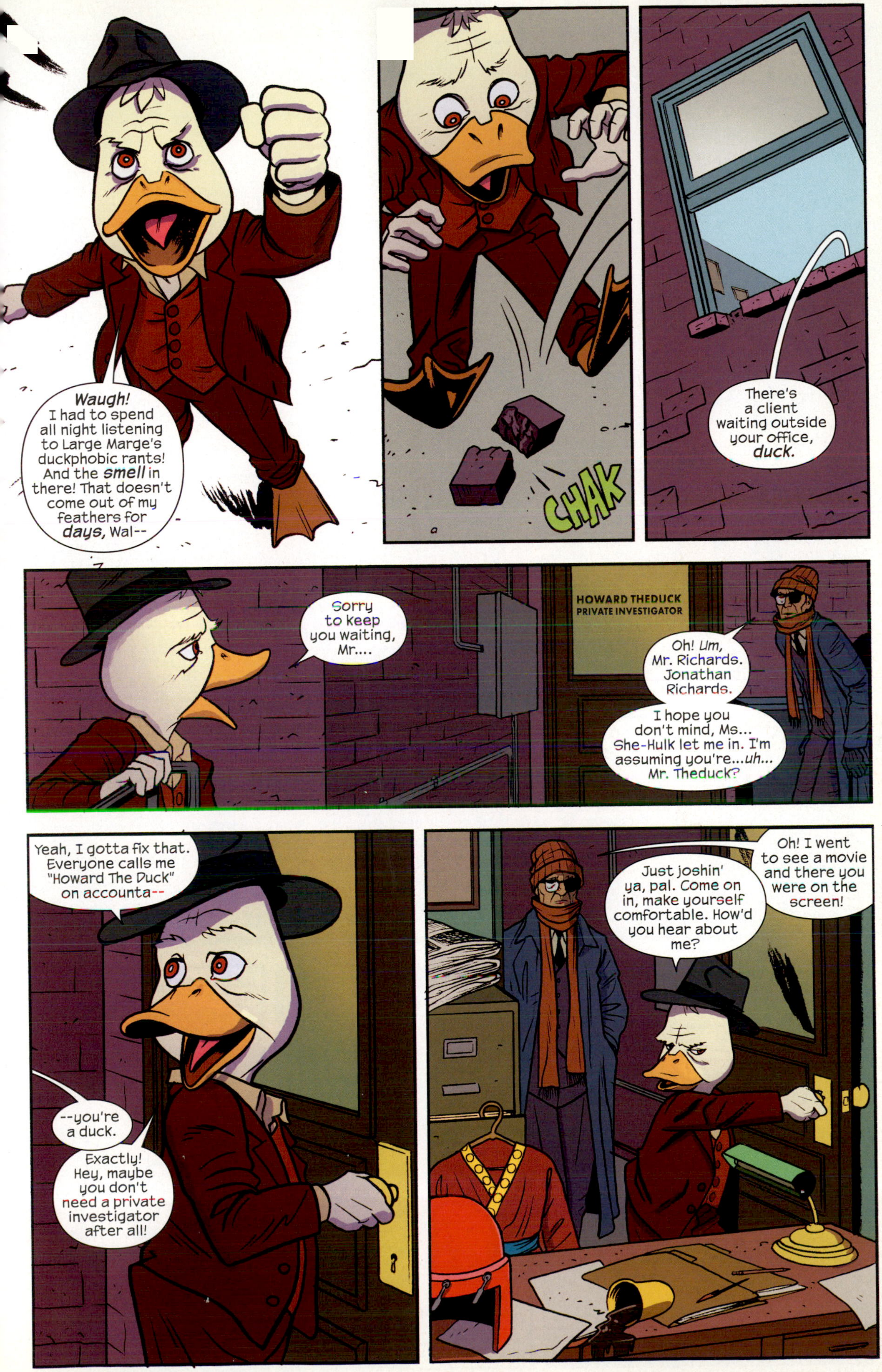

Waugh! I had to spend all night listening to Large Marge's duckphobic rants! And the smell in there! That doesn't come out of my feathers for days, Wal--
CHAK
There's a client waiting outside your office, duck.
Sorry to keep you waiting, Mr....
HOWARD THEDUCK
PRIVATE INVESTIGATOR
Oh! Um, Mr. Richards. Jonathan Richards.
I hope you don't mind, Ms... She-Hulk let me in. I'm assuming you're...uh... Mr. Theduck?
Yeah, I gotta fix that. Everyone calls me "Howard The Duck" on accounta--
--you're a duck.
Exactly! Hey, maybe you don't need a private investigator after all!
Just joshin' ya, pal. Come on in, make yourself comfortable. How'd you hear about me?
Oh! I went to see a movie and there you were on the screen!

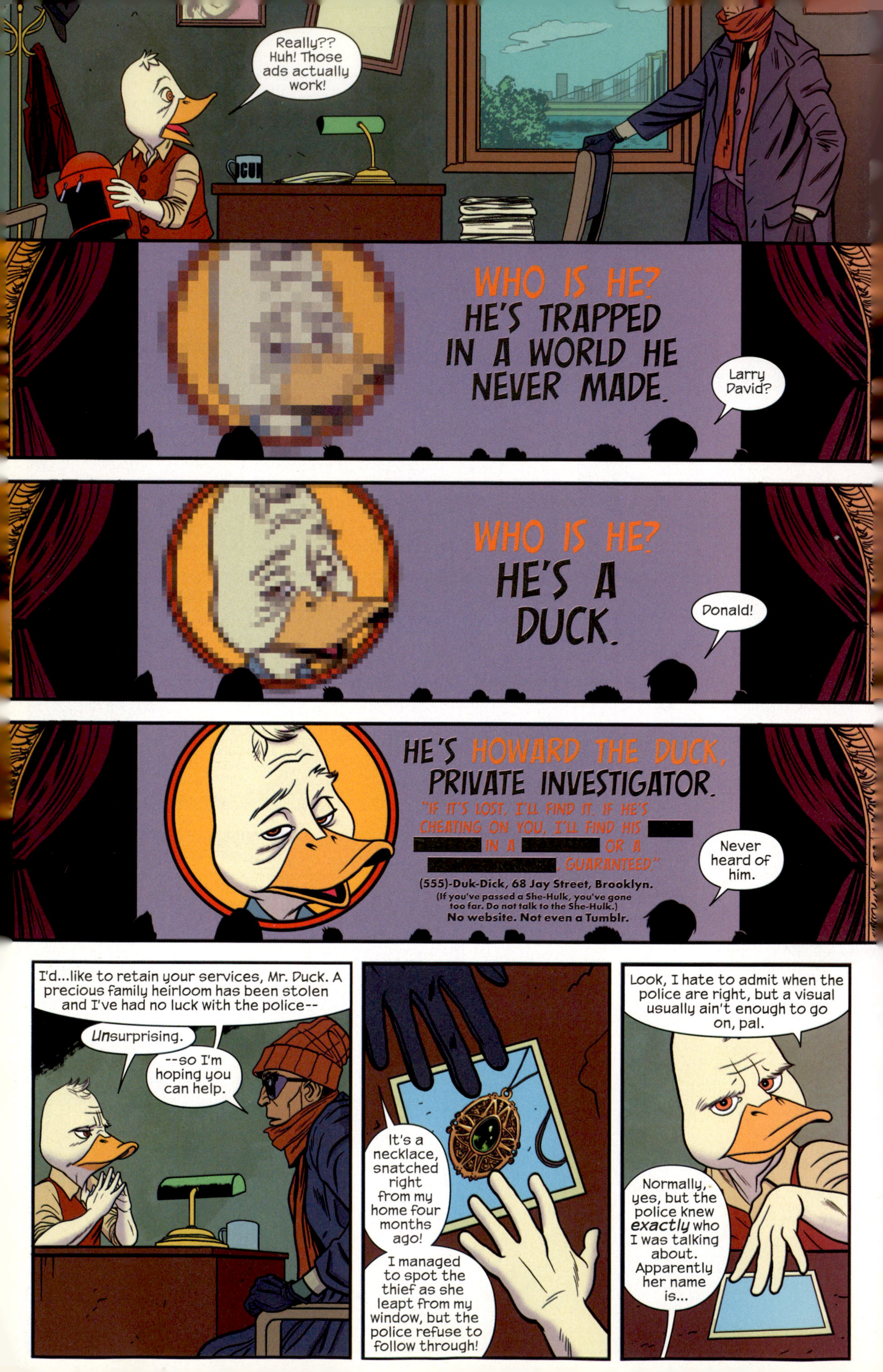

Really?? Huh! Those ads actually work!
CUN
WHO IS HE?
HE'S TRAPPED IN A WORLD HE NEVER MADE.
Larry David?
WHO IS HE?
HE'S A DUCK.
Donald!
HE'S HOWARD THE DUCK, PRIVATE INVESTIGATOR.
"IF IT'S LOST, I'LL FIND IT. IF HE'S CHEATING ON YOU, I'LL FIND HIS [redacted] IN A [redacted] OR A [redacted], GUARANTEED."
(555)-Duk-Dick, 68 Jay Street, Brooklyn.
(If you've passed a She-Hulk, you've gone too far. Do not talk to the She-Hulk.)
No website. Not even a Tumblr.
Never heard of him.
I'd...like to retain your services, Mr. Duck. A precious family heirloom has been stolen and I've had no luck with the police--
Unsurprising.
--so I'm hoping you can help.
It's a necklace, snatched right from my home four months ago!
I managed to spot the thief as she leapt from my window, but the police refuse to follow through!
Look, I hate to admit when the police are right, but a visual usually ain't enough to go on, pal.
Normally, yes, but the police knew *exactly* who I was talking about. Apparently her name is...

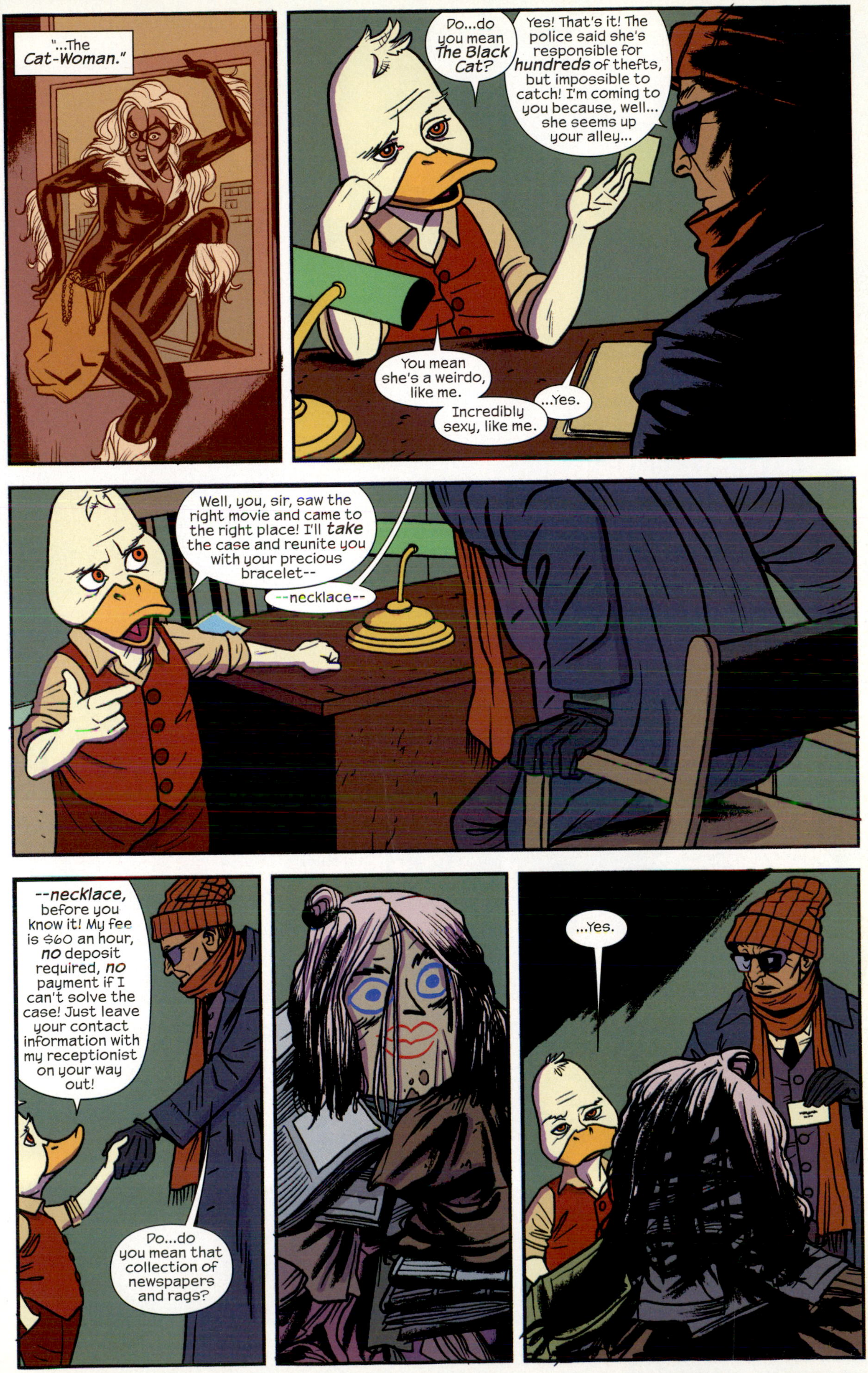
"...The Cat-Woman."
Do...do you mean The Black Cat?
Yes! That's it! The police said she's responsible for hundreds of thefts, but impossible to catch! I'm coming to you because, well... she seems up your alley...
You mean she's a weirdo, like me.
...Yes.
Incredibly sexy, like me.
Well, you, sir, saw the right movie and came to the right place! I'll take the case and reunite you with your precious bracelet--
--necklace--
--necklace, before you know it! My fee is $60 an hour, no deposit required, no payment if I can't solve the case! Just leave your contact information with my receptionist on your way out!
Do...do you mean that collection of newspapers and rags?
...Yes.

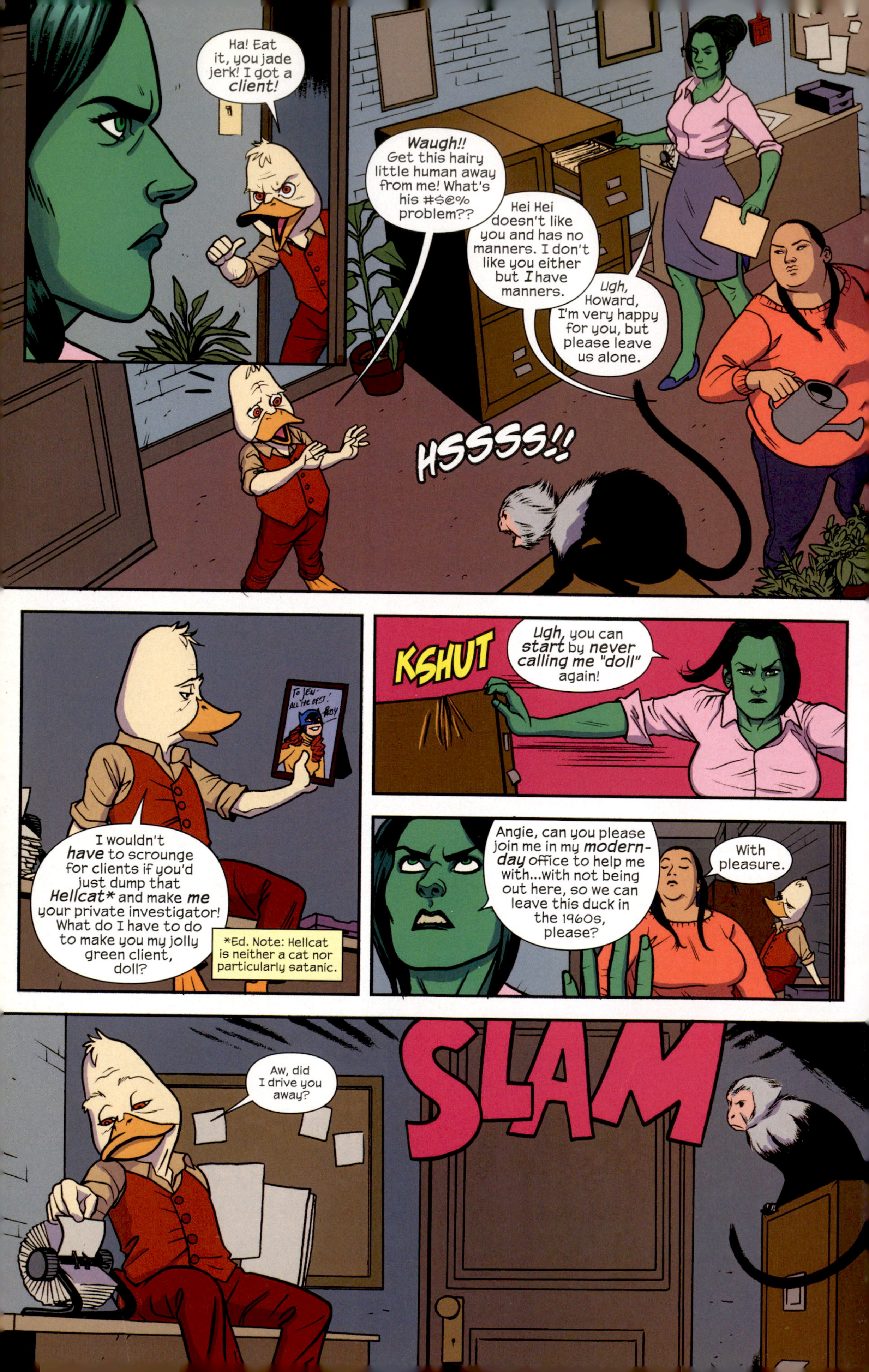

Ha! Eat it, you jade jerk! I got a client!
Waugh!! Get this hairy little human away from me! What's his #$@% problem??
Hei Hei doesn't like you and has no manners. I don't like you either but I have manners.
Ugh, Howard, I'm very happy for you, but please leave us alone.
HSSSS!!
I wouldn't have to scrounge for clients if you'd just dump that Hellcat* and make me your private investigator! What do I have to do to make you my jolly green client, doll?
*Ed. Note: Hellcat is neither a cat nor particularly satanic.
KSHUT
Ugh, you can start by never calling me "doll" again!
Angie, can you please join me in my modern-day office to help me with...with not being out here, so we can leave this duck in the 1960s, please?
With pleasure.
Aw, did I drive you away?
SLAM

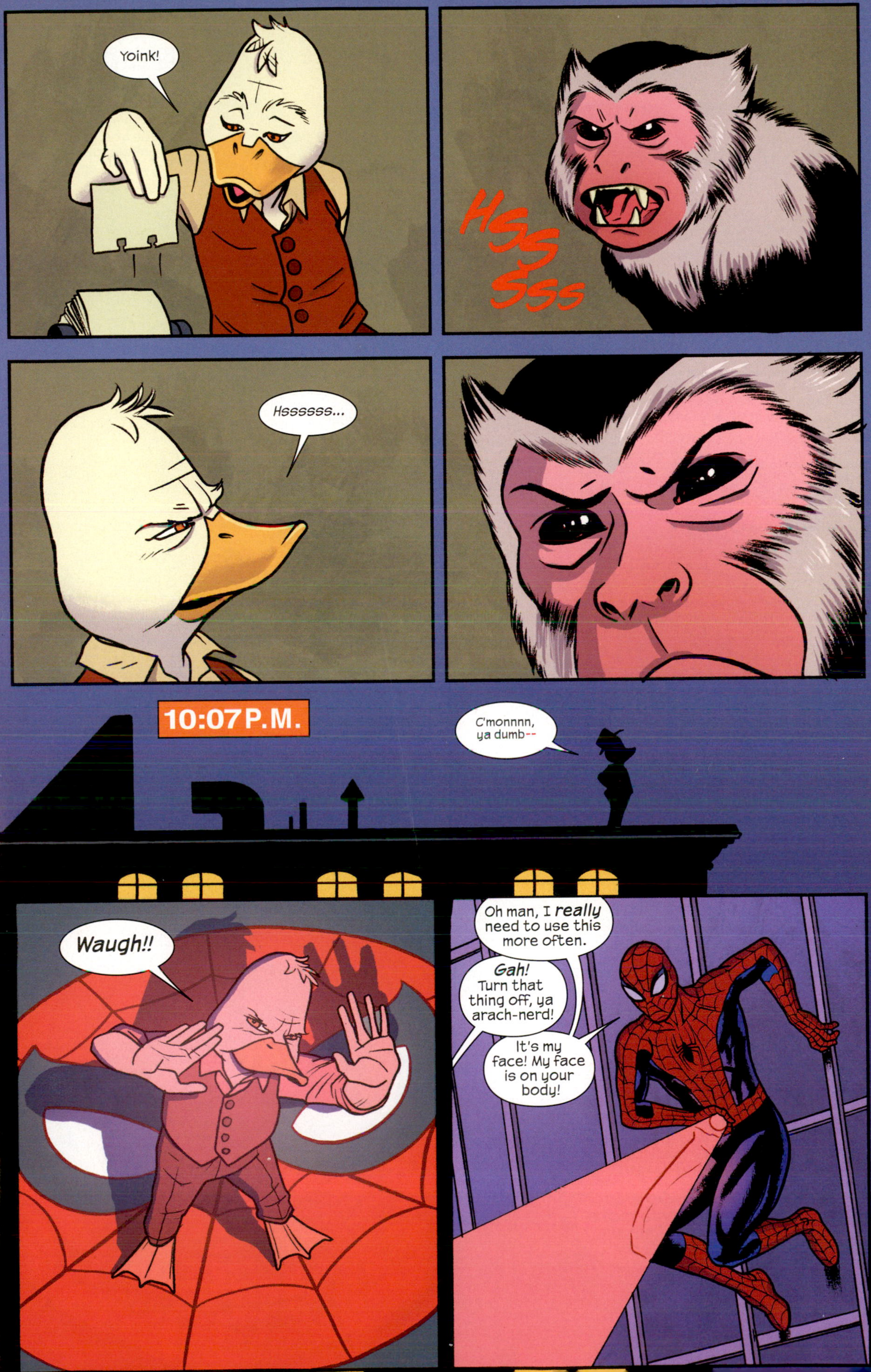
Yoink!
HSSSSS
Hssssss...
10:07 P.M.
C'monnnn, ya dumb--
Waugh!!
Oh man, I *really* need to use this more often.
Gah! Turn that thing off, ya arach-nerd!
It's my face! My face is on your body!

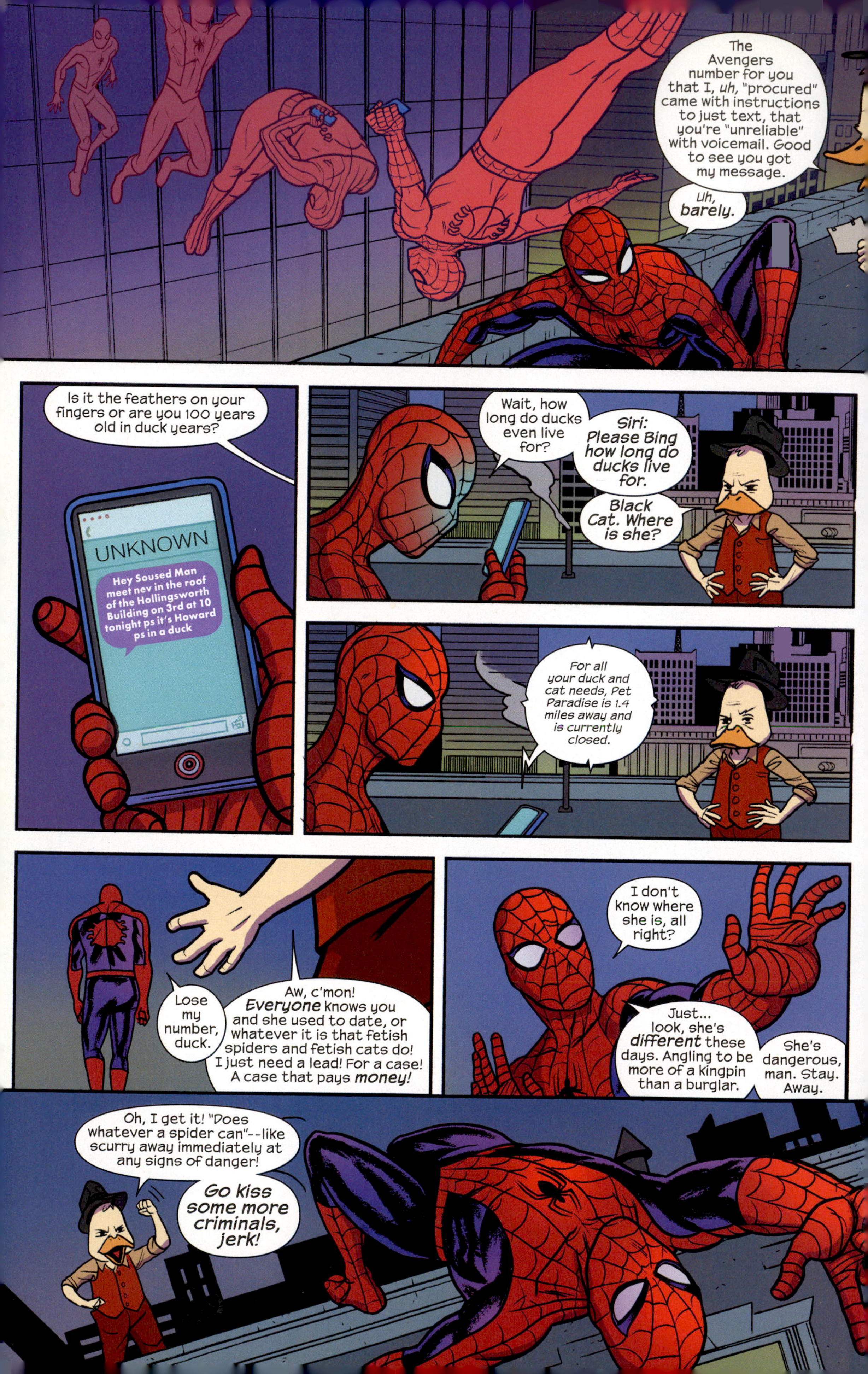
The Avengers number for you that I, uh, "procured" came with instructions to just text, that you're "unreliable" with voicemail. Good to see you got my message.
Uh, barely.
Is it the feathers on your fingers or are you 100 years old in duck years?
UNKNOWN
Hey Soused Man meet nev in the roof of the Hollingsworth Building on 3rd at 10 tonight ps it's Howard ps in a duck
Wait, how long do ducks even live for?
Siri: Please Bing how long do ducks live for.
Black Cat. Where is she?
For all your duck and cat needs, Pet Paradise is 1.4 miles away and is currently closed.
Lose my number, duck.
Aw, c'mon! Everyone knows you and she used to date, or whatever it is that fetish spiders and fetish cats do! I just need a lead! For a case! A case that pays money!
I don't know where she is, all right?
Just... look, she's different these days. Angling to be more of a kingpin than a burglar.
She's dangerous, man. Stay. Away.
Oh, I get it! "Does whatever a spider can"--like scurry away immediately at any signs of danger!
Go kiss some more criminals, jerk!

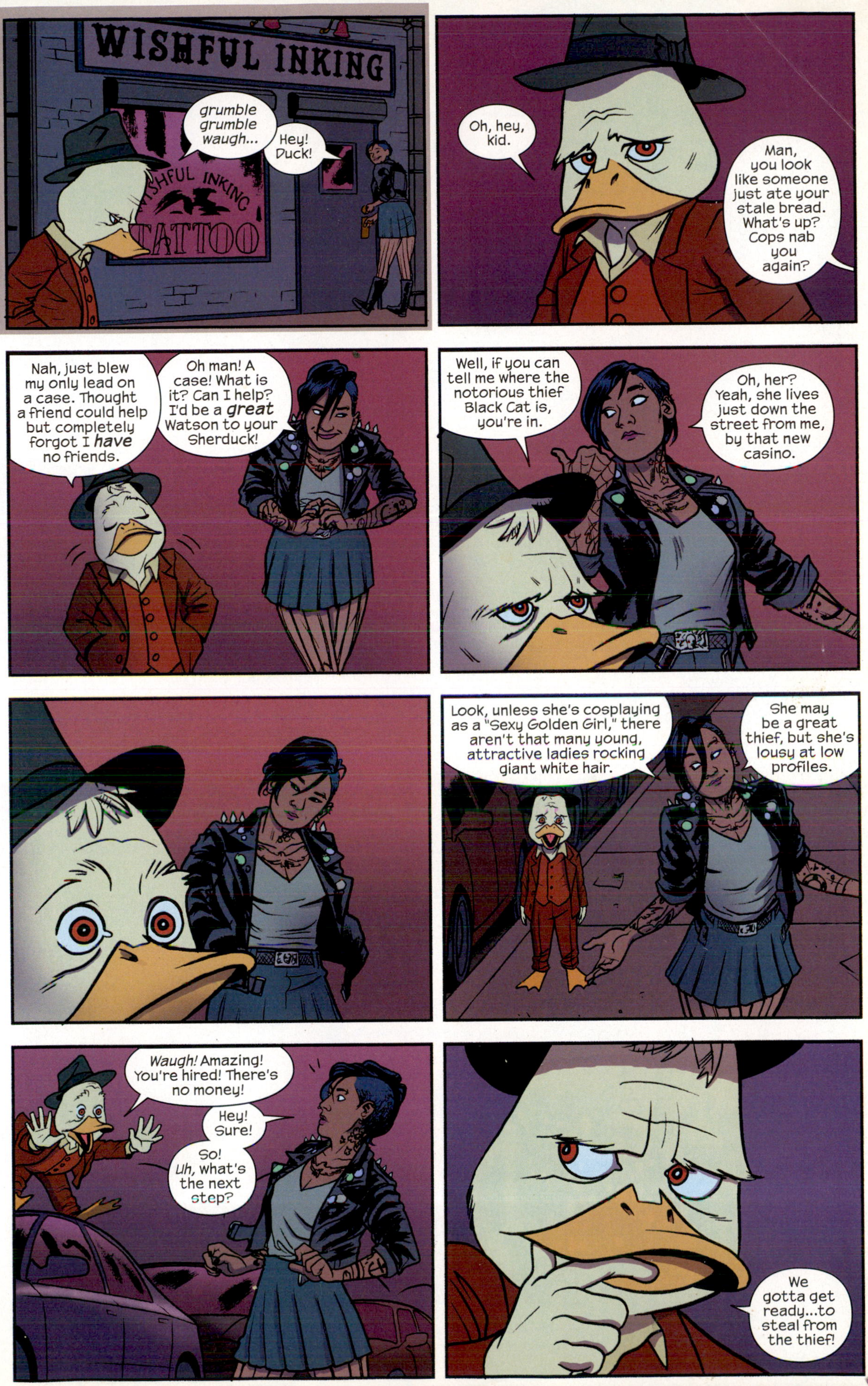
WISHFUL INKING
grumble grumble waugh...
Hey! Duck!
WISHFUL INKING TATTOO
Oh, hey, kid.
Man, you look like someone just ate your stale bread. What's up? Cops nab you again?
Nah, just blew my only lead on a case. Thought a friend could help but completely forgot I *have* no friends.
Oh man! A case! What is it? Can I help? I'd be a ***great*** Watson to your Sherduck!
Well, if you can tell me where the notorious thief Black Cat is, you're in.
Oh, her? Yeah, she lives just down the street from me, by that new casino.
Look, unless she's cosplaying as a "Sexy Golden Girl," there aren't that many young, attractive ladies rocking giant white hair.
She may be a great thief, but she's lousy at low profiles.
Waugh! Amazing! You're hired! There's no money!
Hey! Sure!
So! Uh, what's the next step?
We gotta get ready...to steal from the thief!

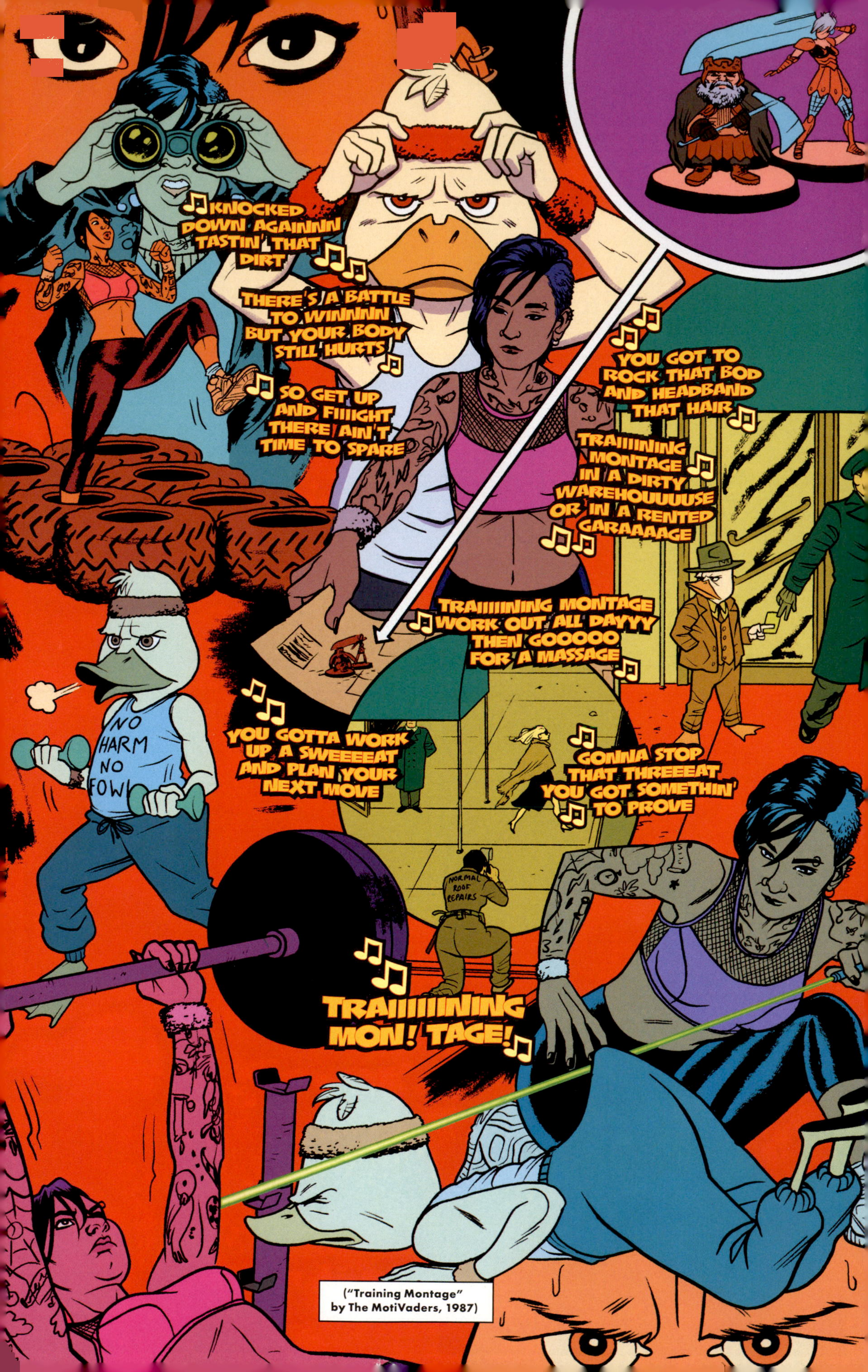
KNOCKED DOWN AGAINNNN TASTIN' THAT DIRT
THERE'S A BATTLE TO WINNNNN BUT YOUR BODY STILL HURTS
SO GET UP AND FIIIGHT THERE AIN'T TIME TO SPARE
YOU GOT TO ROCK THAT BOD AND HEADBAND THAT HAIR
TRAIIIINING MONTAGE IN A DIRTY WAREHOUUUUSE OR IN A RENTED GARAAAAGE
TRAIIIIINING MONTAGE WORK OUT ALL DAYYY THEN GOOOOO FOR A MASSAGE
NO HARM NO FOWL
YOU GOTTA WORK UP A SWEEEEAT AND PLAN YOUR NEXT MOVE
GONNA STOP THAT THREEEAT YOU GOT SOMETHIN' TO PROVE
NORMAL ROOF REPAIRS
TRAIIIIIINING MON! TAGE!
("Training Montage" by The MotiVaders, 1987)

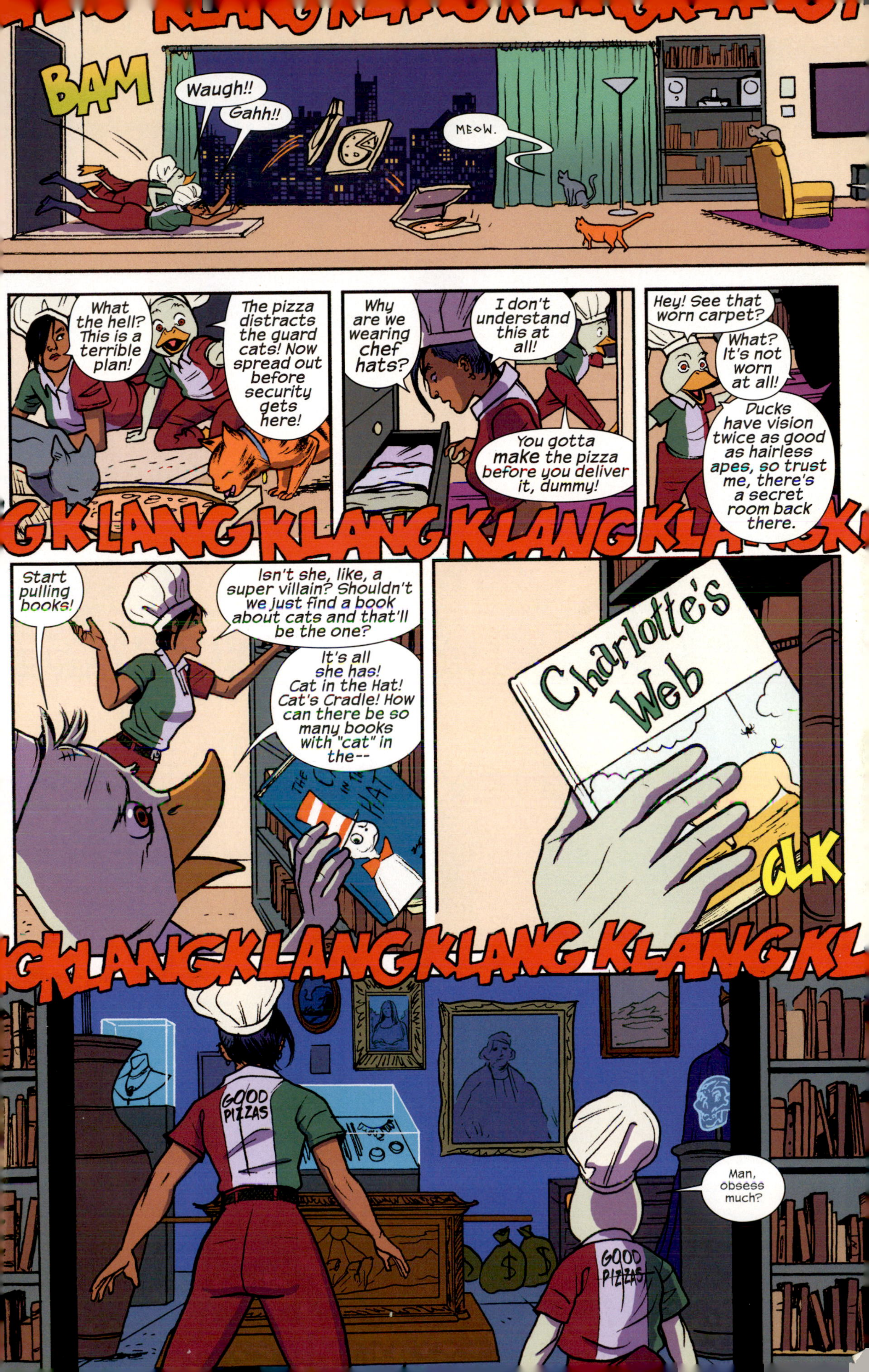
BAM
Waugh!!
Gahh!!
MEOW.
What the hell? This is a terrible plan!
The pizza distracts the guard cats! Now spread out before security gets here!
Why are we wearing chef hats?
I don't understand this at all!
You gotta make the pizza before you deliver it, dummy!
Hey! See that worn carpet?
What? It's not worn at all!
Ducks have vision twice as good as hairless apes, so trust me, there's a secret room back there.
Start pulling books!
Isn't she, like, a super villain? Shouldn't we just find a book about cats and that'll be the one?
It's all she has! Cat in the Hat! Cat's Cradle! How can there be so many books with "cat" in the--
Charlotte's Web
CLK
GOOD PIZZAS
Man, obsess much?
GOOD PIZZAS

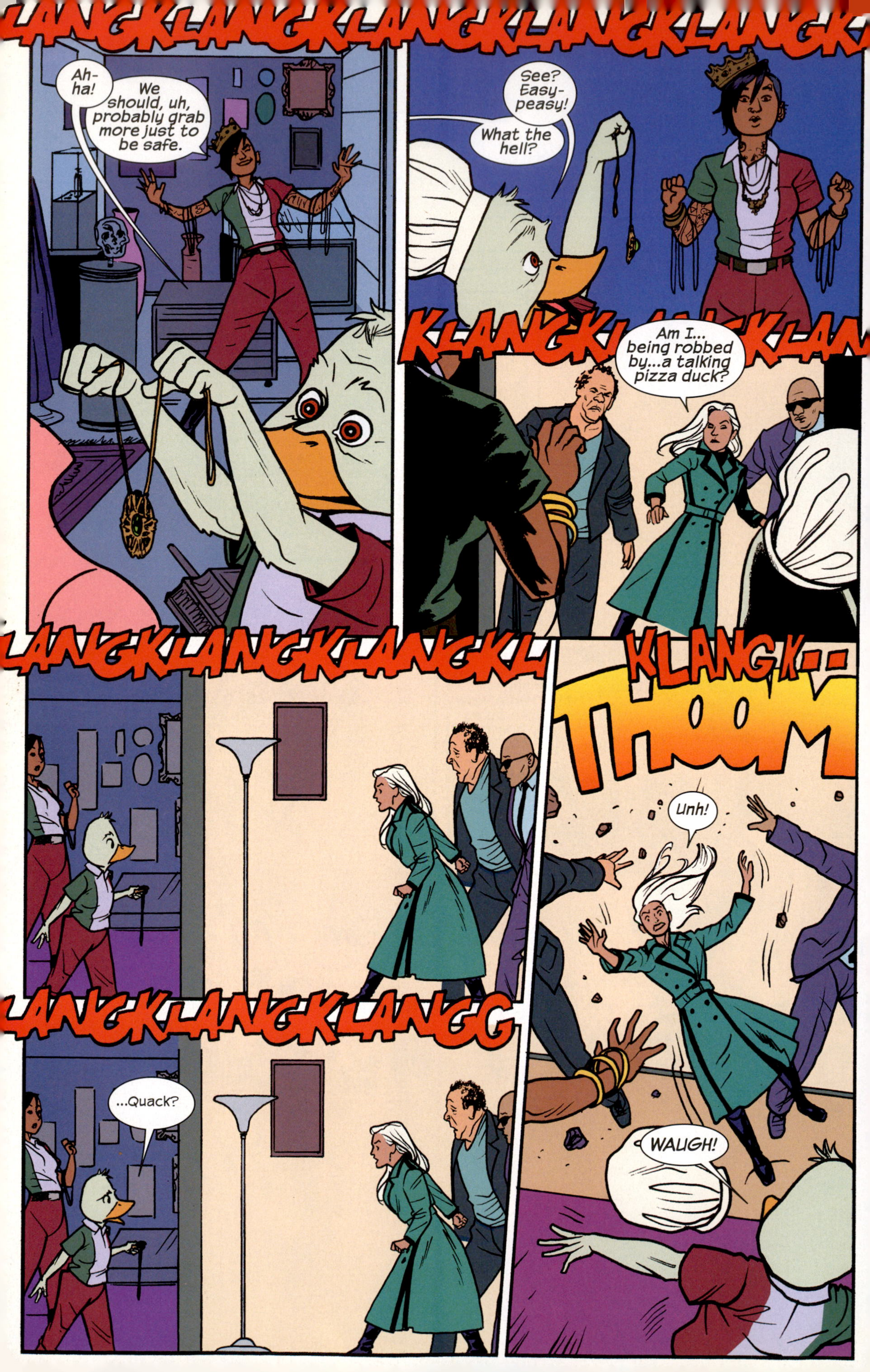
KLANGKLANGKLANGKLANGKLANGKLANGK
Ah-ha!
We should, uh, probably grab more just to be safe.
See? Easy-peasy!
What the hell?
KLANGKLANGKLAN
Am I... being robbed by...a talking pizza duck?
KLANGKLANGKLANGKL
KLANGK..
THOOM
Unh!
KLANGKLANGKLANGG
...Quack?
WAUGH!

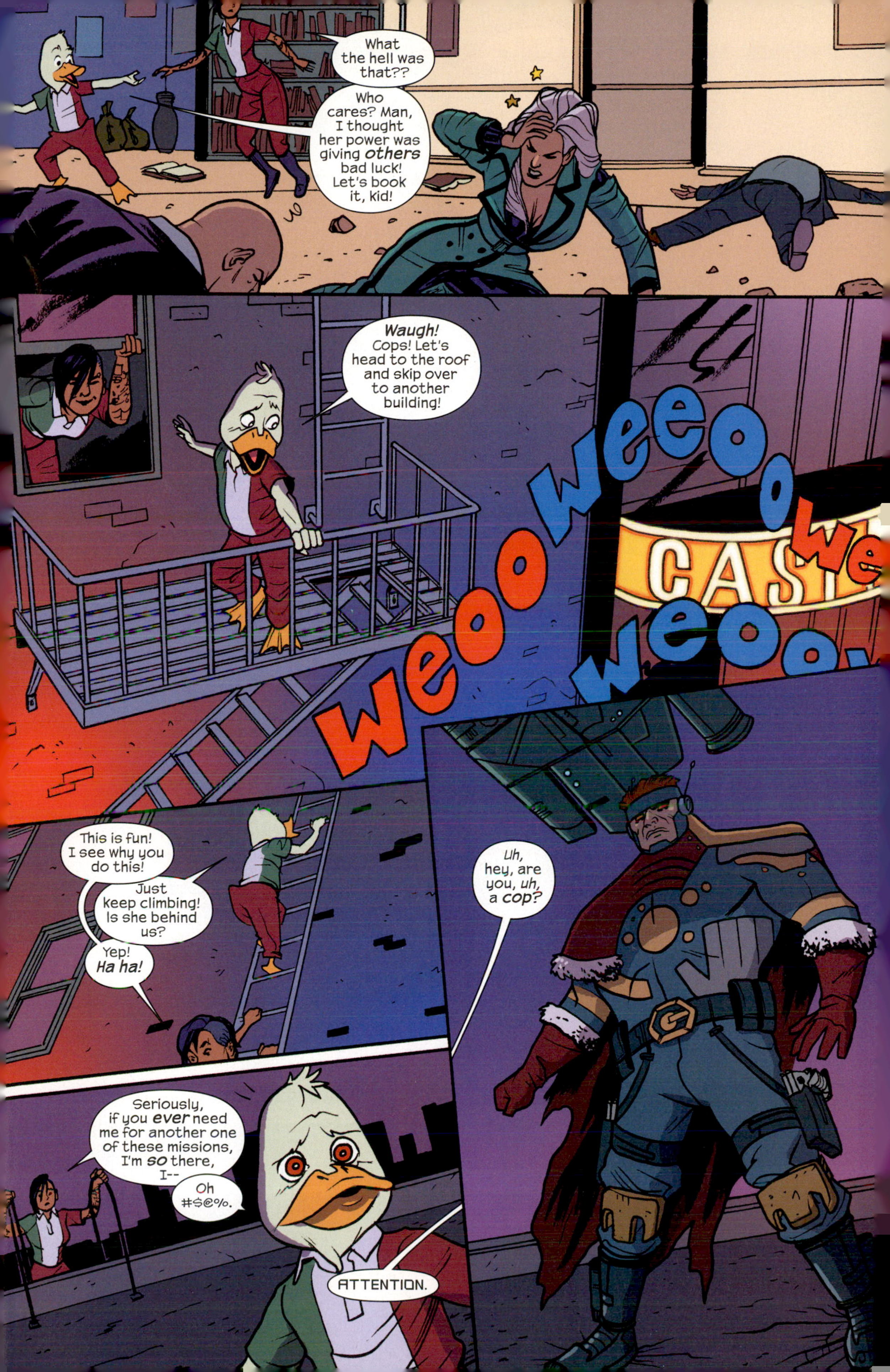
What the hell was that??
Who cares? Man, I thought her power was giving *others* bad luck! Let's book it, kid!
Waugh! Cops! Let's head to the roof and skip over to another building!
weoo weeoo weoo weoo...
This is fun! I see why you do this!
Just keep climbing! Is she behind us?
Yep! *Ha ha!*
Seriously, if you *ever* need me for another one of these missions, I'm *so* there, I--
Oh #$@%.
Uh, hey, are you, uh, a *cop?*
ATTENTION.

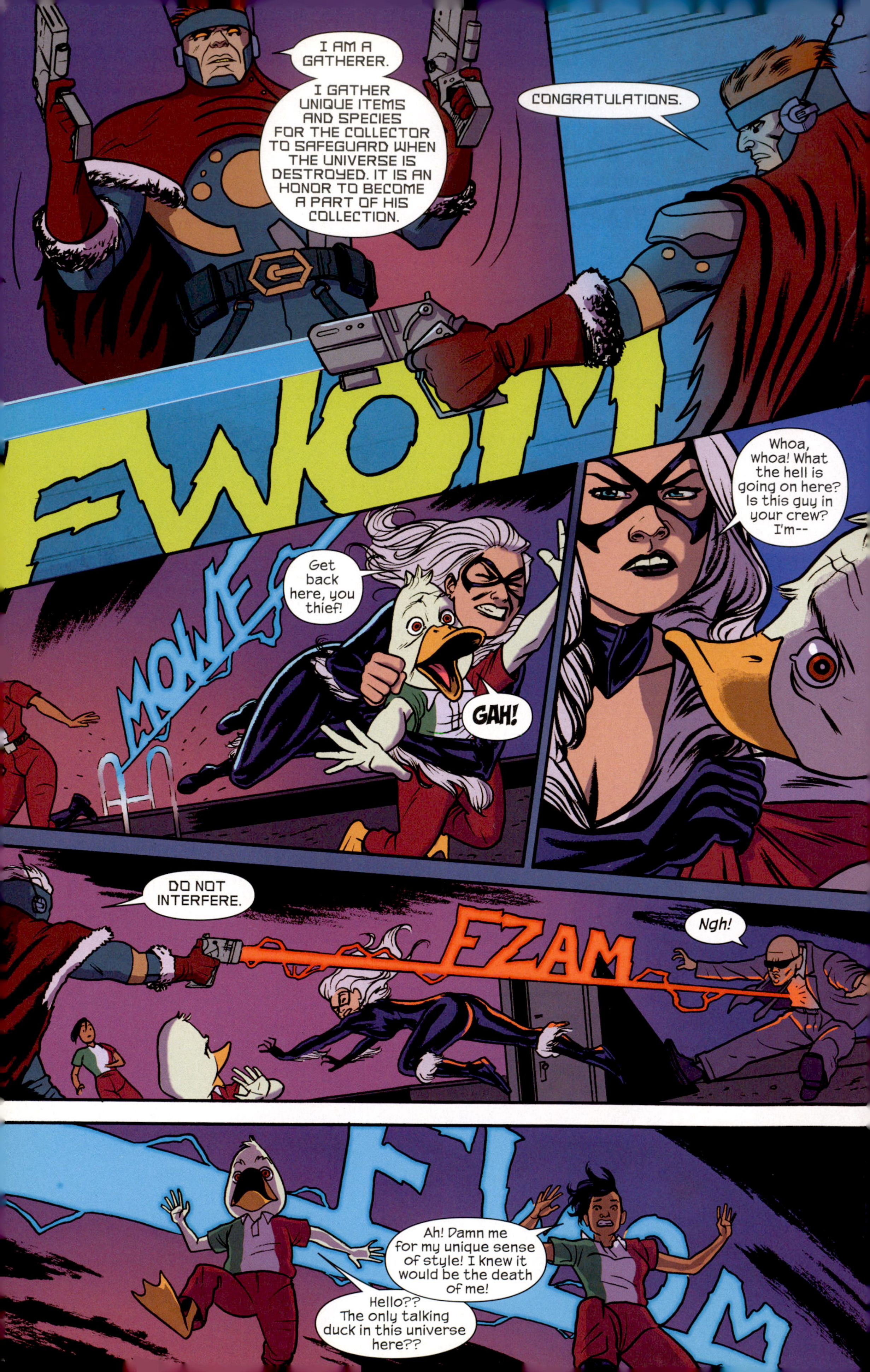
I AM A GATHERER.
I GATHER UNIQUE ITEMS AND SPECIES FOR THE COLLECTOR TO SAFEGUARD WHEN THE UNIVERSE IS DESTROYED. IT IS AN HONOR TO BECOME A PART OF HIS COLLECTION.
CONGRATULATIONS.
FWOM
Whoa, whoa! What the hell is going on here? Is this guy in your crew? I'm--
MOWF
Get back here, you thief!
GAH!
DO NOT INTERFERE.
EZAM
Ngh!
Ah! Damn me for my unique sense of style! I knew it would be the death of me!
Hello?? The only talking duck in this universe here??

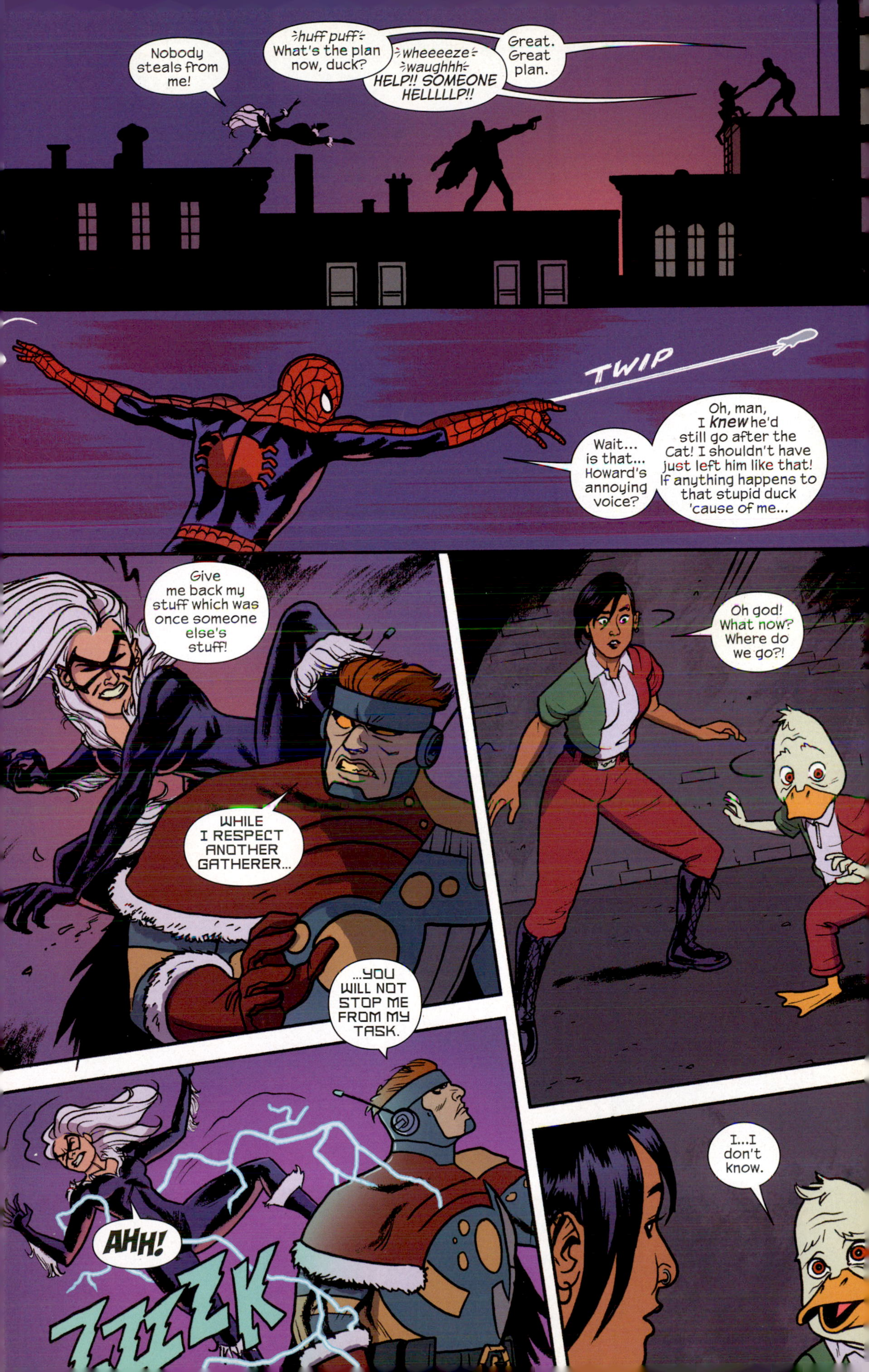
Nobody steals from me!
huff puff What's the plan now, duck?
wheeeeze waughhh HELP!! SOMEONE HELLLLLP!!
Great. Great plan.
TWIP
Wait... is that... Howard's annoying voice?
Oh, man, I knew he'd still go after the Cat! I shouldn't have just left him like that! If anything happens to that stupid duck 'cause of me...
Give me back my stuff which was once someone else's stuff!
WHILE I RESPECT ANOTHER GATHERER...
...YOU WILL NOT STOP ME FROM MY TASK.
Oh god! What now? Where do we go?!
AHH!
ZZZZK
I...I don't know.

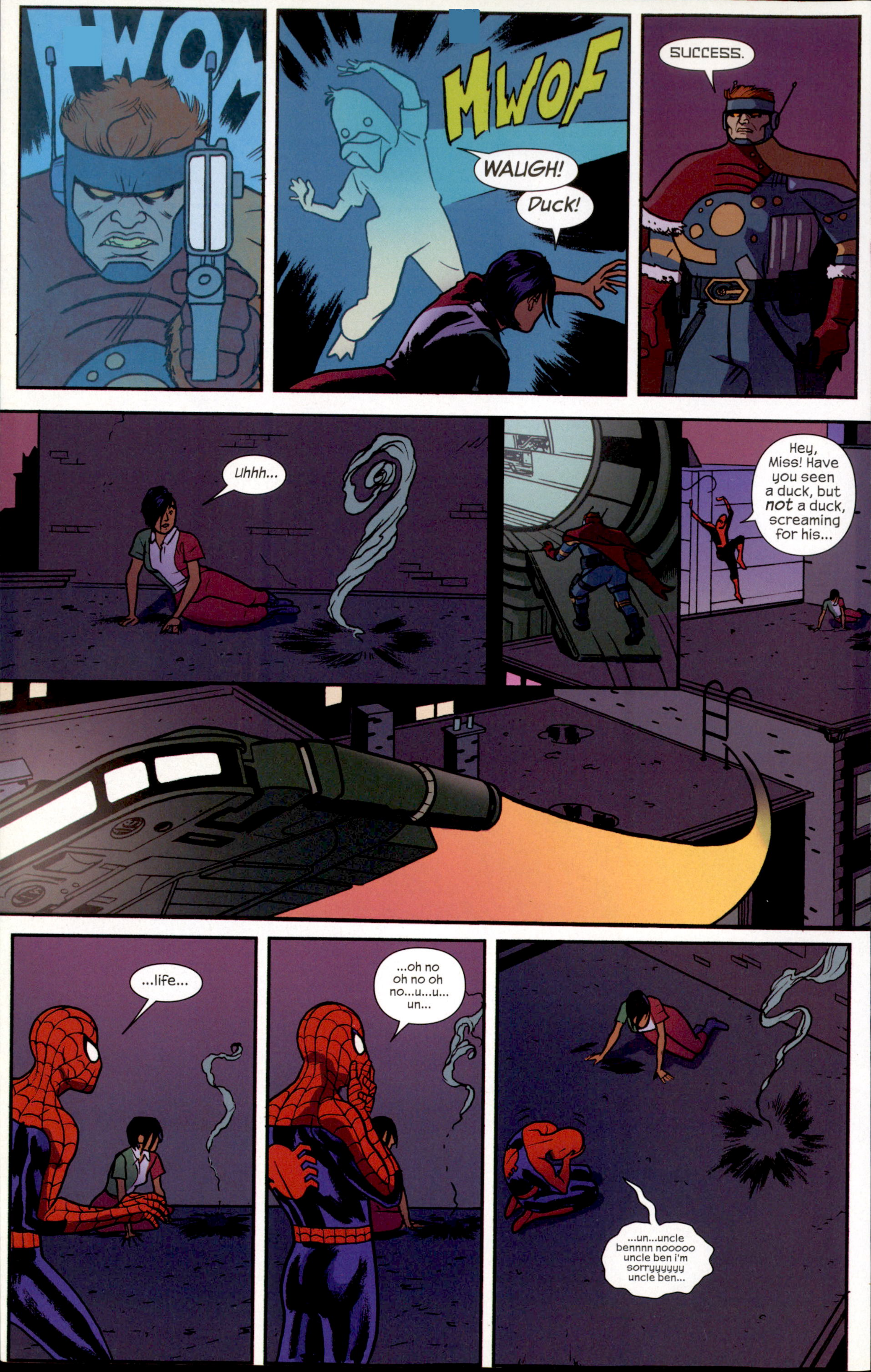
WOM
MWOF
WAUGH!
Duck!
SUCCESS.
Uhhh...
Hey, Miss! Have you seen a duck, but **not** a duck, screaming for his...
...life...
...oh no oh no oh no...u...u... un...
...un...uncle bennnn nooooo uncle ben i'm sorryyyyyy uncle ben...

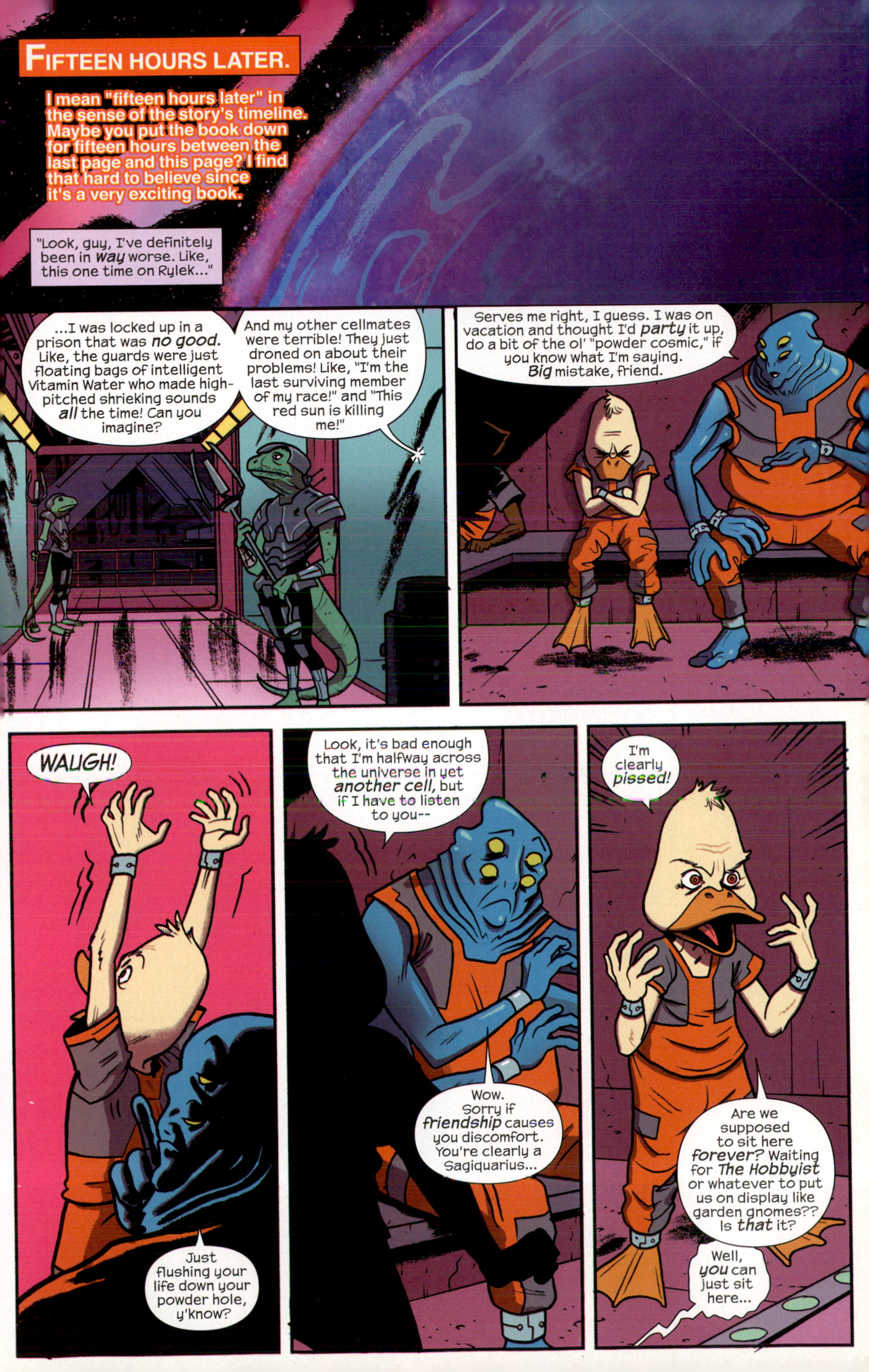
FIFTEEN HOURS LATER.
I mean "fifteen hours later" in the sense of the story's timeline. Maybe you put the book down for fifteen hours between the last page and this page? I find that hard to believe since it's a very exciting book.
"Look, guy, I've definitely been in way worse. Like, this one time on Rylek..."
...I was locked up in a prison that was no good. Like, the guards were just floating bags of intelligent Vitamin Water who made high-pitched shrieking sounds all the time! Can you imagine?
And my other cellmates were terrible! They just droned on about their problems! Like, "I'm the last surviving member of my race!" and "This red sun is killing me!"
Serves me right, I guess. I was on vacation and thought I'd party it up, do a bit of the ol' "powder cosmic," if you know what I'm saying. Big mistake, friend.
WAUGH!
Just flushing your life down your powder hole, y'know?
Look, it's bad enough that I'm halfway across the universe in yet another cell, but if I have to listen to you--
Wow. Sorry if friendship causes you discomfort. You're clearly a Sagiquarius...
I'm clearly pissed!
Are we supposed to sit here forever? Waiting for The Hobbyist or whatever to put us on display like garden gnomes?? Is that it?
Well, you can just sit here...

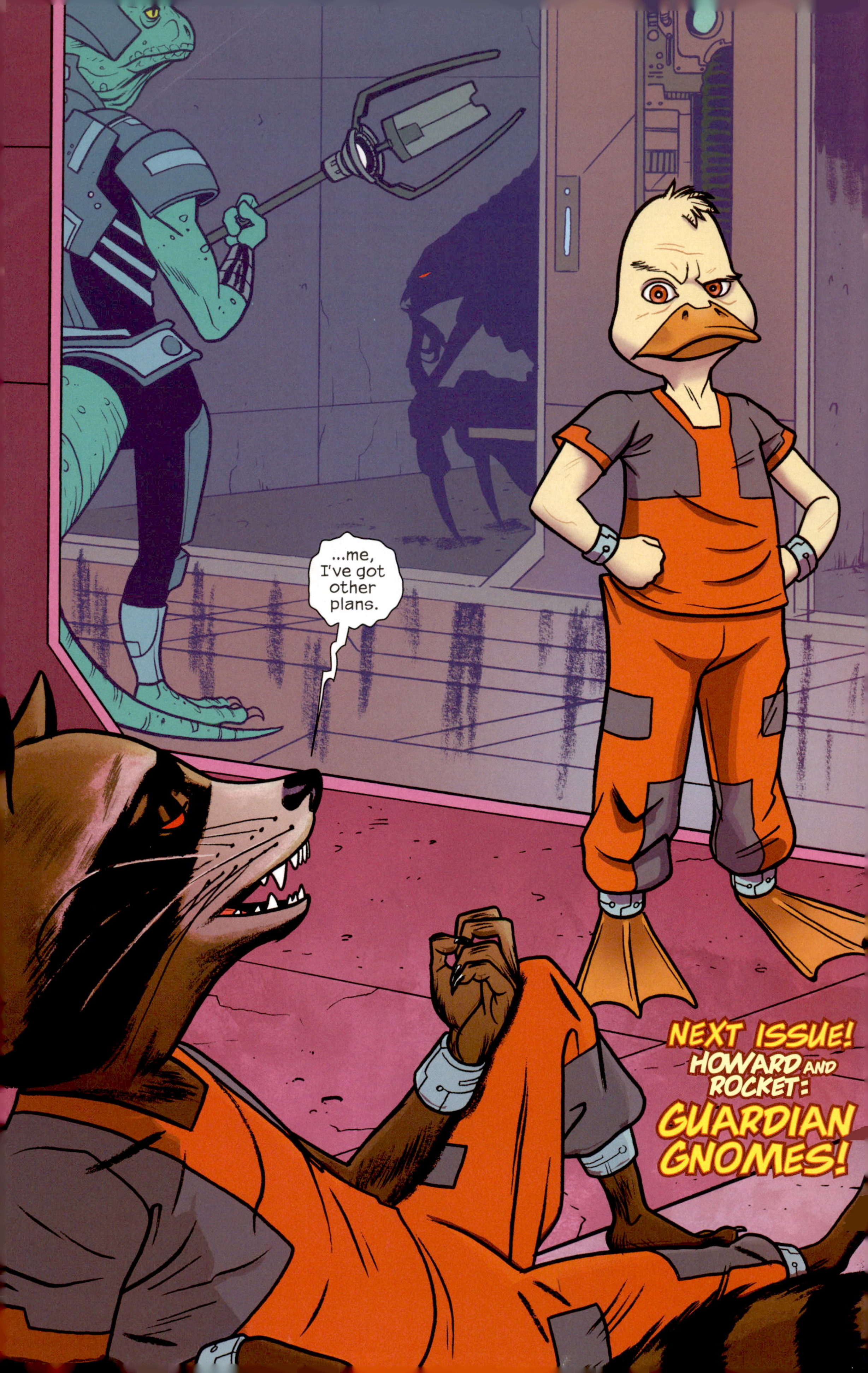
...me, I've got other plans.
NEXT ISSUE! HOWARD AND ROCKET: GUARDIAN GNOMES!

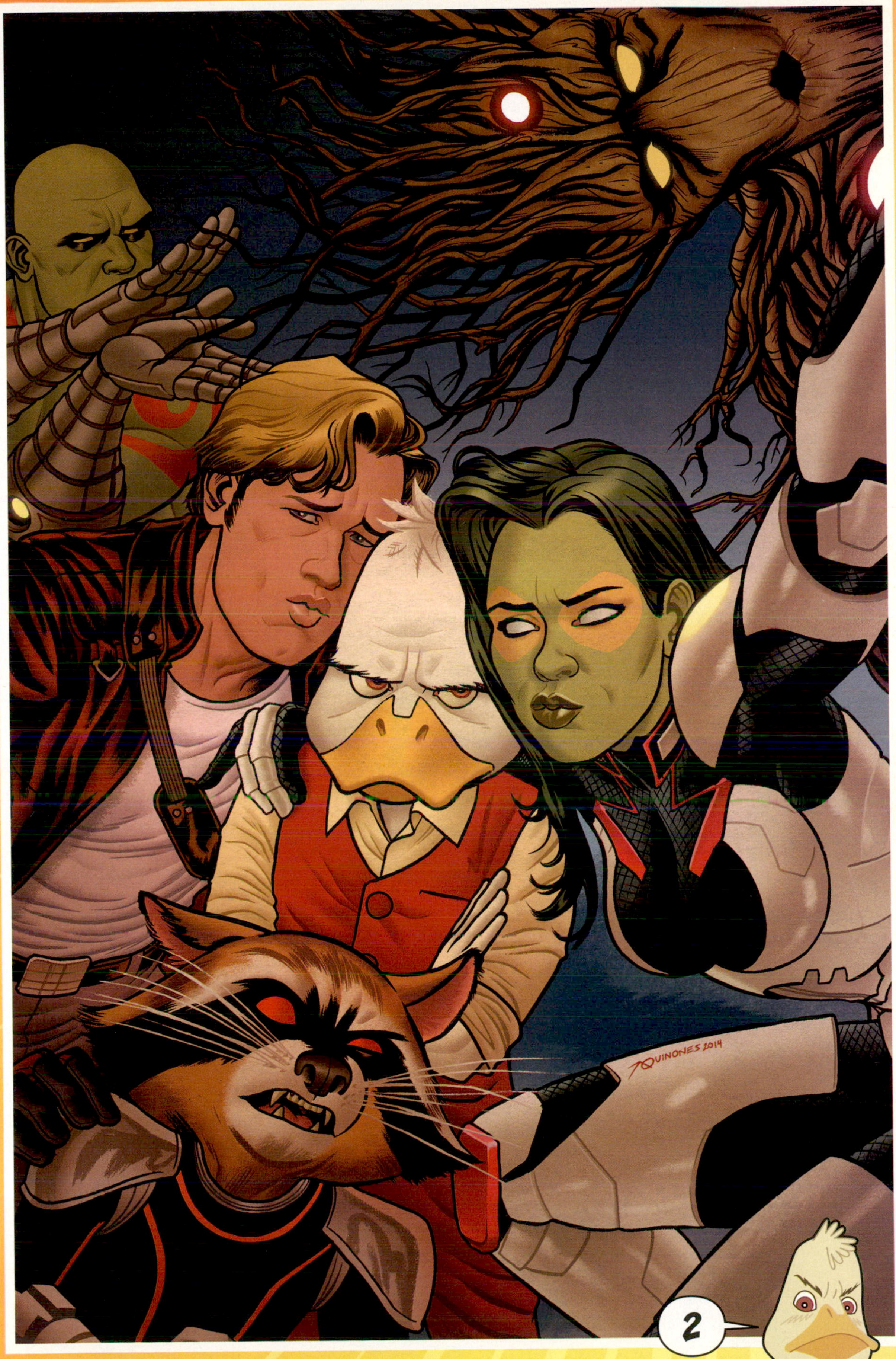
QUINONES 2014

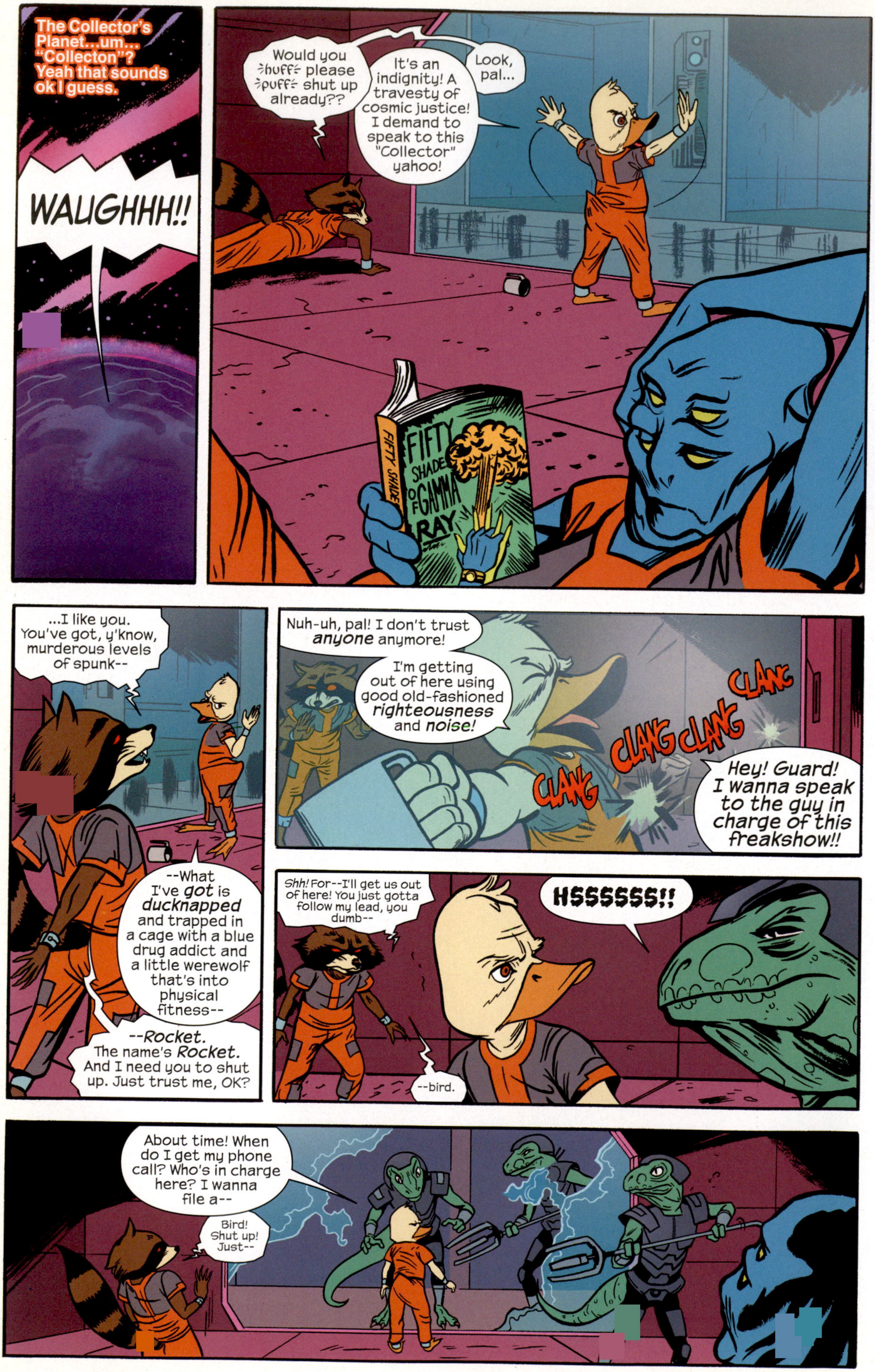
The Collector's Planet...um... "Collecton"? Yeah that sounds ok I guess.
WAUGHHH!!
Would you ≈huff≈ please ≈puff≈ shut up already??
Look, pal...
It's an indignity! A travesty of cosmic justice! I demand to speak to this "Collector" yahoo!
FIFTY SHADES OF GAMMA RAY
...I like you. You've got, y'know, murderous levels of spunk--
--What I've *got* is ***ducknapped*** and trapped in a cage with a blue drug addict and a little werewolf that's into physical fitness--
--Rocket. The name's *Rocket.* And I need you to shut up. Just trust me, OK?
Nuh-uh, pal! I don't trust ***anyone*** anymore!
I'm getting out of here using good old-fashioned ***righteousness*** and ***noise!***
CLANG
CLANG CLANG
CLANG
Hey! Guard! I wanna speak to the guy in charge of this freakshow!!
Shh! For--I'll get us out of here! You just gotta follow my lead, you dumb--
--bird.
HSSSSSS!!
About time! When do I get my phone call? Who's in charge here? I wanna file a--
Bird! Shut up! Just--

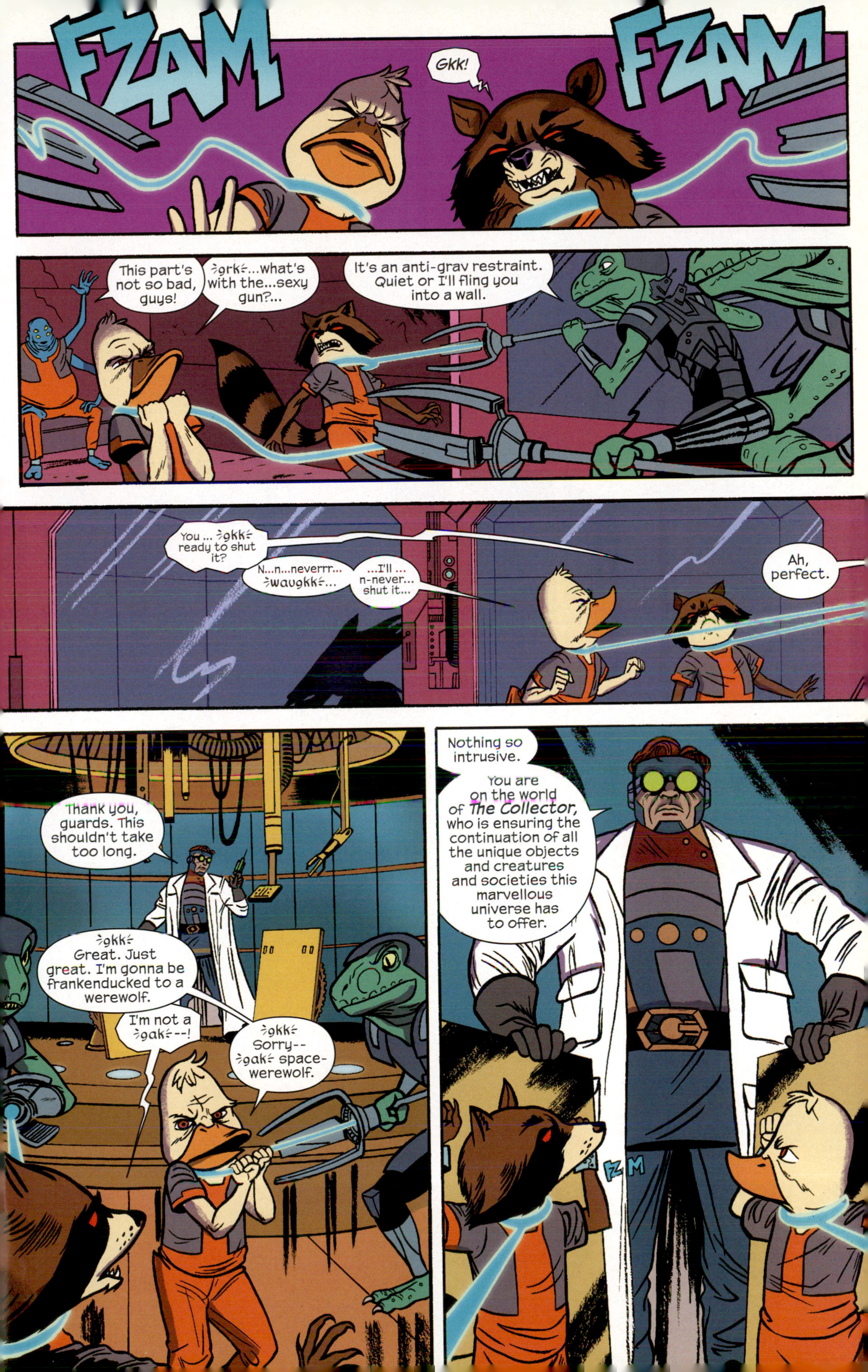
FZAM
Gkk!
FZAM
This part's not so bad, guys!
⚡grk⚡...what's with the...sexy gun?...
It's an anti-grav restraint. Quiet or I'll fling you into a wall.
You ... ⚡gkk⚡ ready to shut it?
N...n...neverrr... ⚡waugkk⚡...
...I'll ... n-never... shut it...
Ah, perfect.
Thank you, guards. This shouldn't take too long.
⚡gkk⚡ Great. Just great. I'm gonna be frankenducked to a werewolf.
I'm not a ⚡gak⚡--!
⚡gkk⚡ Sorry-- ⚡gak⚡ space-werewolf.
Nothing so intrusive.
You are on the world of The Collector, who is ensuring the continuation of all the unique objects and creatures and societies this marvellous universe has to offer.
FZM

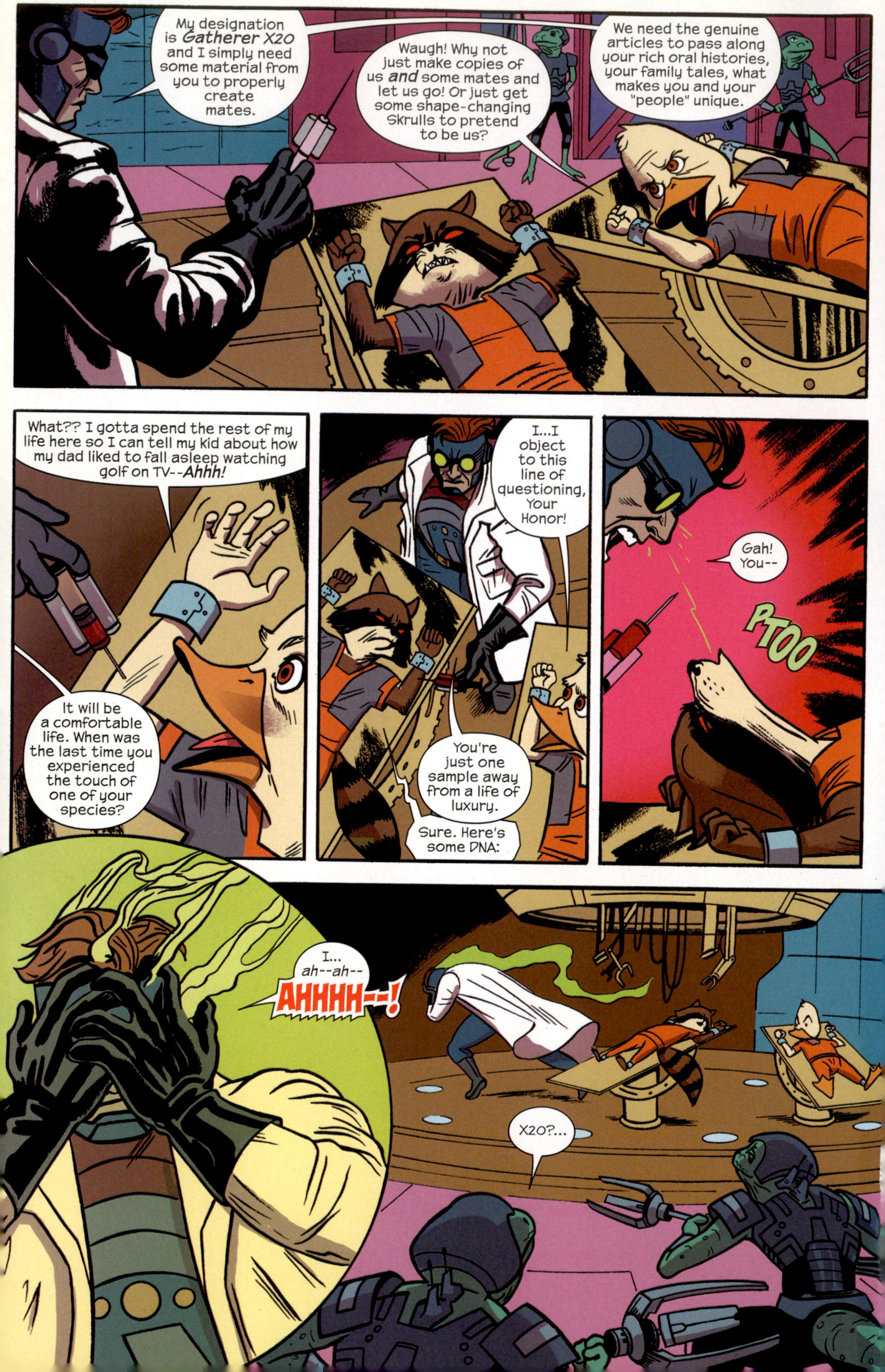

My designation is Gatherer X20 and I simply need some material from you to properly create mates.
Waugh! Why not just make copies of us *and* some mates and let us go! Or just get some shape-changing Skrulls to pretend to be us?
We need the genuine articles to pass along your rich oral histories, your family tales, what makes you and your "people" unique.
What?? I gotta spend the rest of my life here so I can tell my kid about how my dad liked to fall asleep watching golf on TV--*Ahhh!*
It will be a comfortable life. When was the last time you experienced the touch of one of your species?
I...I object to this line of questioning, Your Honor!
You're just one sample away from a life of luxury.
Sure. Here's some DNA:
Gah! You--
PTOO
I... ah--ah--
AHHHH--!
X20?...

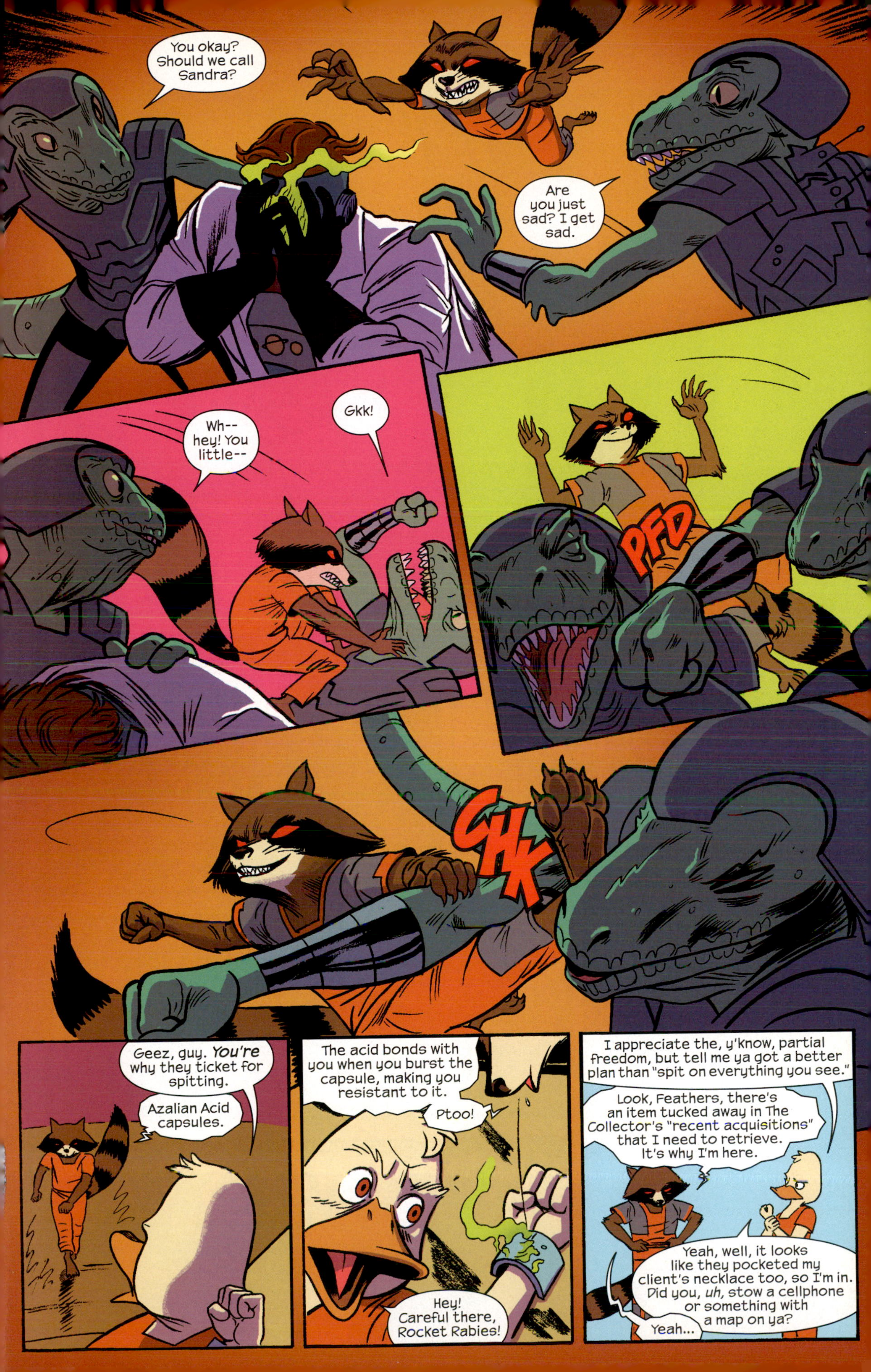
You okay? Should we call Sandra?
Are you just sad? I get sad.
Wh-- hey! You little--
Gkk!
PFD
CHK
Geez, guy. *You're* why they ticket for spitting.
Azalian Acid capsules.
The acid bonds with you when you burst the capsule, making you resistant to it.
Ptoo!
Hey! Careful there, Rocket Rabies!
I appreciate the, y'know, partial freedom, but tell me ya got a better plan than "spit on everything you see."
Look, Feathers, there's an item tucked away in The Collector's "recent acquisitions" that I need to retrieve. It's why I'm here.
Yeah, well, it looks like they pocketed my client's necklace too, so I'm in. Did you, *uh,* stow a cellphone or something with a map on ya?
Yeah...

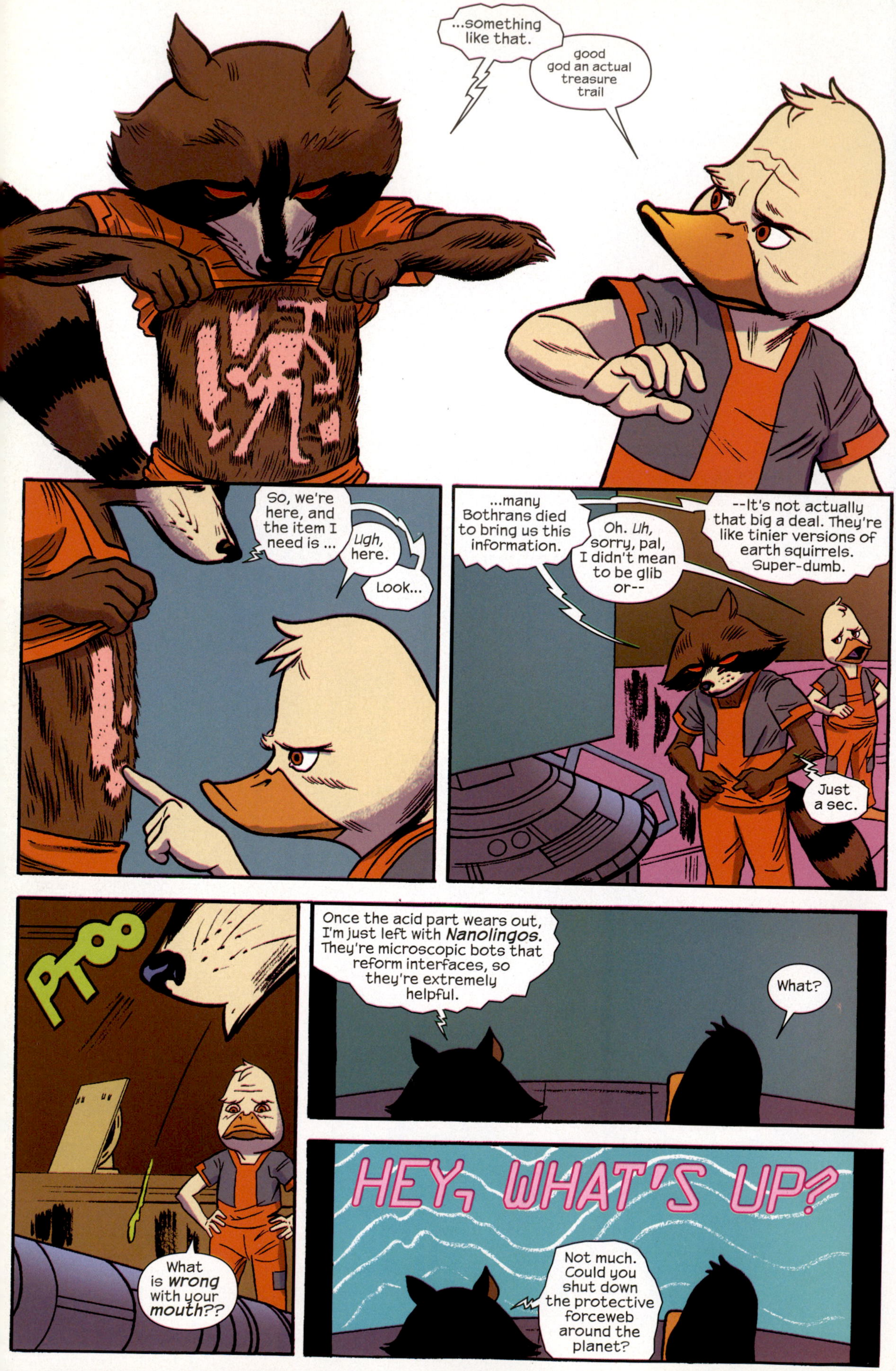
...something like that.
good god an actual treasure trail
So, we're here, and the item I need is ...
Ugh, here.
Look...
...many Bothrans died to bring us this information.
Oh. Uh, sorry, pal, I didn't mean to be glib or--
--It's not actually that big a deal. They're like tinier versions of earth squirrels. Super-dumb.
Just a sec.
PTOO
What is *wrong* with your *mouth*??
Once the acid part wears out, I'm just left with *Nanolingos.* They're microscopic bots that reform interfaces, so they're extremely helpful.
What?
HEY, WHAT'S UP?
Not much. Could you shut down the protective forceweb around the planet?

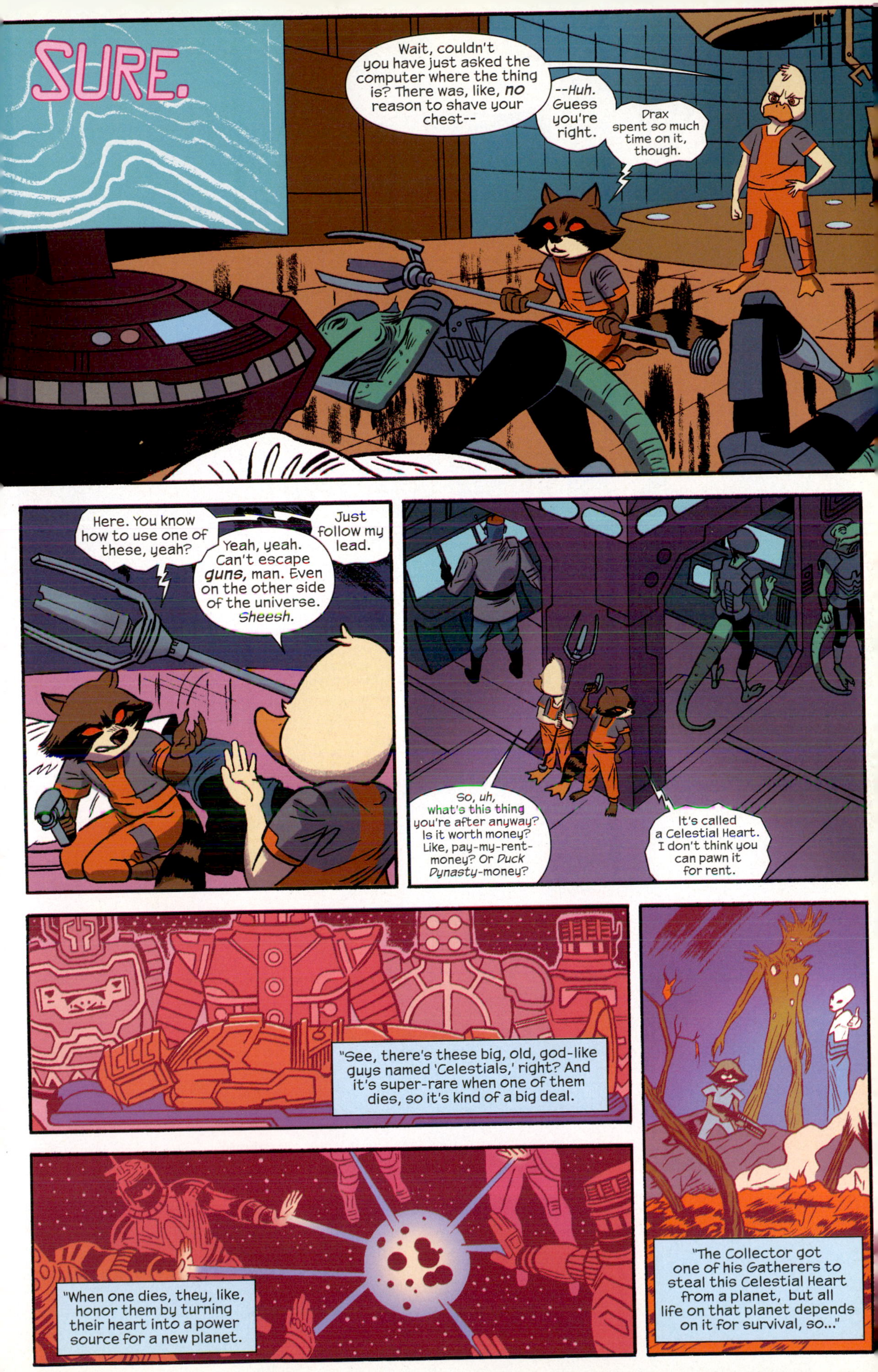
SURE.
Wait, couldn't you have just asked the computer where the thing is? There was, like, no reason to shave your chest--
--Huh. Guess you're right.
Drax spent so much time on it, though.
Here. You know how to use one of these, yeah?
Yeah, yeah. Can't escape guns, man. Even on the other side of the universe. Sheesh.
Just follow my lead.
So, uh, what's this thing you're after anyway? Is it worth money? Like, pay-my-rent-money? Or Duck Dynasty-money?
It's called a Celestial Heart. I don't think you can pawn it for rent.
"See, there's these big, old, god-like guys named 'Celestials,' right? And it's super-rare when one of them dies, so it's kind of a big deal.
"When one dies, they, like, honor them by turning their heart into a power source for a new planet.
"The Collector got one of his Gatherers to steal this Celestial Heart from a planet, but all life on that planet depends on it for survival, so..."

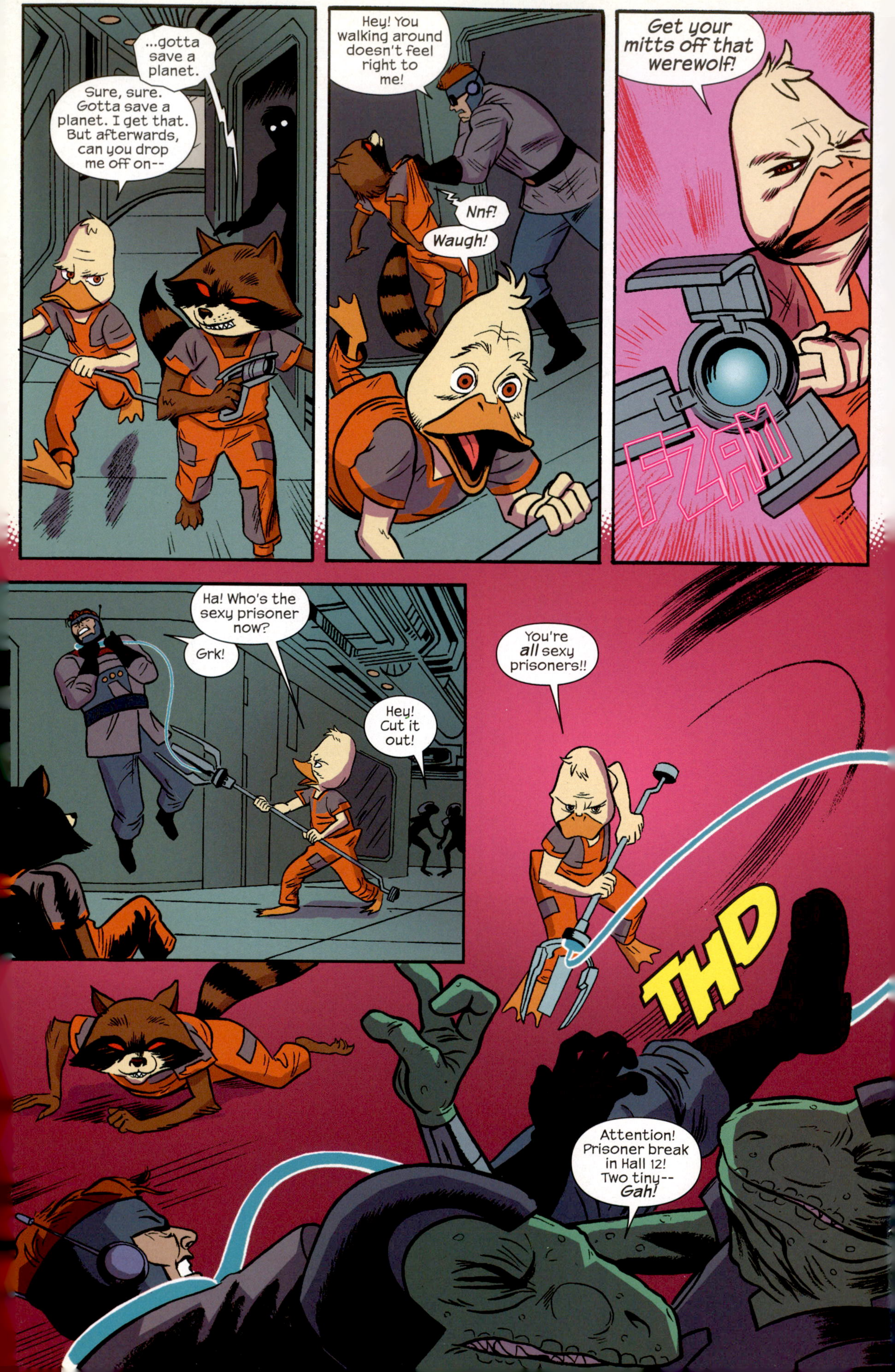

Sure, sure. Gotta save a planet. I get that. But afterwards, can you drop me off on--
...gotta save a planet.
Hey! You walking around doesn't feel right to me!
Nnf!
Waugh!
Get your mitts off that werewolf!
FZAM
Ha! Who's the sexy prisoner now?
Grk!
Hey! Cut it out!
You're all sexy prisoners!!
THD
Attention! Prisoner break in Hall 12! Two tiny-- Gah!

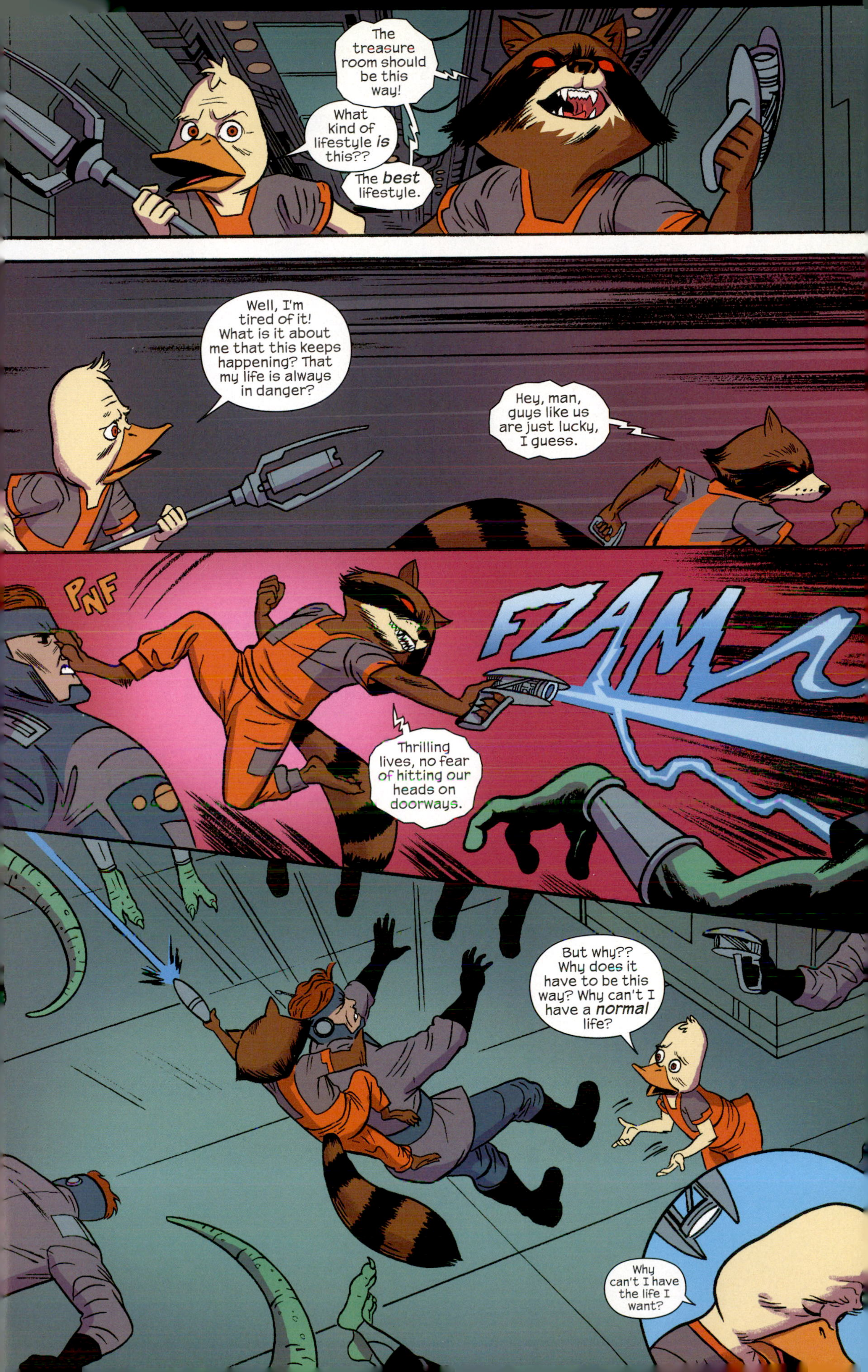
The treasure room should be this way!
What kind of lifestyle *is* this??
The *best* lifestyle.
Well, I'm tired of it! What is it about me that this keeps happening? That my life is always in danger?
Hey, man, guys like us are just lucky, I guess.
PNF
FZAM
Thrilling lives, no fear of hitting our heads on doorways.
But why?? Why does it have to be this way? Why can't I have a *normal* life?
Why can't I have the life I want?

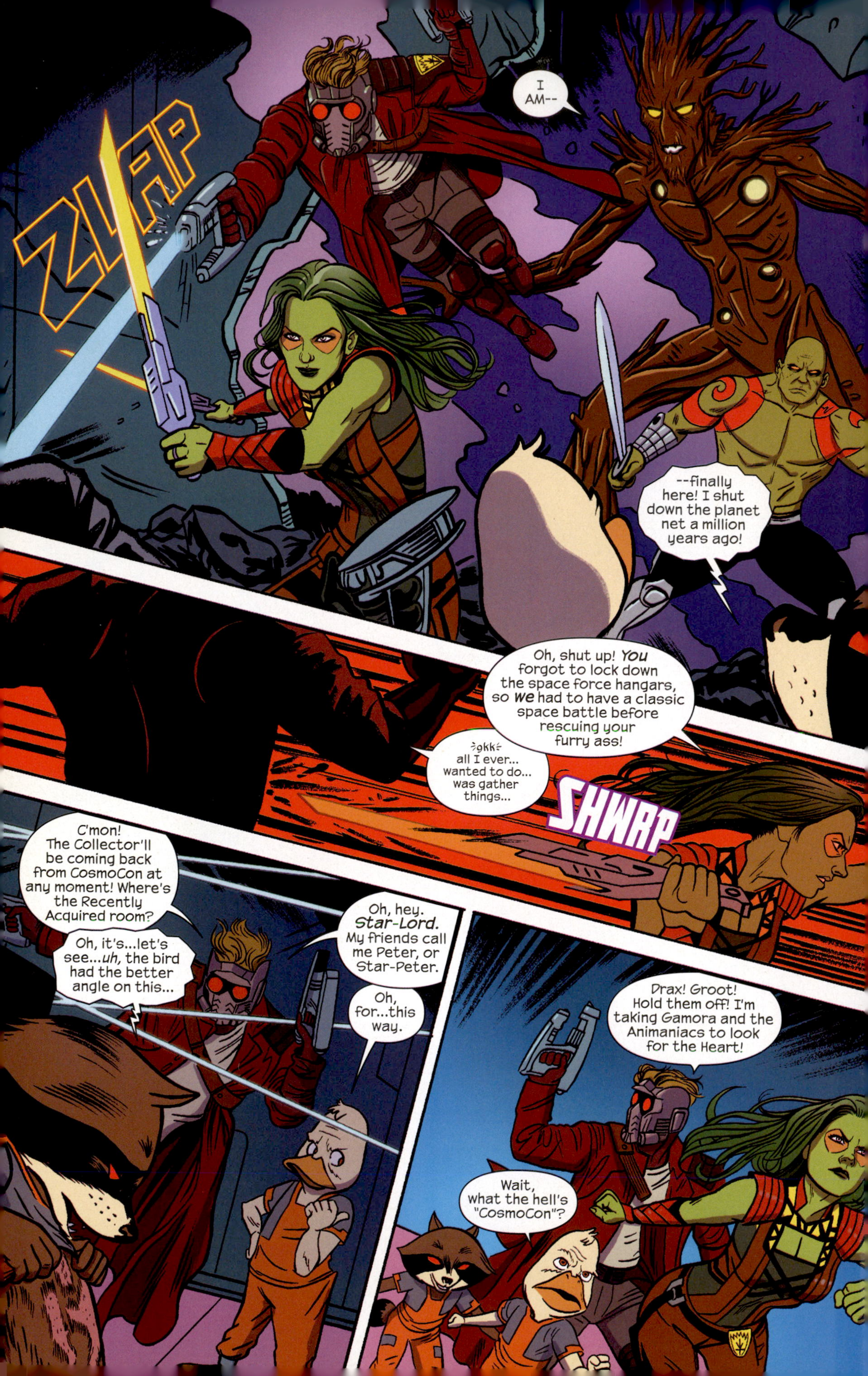

ZIIAP
I AM--
--finally here! I shut down the planet net a million years ago!
Oh, shut up! *You* forgot to lock down the space force hangars, so *we* had to have a classic space battle before rescuing your furry ass!
gkk all I ever... wanted to do... was gather things...
SHWRP
C'mon! The Collector'll be coming back from CosmoCon at any moment! Where's the Recently Acquired room?
Oh, it's...let's see...*uh,* the bird had the better angle on this...
Oh, hey. *Star-Lord.* My friends call me Peter, or Star-Peter.
Oh, for...this way.
Drax! Groot! Hold them off! I'm taking Gamora and the Animaniacs to look for the Heart!
Wait, what the hell's "CosmoCon"?

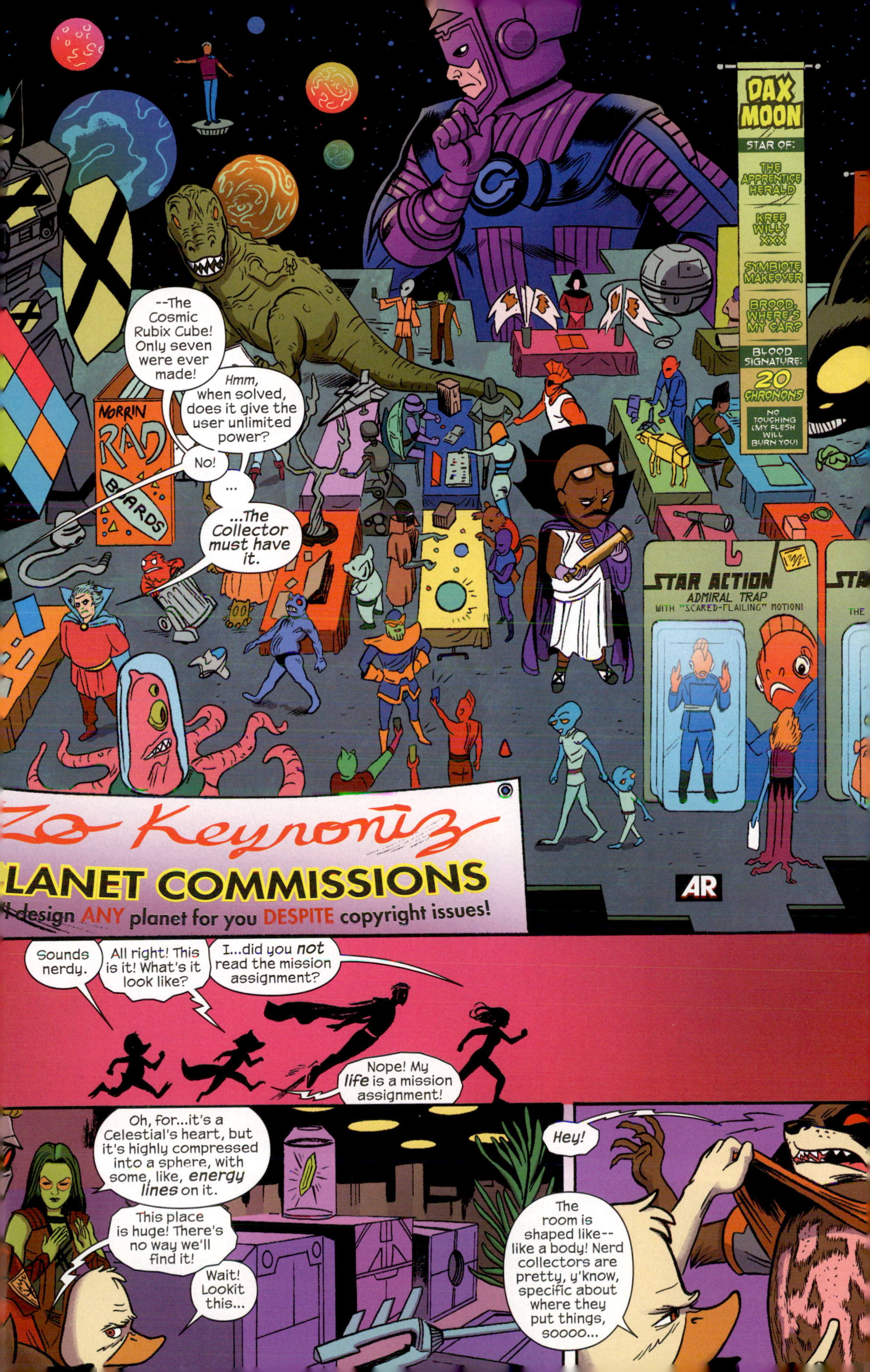
DAX MOON
STAR OF:
THE APPRENTICE HERALD
KREE WILLY XXX
SYMBIOTE MAKEOVER
BROOD, WHERE'S MY CAR?
BLOOD SIGNATURE: 20 CHRONONS
NO TOUCHING (MY FLESH WILL BURN YOU)
--The Cosmic Rubix Cube! Only seven were ever made!
Hmm, when solved, does it give the user unlimited power?
No!
...
...The Collector must have it.
NORRIN RAD BOARDS
STAR ACTION
ADMIRAL TRAP
WITH "SCARED-FLAILING" MOTION!
Zo Keynoniz
LANET COMMISSIONS
design ANY planet for you DESPITE copyright issues!
AR
Sounds nerdy.
All right! This is it! What's it look like?
I...did you not read the mission assignment?
Nope! My life is a mission assignment!
Oh, for...it's a Celestial's heart, but it's highly compressed into a sphere, with some, like, energy lines on it.
This place is huge! There's no way we'll find it!
Wait! Lookit this...
Hey!
The room is shaped like--like a body! Nerd collectors are pretty, y'know, specific about where they put things, soooo...

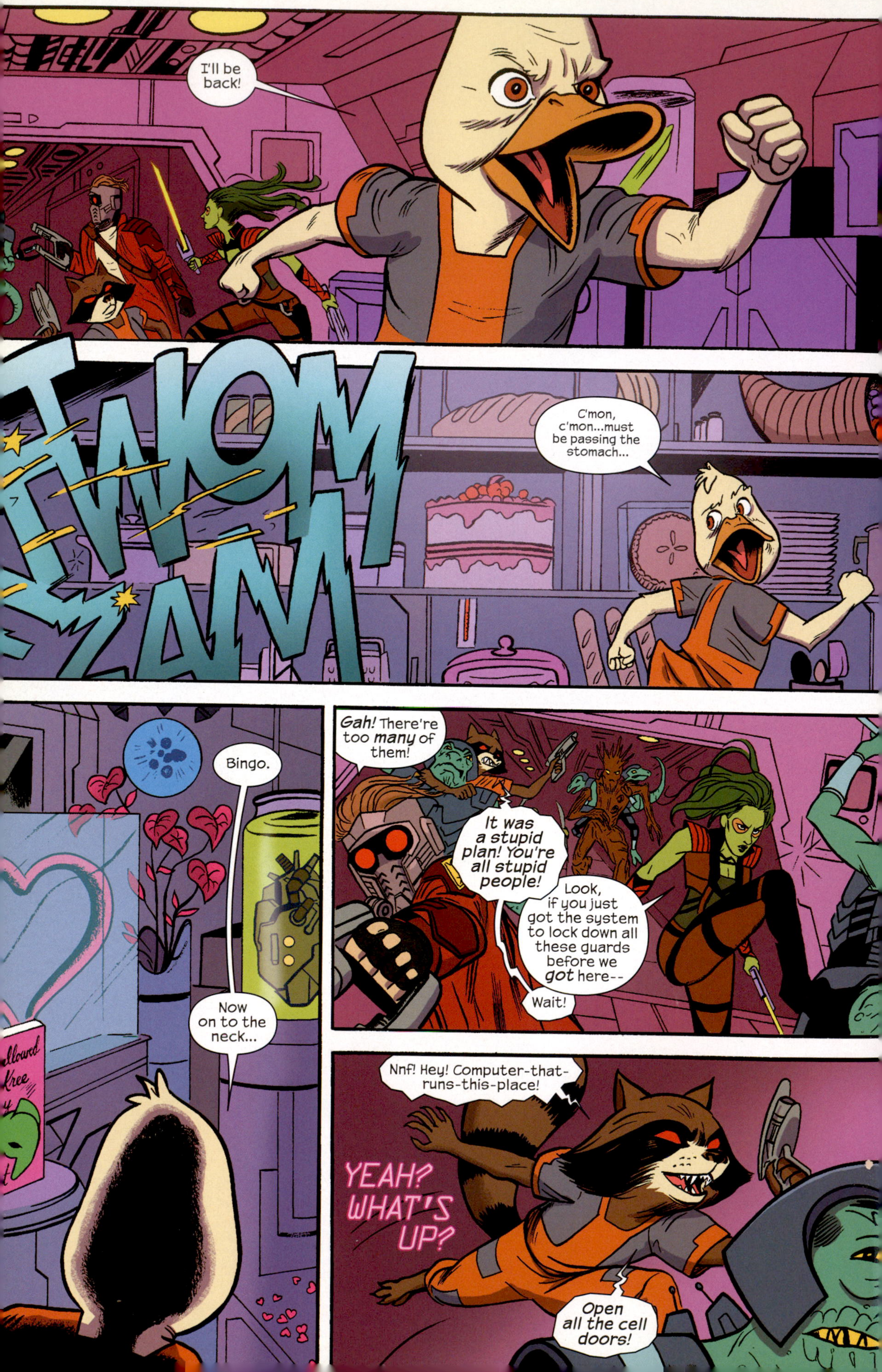
I'll be back!
ZAM
C'mon, c'mon...must be passing the stomach...
Bingo.
Now on to the neck...
Gah! There're too *many* of them!
It was a stupid plan! You're all stupid people!
Look, if you just got the system to lock down all these guards before we *got* here--
Wait!
Nnf! Hey! Computer-that-runs-this-place!
YEAH? WHAT'S UP?
Open all the cell doors!

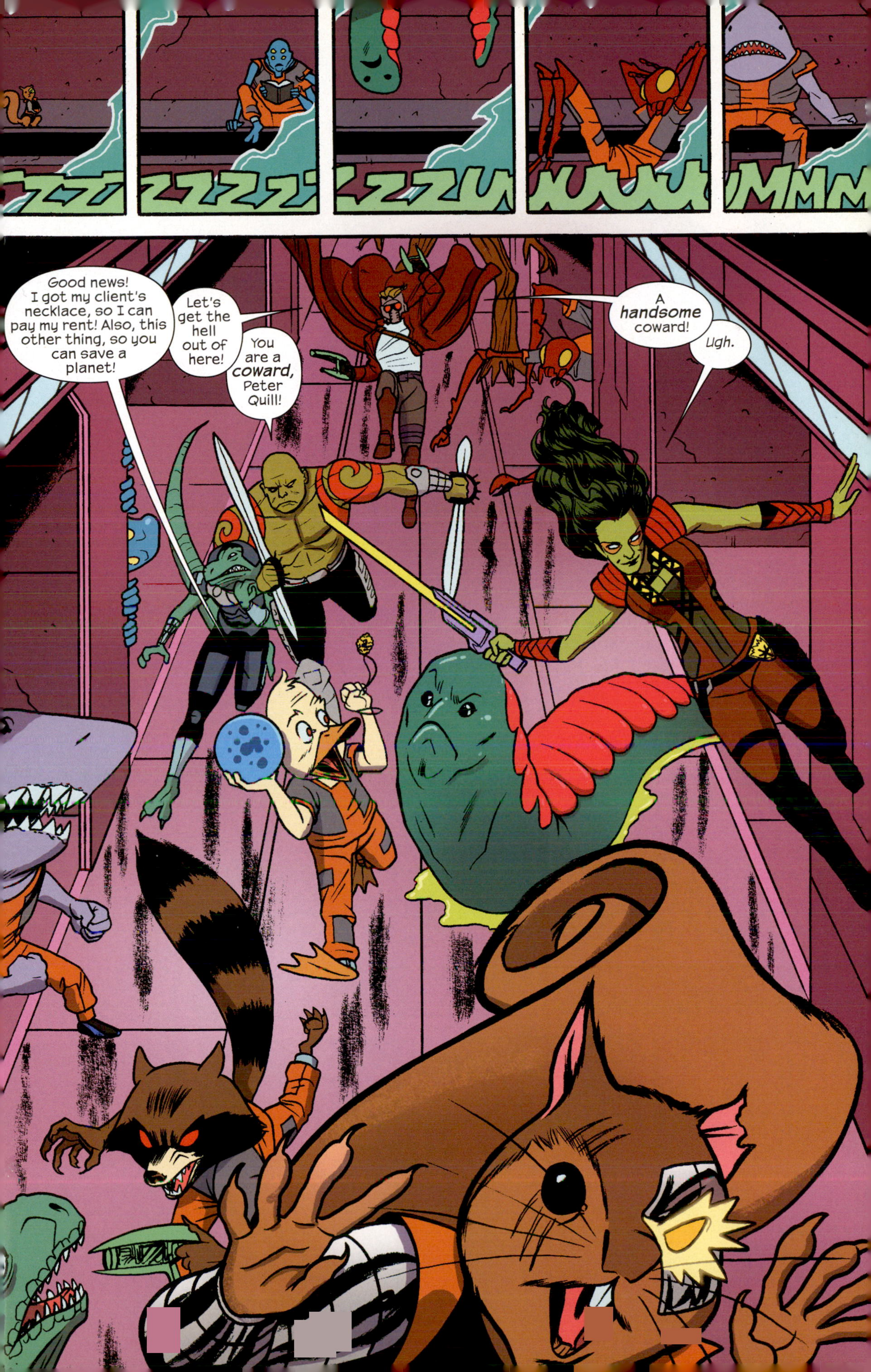
ZZZZZZZZZZZZZZUUUUUUMMM
Good news! I got my client's necklace, so I can pay my rent! Also, this other thing, so you can save a planet!
Let's get the hell out of here!
You are a *coward,* Peter Quill!
A *handsome* coward!
Ugh.

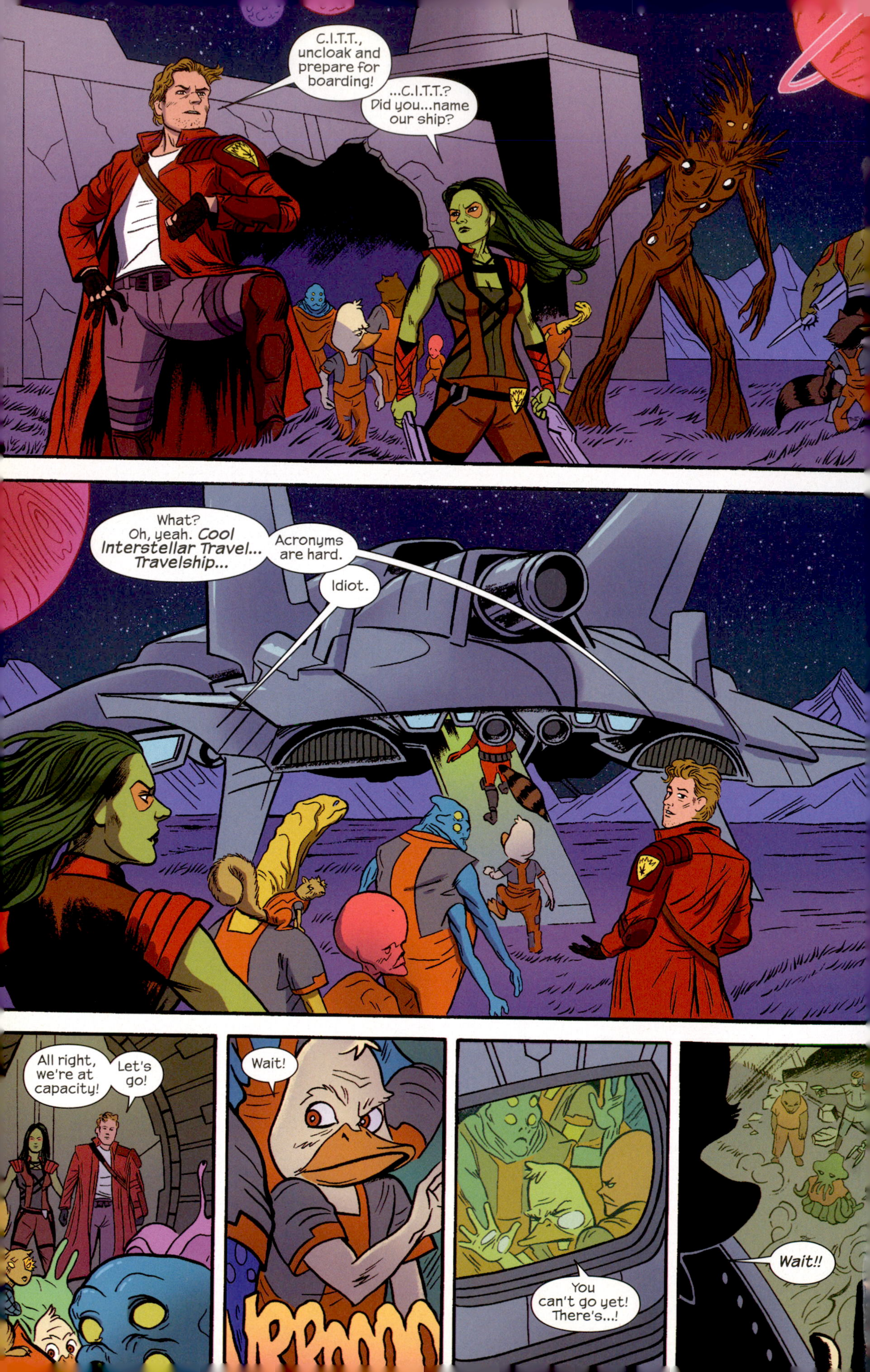

C.I.T.T., uncloak and prepare for boarding!
...C.I.T.T.? Did you...name our ship?
What? Oh, yeah. *Cool Interstellar Travel... Travelship...*
Acronyms are hard.
Idiot.
All right, we're at capacity!
Let's go!
Wait!
You can't go yet! There's...!
Wait!!

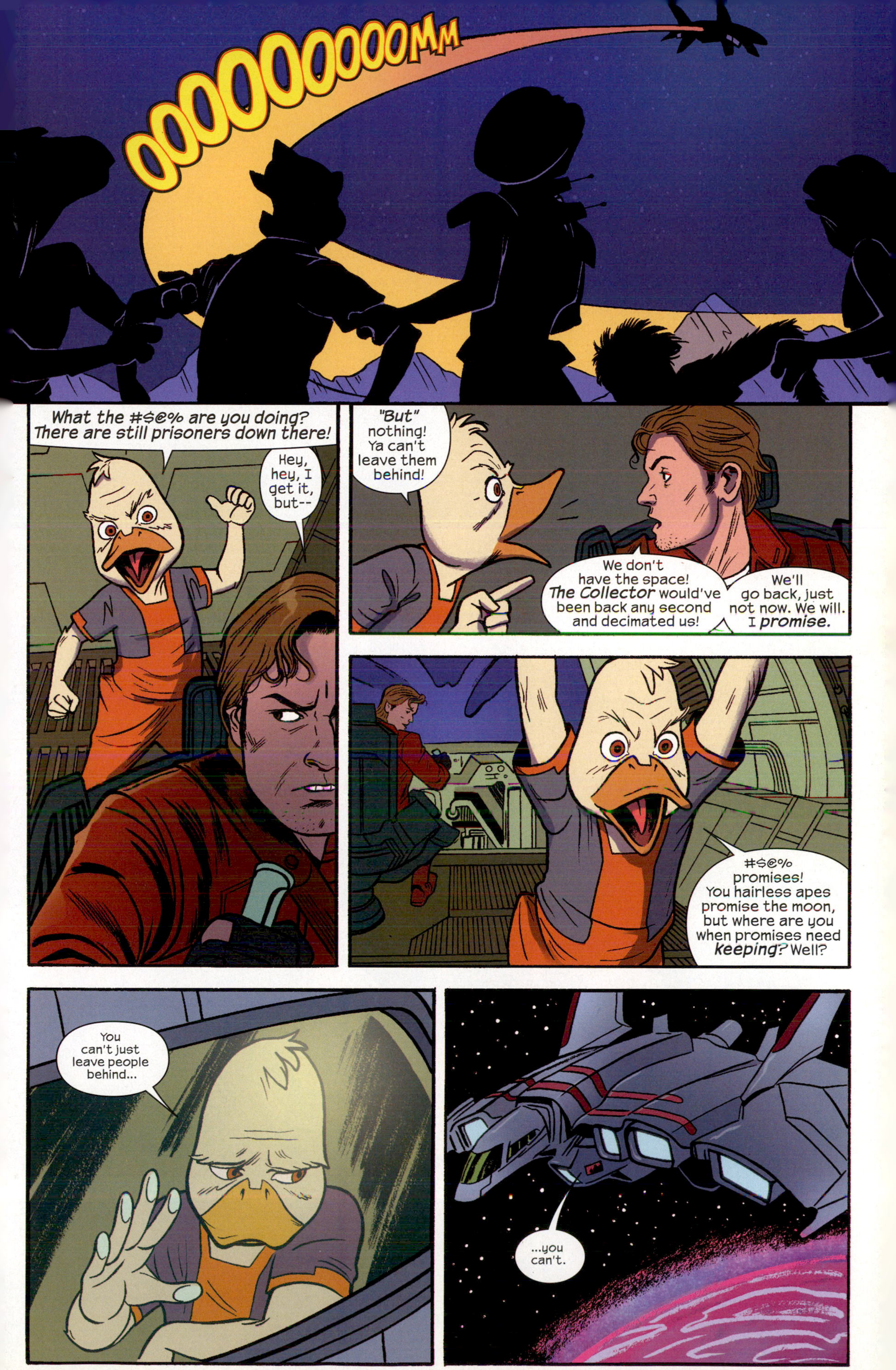
OOOOOOOOOOMM
What the #$@% are you doing? There are still prisoners down there!
Hey, hey, I get it, but--
"But" nothing! Ya can't leave them behind!
We don't have the space! The Collector would've been back any second and decimated us!
We'll go back, just not now. We will. I promise.
#$@% promises! You hairless apes promise the moon, but where are you when promises need keeping? Well?
You can't just leave people behind...
...you can't.

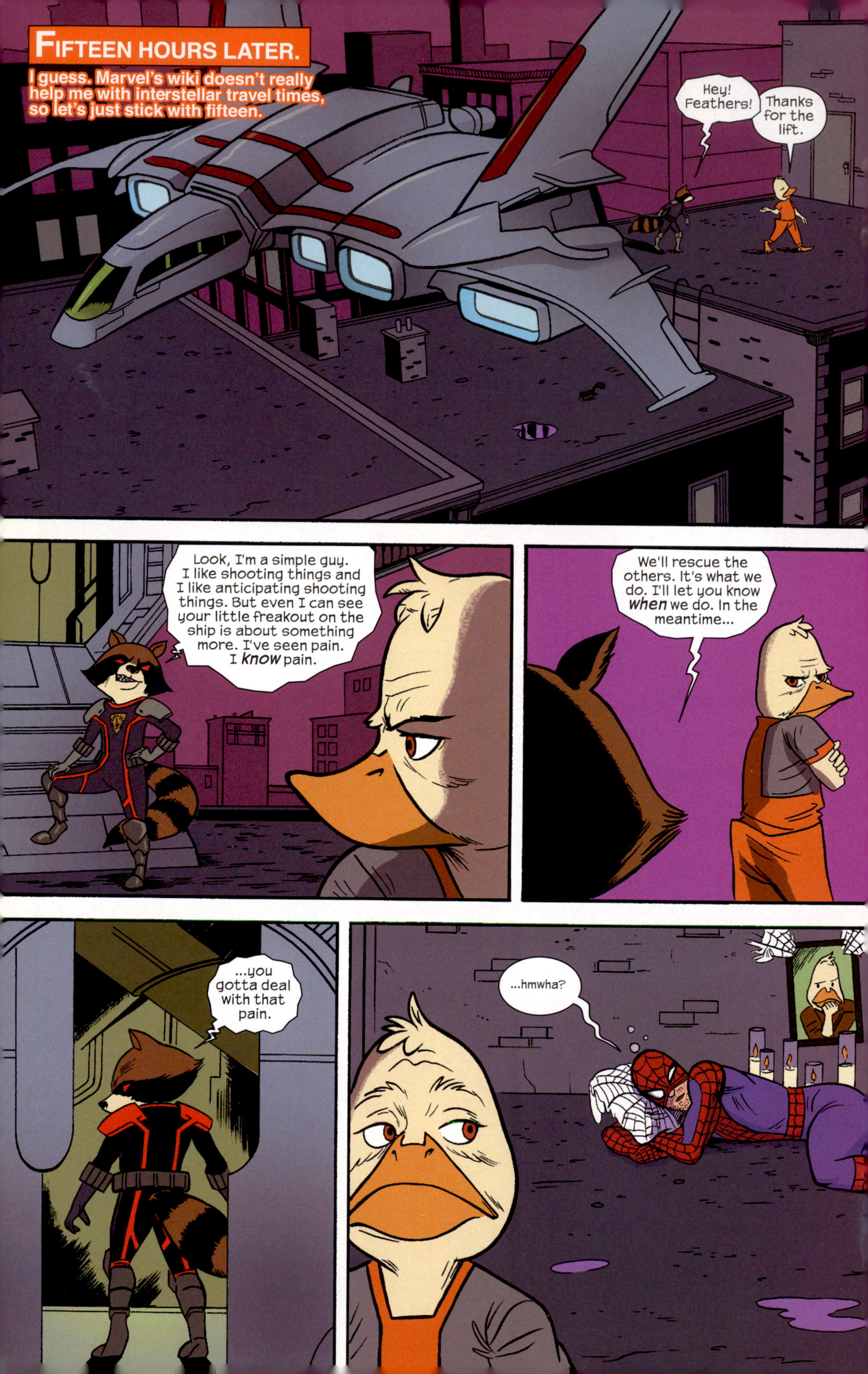
FIFTEEN HOURS LATER.
I guess. Marvel's wiki doesn't really help me with interstellar travel times, so let's just stick with fifteen.
Hey! Feathers!
Thanks for the lift.
Look, I'm a simple guy. I like shooting things and I like anticipating shooting things. But even I can see your little freakout on the ship is about something more. I've seen pain. I *know* pain.
We'll rescue the others. It's what we do. I'll let you know *when* we do. In the meantime...
...you gotta deal with that pain.
...hmwha?

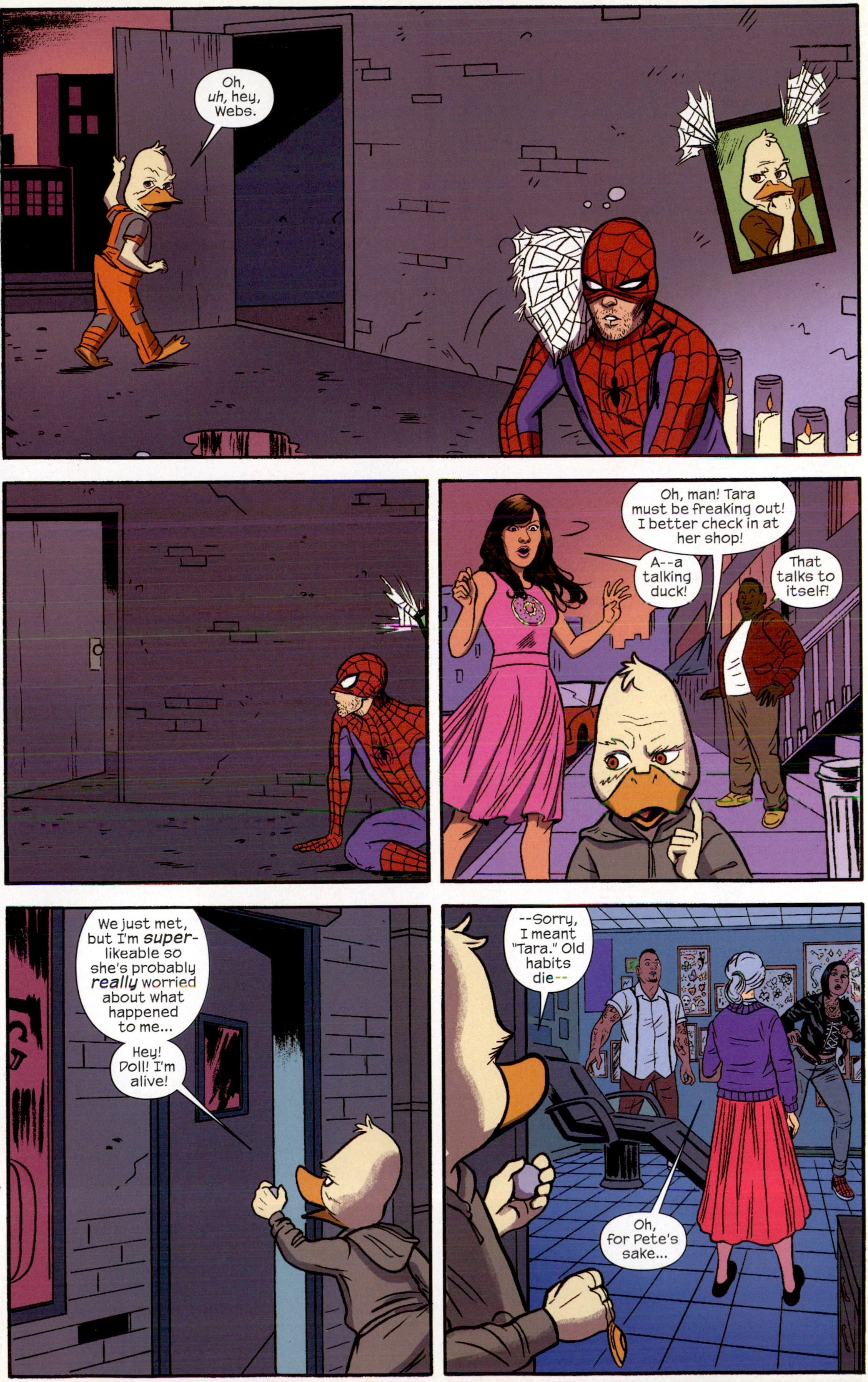
Oh, uh, hey, Webs.
Oh, man! Tara must be freaking out! I better check in at her shop!
A--a talking duck!
That talks to itself!
We just met, but I'm super-likeable so she's probably really worried about what happened to me...
Hey! Doll! I'm alive!
--Sorry, I meant "Tara." Old habits die--
Oh, for Pete's sake...

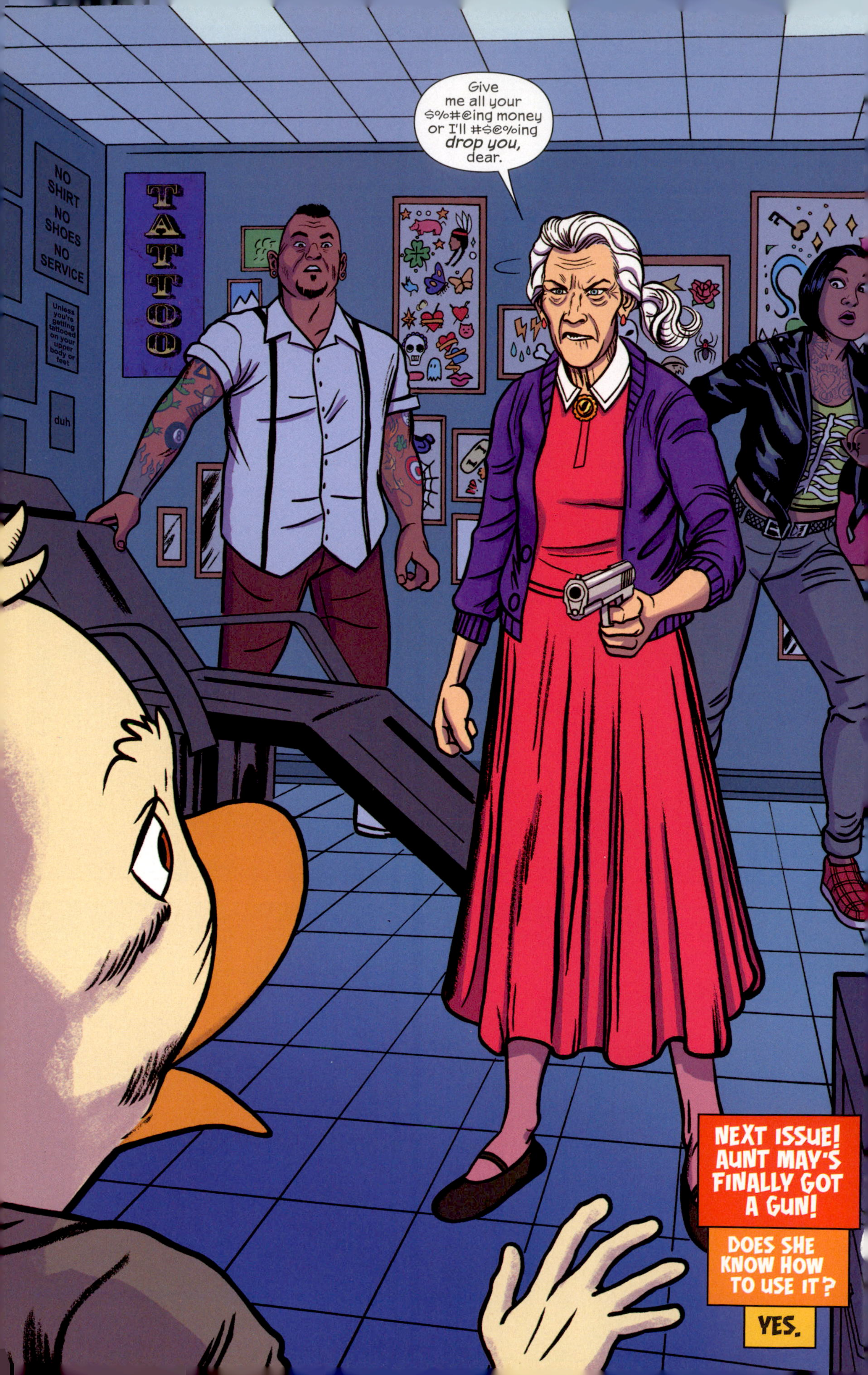
NO SHIRT NO SHOES NO SERVICE
Unless you're getting tattooed on your upper body or feet
duh
TATTOO
Give me all your $%#@ing money or I'll #$@%ing *drop you,* dear.
NEXT ISSUE! AUNT MAY'S FINALLY GOT A GUN!
DOES SHE KNOW HOW TO USE IT?
YES.

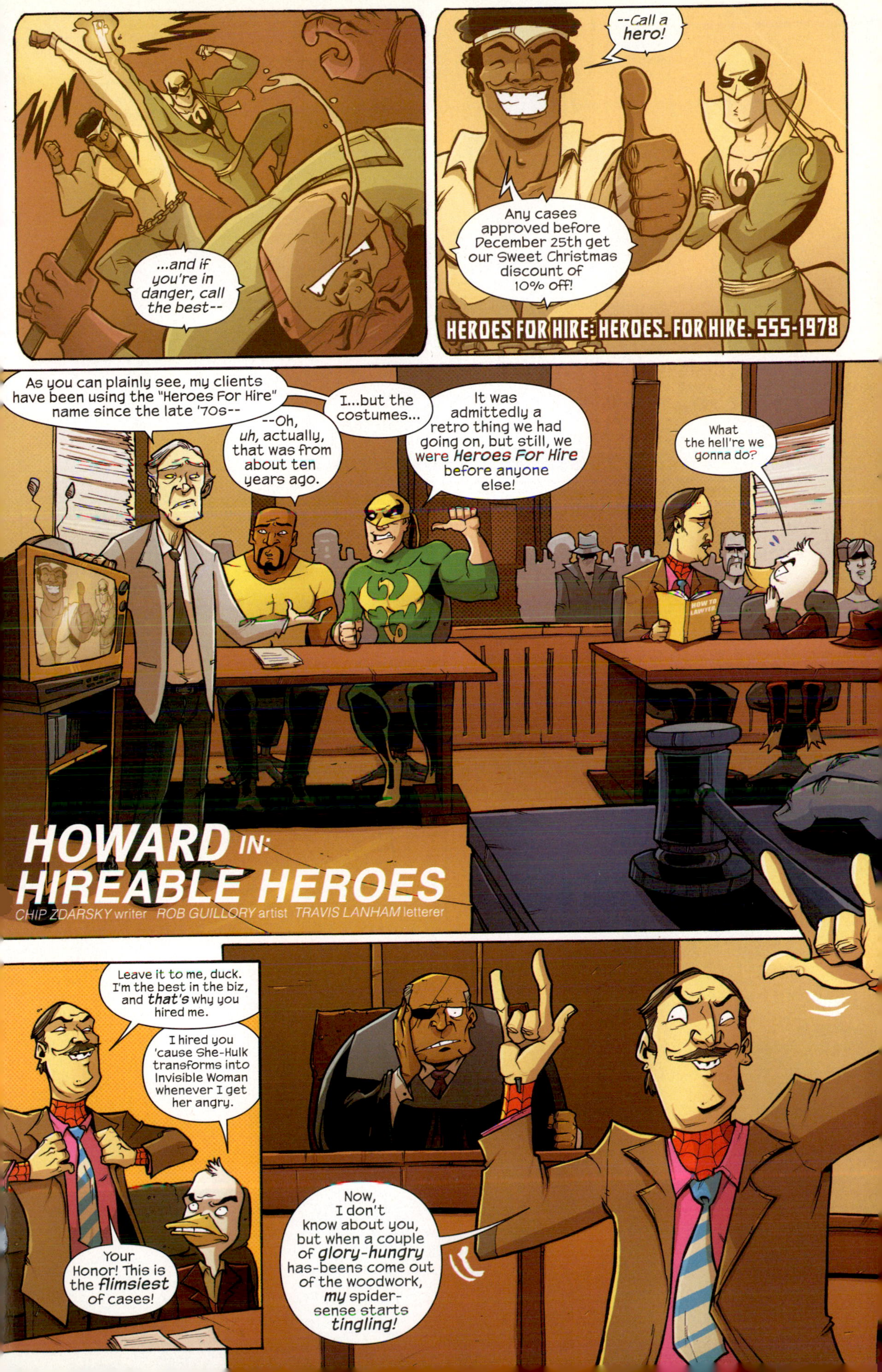

...and if you're in danger, call the best--
--Call a hero!
Any cases approved before December 25th get our Sweet Christmas discount of 10% off!
HEROES FOR HIRE: HEROES. FOR HIRE. 555-1978
As you can plainly see, my clients have been using the "Heroes For Hire" name since the late '70s--
--Oh, uh, actually, that was from about ten years ago.
I...but the costumes...
It was admittedly a retro thing we had going on, but still, we were Heroes For Hire before anyone else!
What the hell're we gonna do?
HOW TO LAWYER
HOWARD IN: HIREABLE HEROES
CHIP ZDARSKY writer ROB GUILLORY artist TRAVIS LANHAM letterer
Leave it to me, duck. I'm the best in the biz, and that's why you hired me.
I hired you 'cause She-Hulk transforms into Invisible Woman whenever I get her angry.
Your Honor! This is the flimsiest of cases!
Now, I don't know about you, but when a couple of glory-hungry has-beens come out of the woodwork, my spider-sense starts tingling!

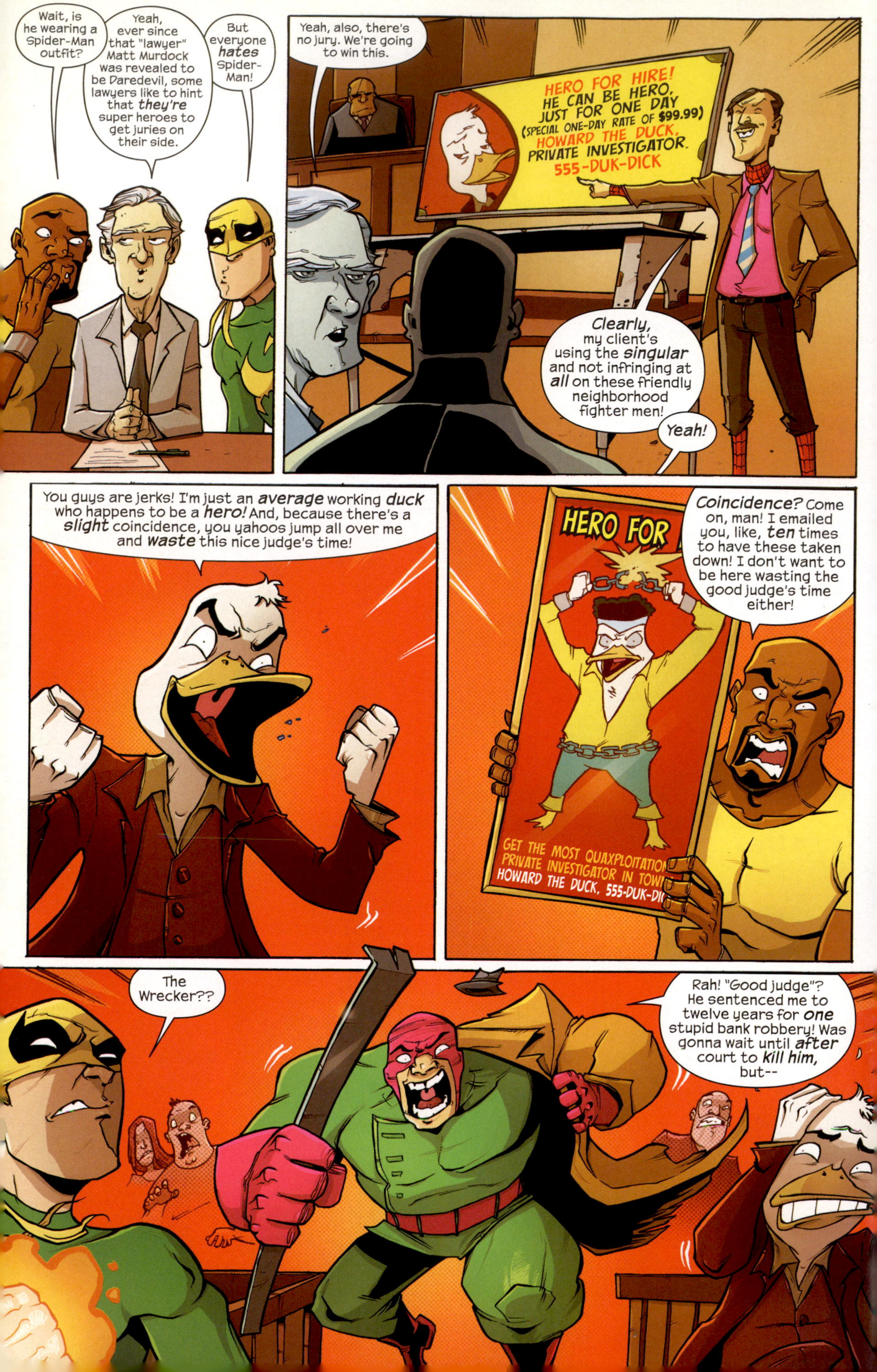

Wait, is he wearing a Spider-Man outfit?
Yeah, ever since that "lawyer" Matt Murdock was revealed to be Daredevil, some lawyers like to hint that *they're* super heroes to get juries on their side.
But everyone *hates* Spider-Man!
Yeah, also, there's no jury. We're going to win this.
HERO FOR HIRE! HE CAN BE HERO, JUST FOR ONE DAY (SPECIAL ONE-DAY RATE OF $99.99) HOWARD THE DUCK, PRIVATE INVESTIGATOR 555-DUK-DICK
Clearly, my client's using the *singular* and not infringing at *all* on these friendly neighborhood fighter men!
Yeah!
You guys are jerks! I'm just an *average* working *duck* who happens to be a *hero!* And, because there's a *slight* coincidence, you yahoos jump all over me and *waste* this nice judge's time!
HERO FOR
GET THE MOST QUAXPLOITATION PRIVATE INVESTIGATOR IN TOWN HOWARD THE DUCK, 555-DUK-DI
Coincidence? Come on, man! I emailed you, like, *ten* times to have these taken down! I don't want to be here wasting the good judge's time either!
The Wrecker??
Rah! "Good judge"? He sentenced me to twelve years for *one* stupid bank robbery! Was gonna wait until *after* court to *kill him,* but--

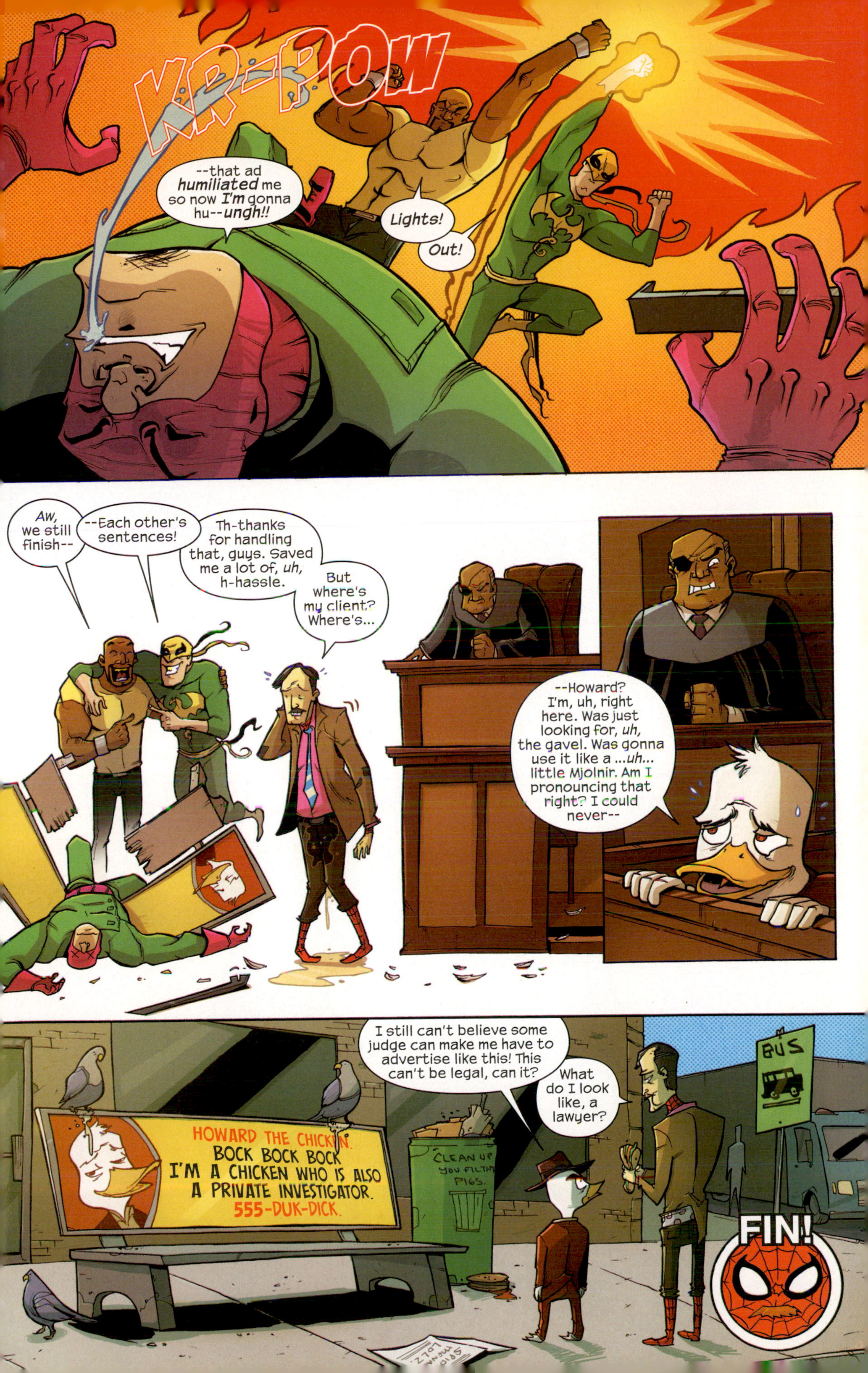

KR-POW
--that ad *humiliated* me so now *I'm* gonna hu--*ungh!!*
Lights!
Out!
Aw, we still finish--
--Each other's sentences!
Th-thanks for handling that, guys. Saved me a lot of, *uh,* h-hassle.
But where's my client? Where's...
--Howard? I'm, uh, right here. Was just looking for, *uh,* the gavel. Was gonna use it like a ...*uh...* little Mjolnir. Am I pronouncing that right? I could never--
HOWARD THE CHICKEN.
BOCK BOCK BOCK
I'M A CHICKEN WHO IS ALSO A PRIVATE INVESTIGATOR.
555-DUK-DICK
CLEAN UP YOU FILTHY PIGS.
I still can't believe some judge can make me have to advertise like this! This can't be legal, can it?
What do I look like, a lawyer?
BUS
FIN!

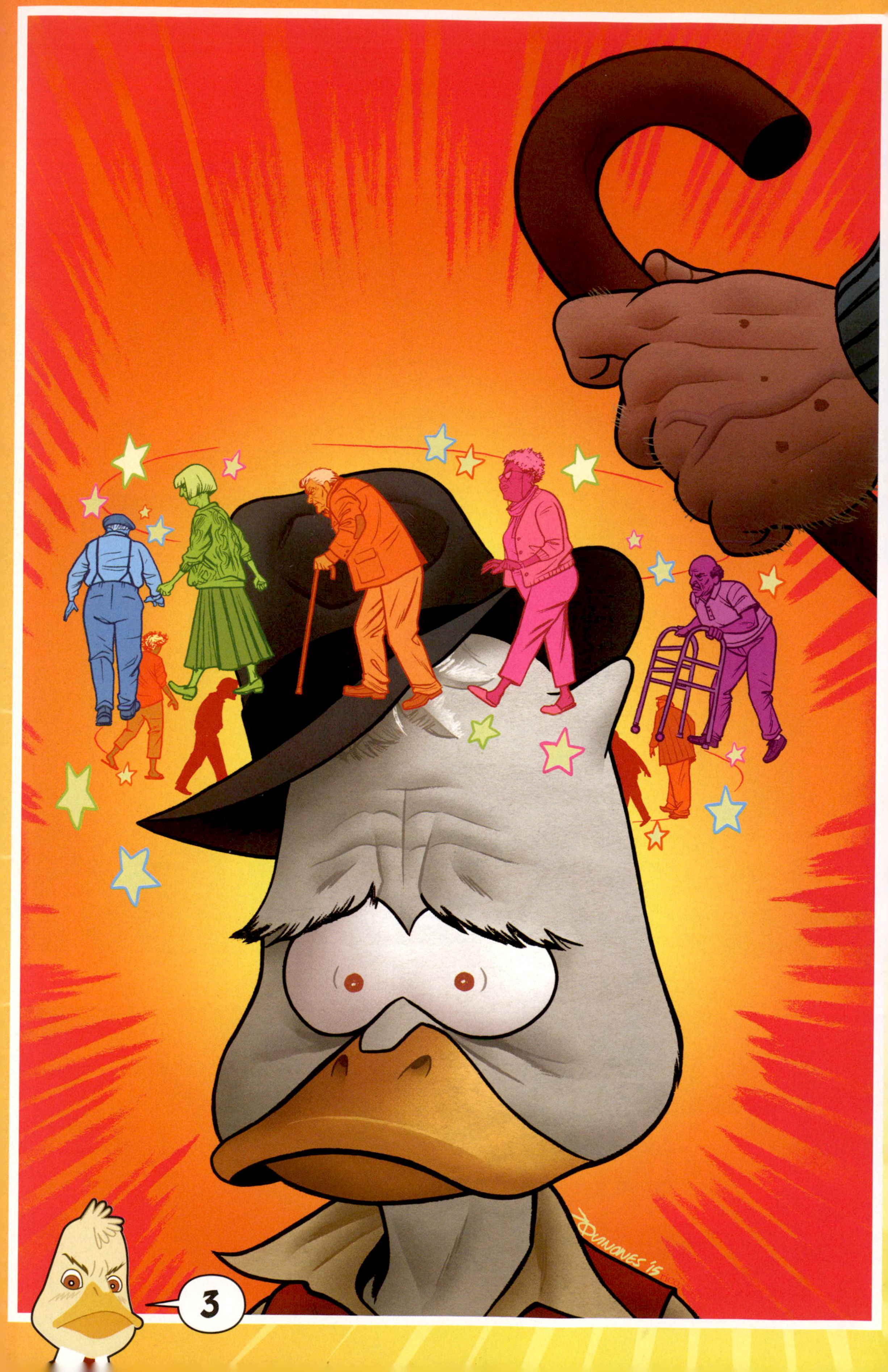
3

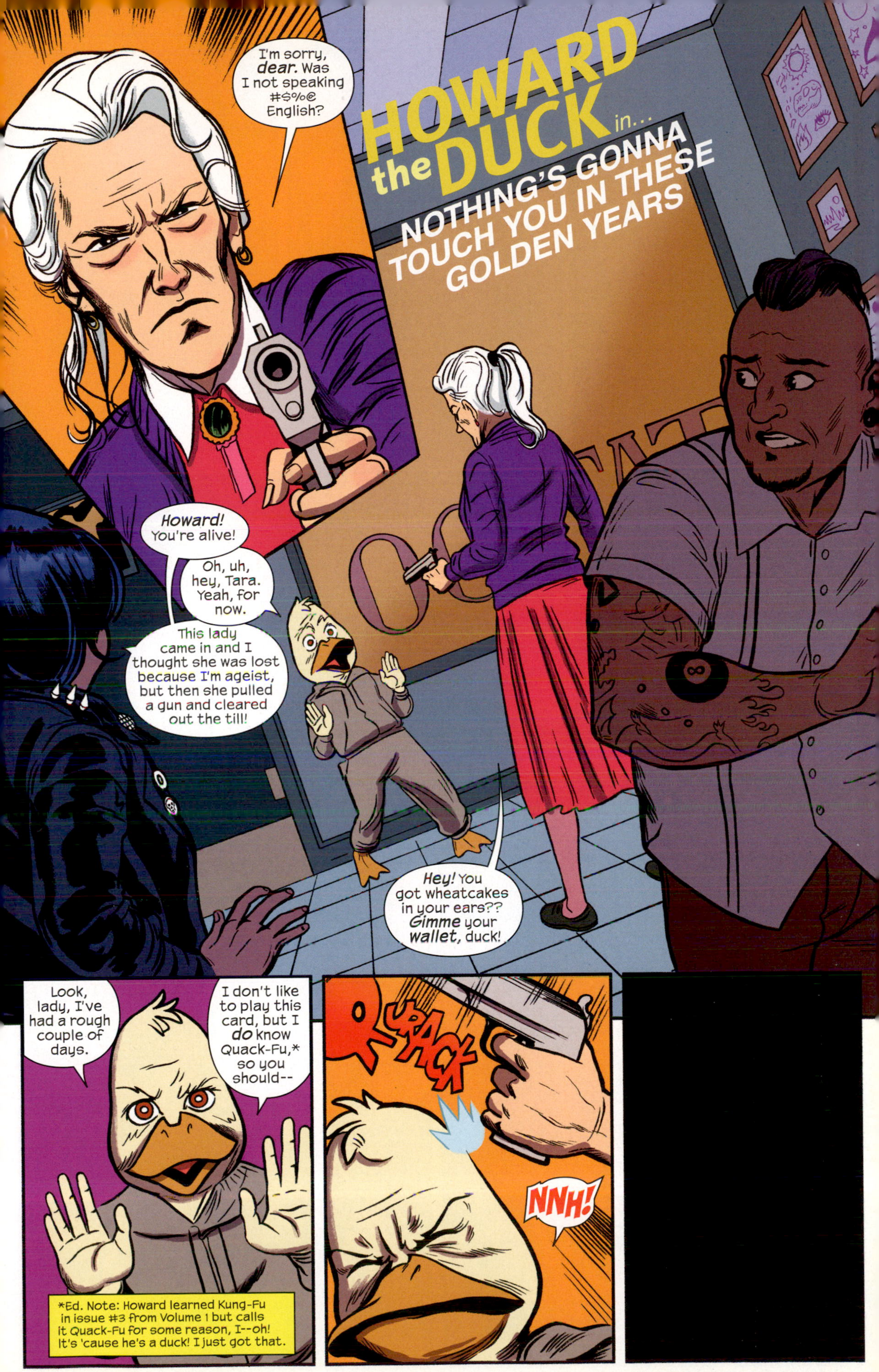

HOWARD the DUCK in...
NOTHING'S GONNA TOUCH YOU IN THESE GOLDEN YEARS
I'm sorry, dear. Was I not speaking #$%@ English?
Howard! You're alive!
Oh, uh, hey, Tara. Yeah, for now.
This lady came in and I thought she was lost because I'm ageist, but then she pulled a gun and cleared out the till!
Hey! You got wheatcakes in your ears?? Gimme your wallet, duck!
Look, lady, I've had a rough couple of days.
I don't like to play this card, but I do know Quack-Fu,* so you should--
*Ed. Note: Howard learned Kung-Fu in issue #3 from Volume 1 but calls it Quack-Fu for some reason, I--oh! It's 'cause he's a duck! I just got that.
QURACK
NNH!

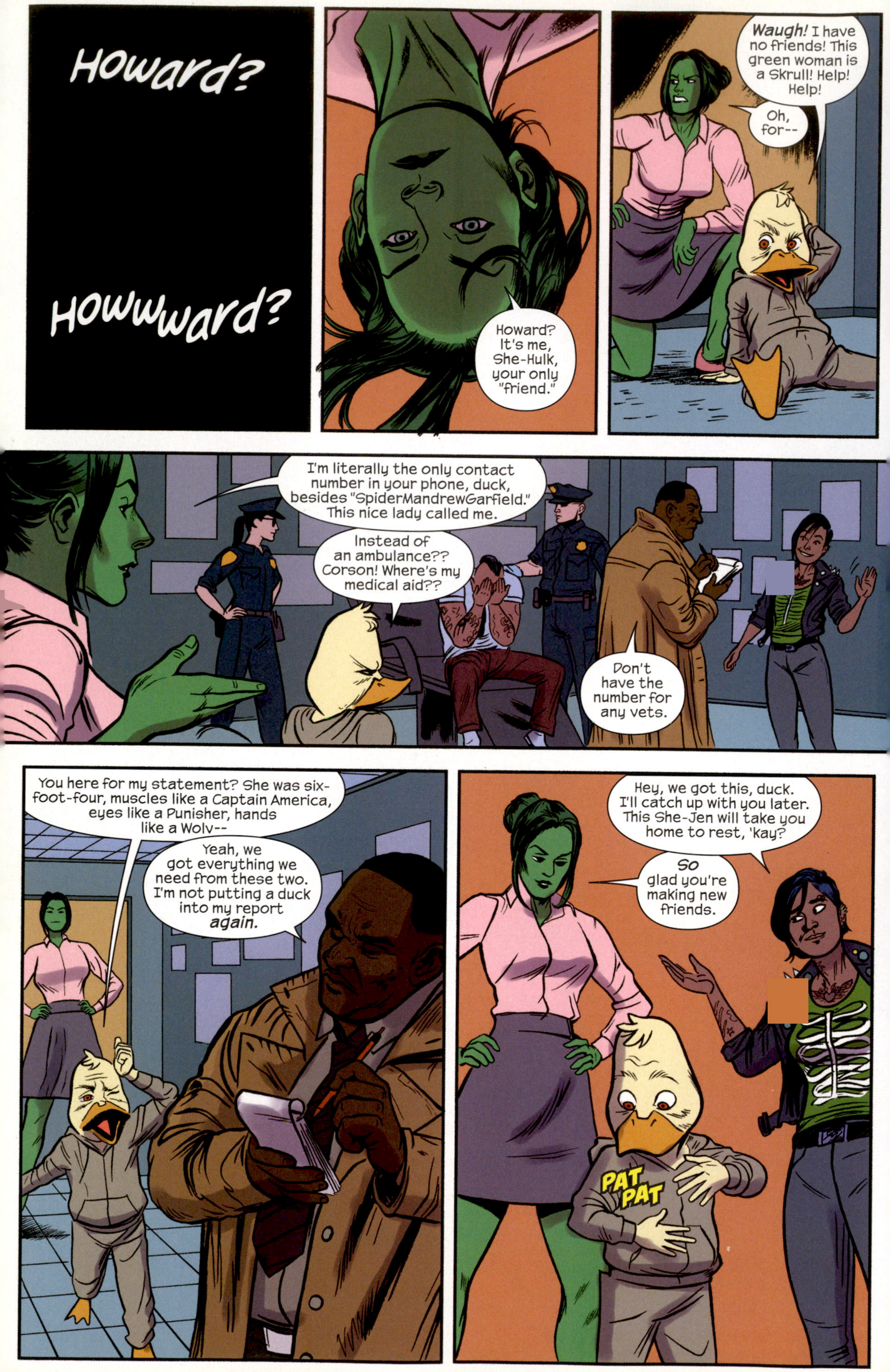
Howard?
Howwward?
Howard? It's me, She-Hulk, your only "friend."
Waugh! I have no friends! This green woman is a Skrull! Help! Help!
Oh, for--
I'm literally the only contact number in your phone, duck, besides "SpiderMandrewGarfield." This nice lady called me.
Instead of an ambulance?? Corson! Where's my medical aid??
Don't have the number for any vets.
You here for my statement? She was six-foot-four, muscles like a Captain America, eyes like a Punisher, hands like a Wolv--
Yeah, we got everything we need from these two. I'm not putting a duck into my report again.
Hey, we got this, duck. I'll catch up with you later. This She-Jen will take you home to rest, 'kay?
So glad you're making new friends.
PAT PAT

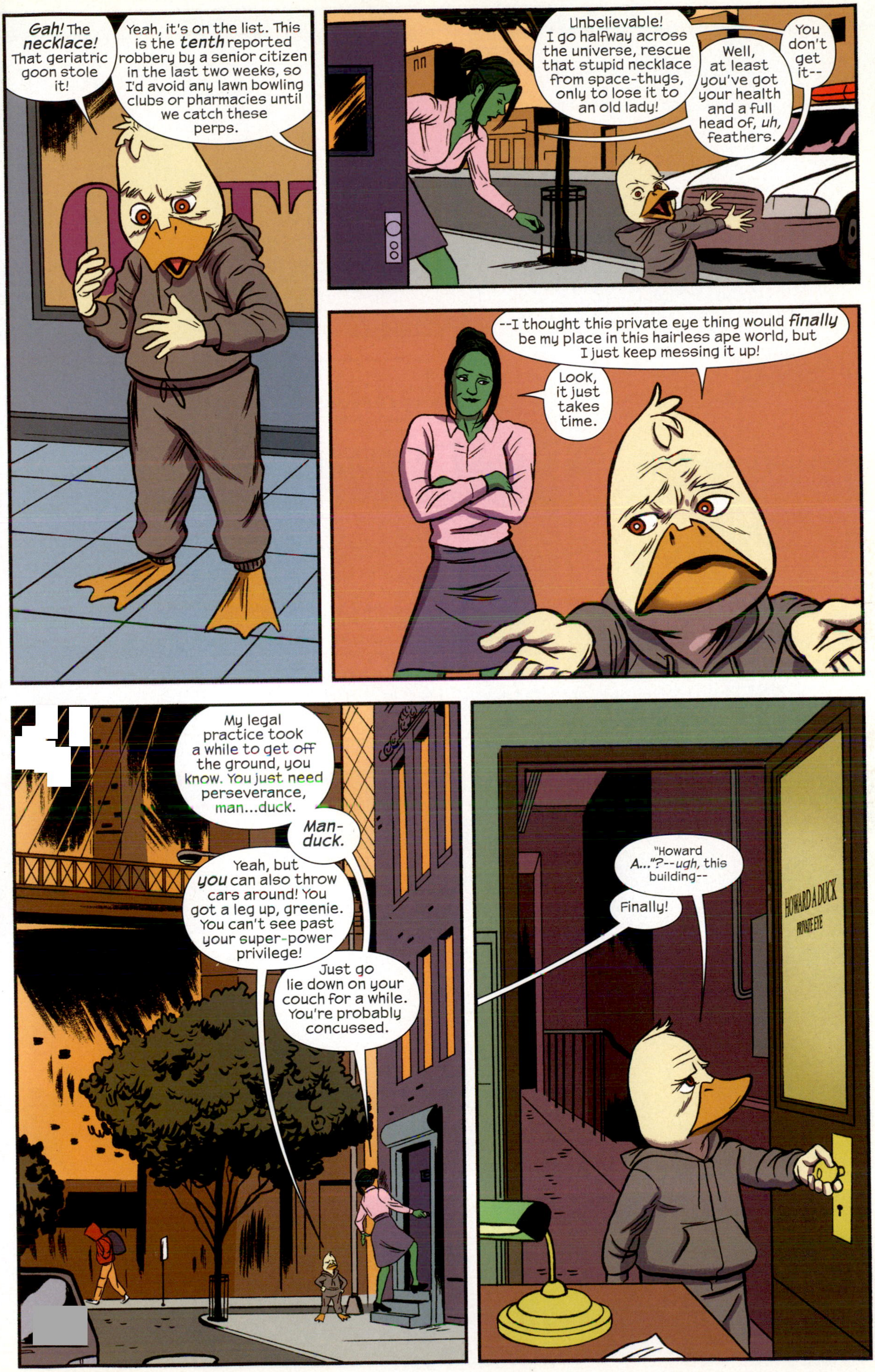

Gah! The *necklace!* That geriatric goon stole it!
Yeah, it's on the list. This is the *tenth* reported robbery by a senior citizen in the last two weeks, so I'd avoid any lawn bowling clubs or pharmacies until we catch these perps.
Unbelievable! I go halfway across the universe, rescue that stupid necklace from space-thugs, only to lose it to an old lady!
Well, at least you've got your health and a full head of, *uh,* feathers.
You don't get it--
--I thought this private eye thing would *finally* be my place in this hairless ape world, but I just keep messing it up!
Look, it just takes time.
My legal practice took a while to get off the ground, you know. You just need perseverance, man...duck.
Man-duck.
Yeah, but *you* can also throw cars around! You got a leg up, greenie. You can't see past your super-power privilege!
Just go lie down on your couch for a while. You're probably concussed.
"Howard A..."?--*ugh,* this building--
Finally!
HOWARD A DUCK
PRIVATE EYE

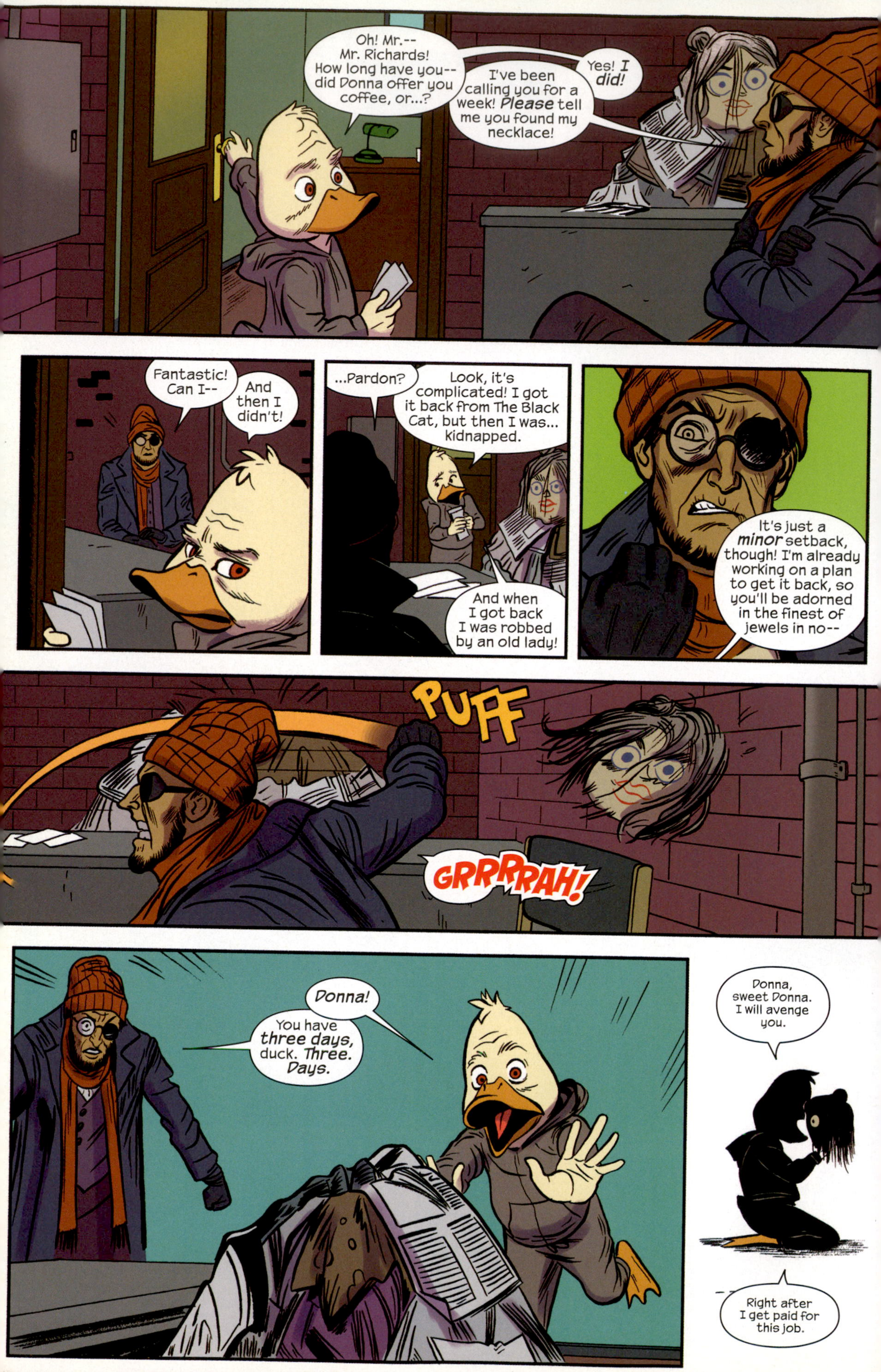

Oh! Mr.-- Mr. Richards! How long have you-- did Donna offer you coffee, or...?
Yes! I did!
I've been calling you for a week! Please tell me you found my necklace!
Fantastic! Can I--
And then I didn't!
...Pardon?
Look, it's complicated! I got it back from The Black Cat, but then I was... kidnapped.
And when I got back I was robbed by an old lady!
It's just a minor setback, though! I'm already working on a plan to get it back, so you'll be adorned in the finest of jewels in no--
PUFF
GRRRRAH!
Donna!
You have three days, duck. Three. Days.
Donna, sweet Donna. I will avenge you.
Right after I get paid for this job.

QUACK

Quack!

Quack!

Quack!
Quack!

Duck! Are you *still* doing this?

Shh! You'll blow my cover!

You've gained, like, five pounds in a week!

What? I've just been eating bread!

Bread makes you fat! I read it somewhere!

That's insa--*Waugh! It's her!*

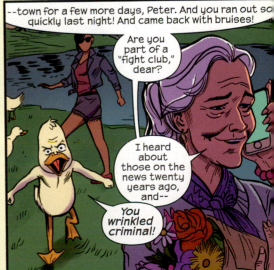

--town for a few more days, Peter. And you ran out so quickly last night! And came back with bruises!

Are you part of a "fight club," dear?

I heard about those on the news twenty years ago, and--

You wrinkled criminal!

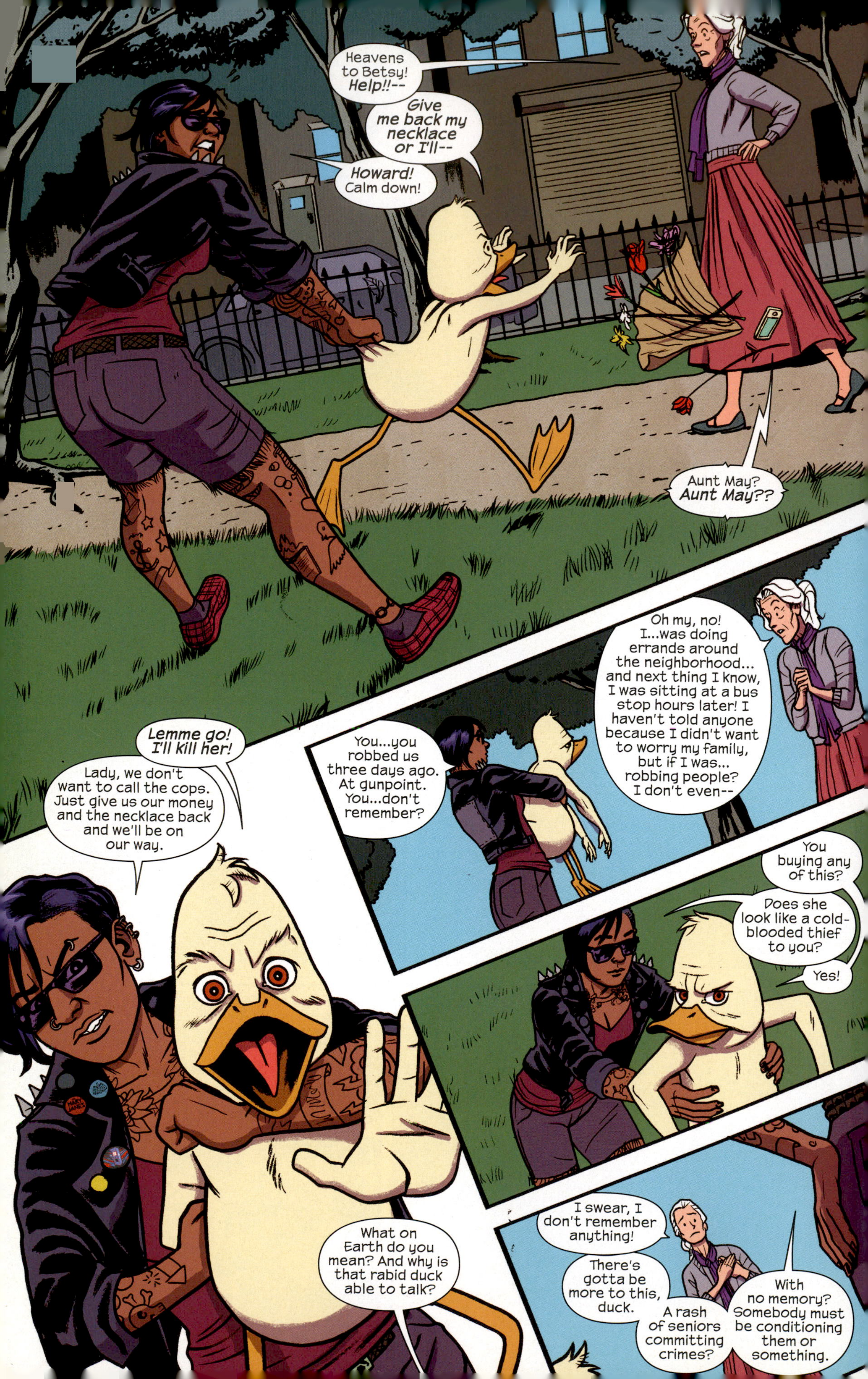
Heavens to Betsy! Help!!--
Give me back my necklace or I'll--
Howard! Calm down!
Aunt May? Aunt May??
Lemme go! I'll kill her!
Lady, we don't want to call the cops. Just give us our money and the necklace back and we'll be on our way.
What on Earth do you mean? And why is that rabid duck able to talk?
You...you robbed us three days ago. At gunpoint. You...don't remember?
Oh my, no! I...was doing errands around the neighborhood... and next thing I know, I was sitting at a bus stop hours later! I haven't told anyone because I didn't want to worry my family, but if I was... robbing people? I don't even--
You buying any of this?
Does she look like a cold-blooded thief to you?
Yes!
I swear, I don't remember anything!
There's gotta be more to this, duck.
A rash of seniors committing crimes?
With no memory? Somebody must be conditioning them or something.

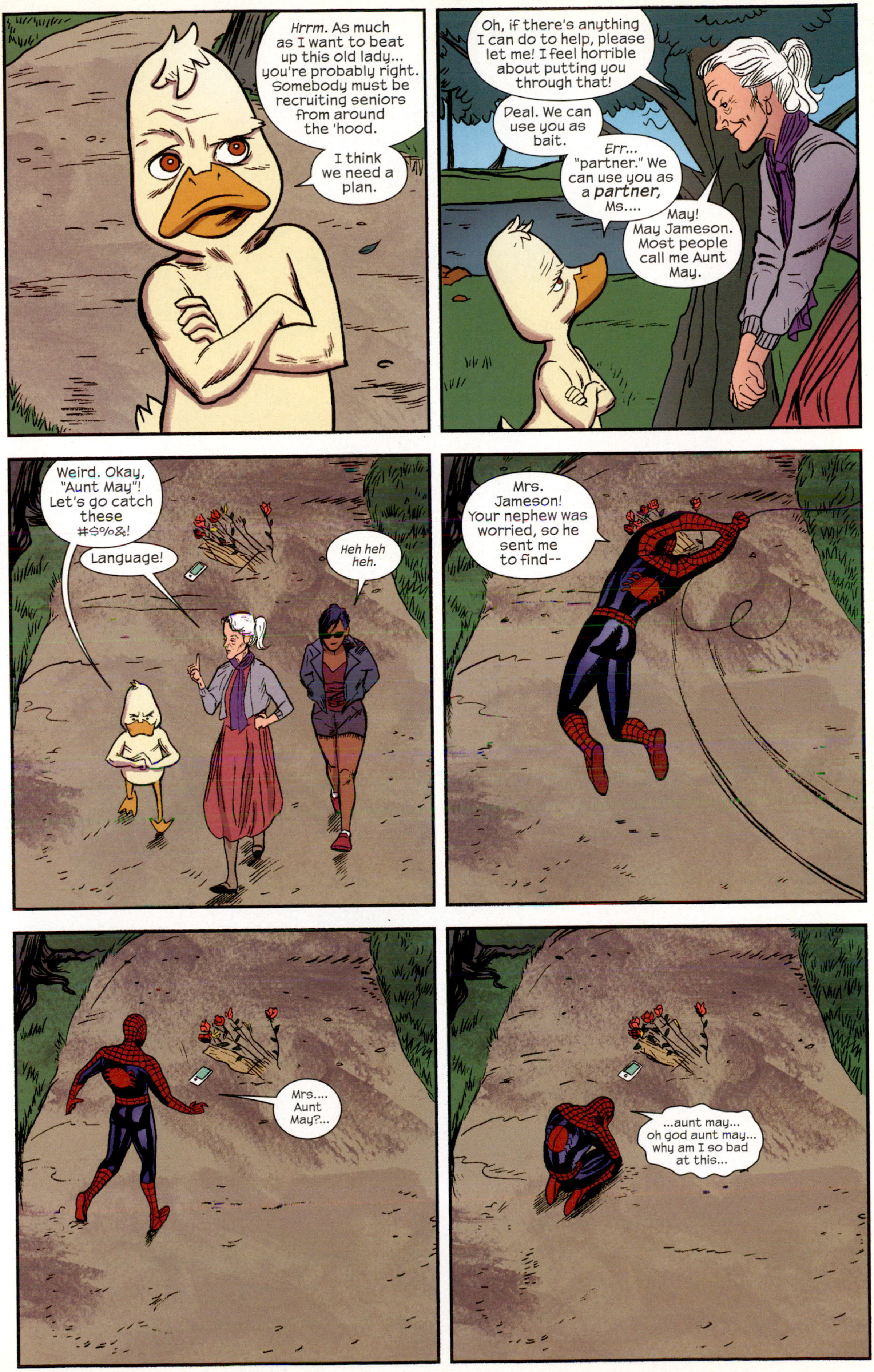
Hrrm. As much as I want to beat up this old lady... you're probably right. Somebody must be recruiting seniors from around the 'hood.
I think we need a plan.
Oh, if there's anything I can do to help, please let me! I feel horrible about putting you through that!
Deal. We can use you as bait.
Err... "partner." We can use you as a partner, Ms....
May! May Jameson. Most people call me Aunt May.
Weird. Okay, "Aunt May"! Let's go catch these #$%&!
Language!
Heh heh heh.
Mrs. Jameson! Your nephew was worried, so he sent me to find--
Mrs.... Aunt May?...
...aunt may... oh god aunt may... why am I so bad at this...

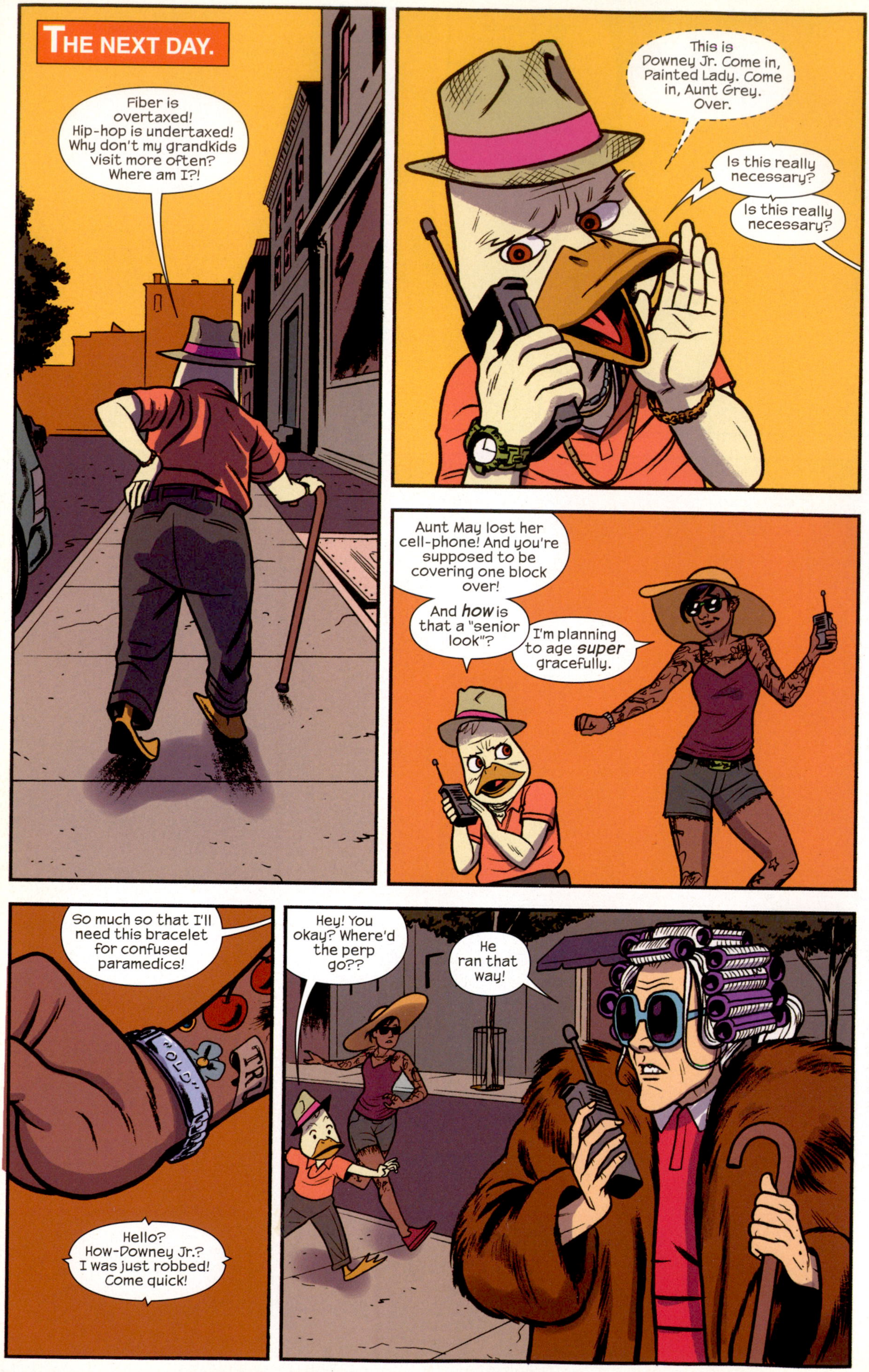
THE NEXT DAY.
Fiber is overtaxed! Hip-hop is undertaxed! Why don't my grandkids visit more often? Where am I?!
This is Downey Jr. Come in, Painted Lady. Come in, Aunt Grey. Over.
Is this really necessary?
Is this really necessary?
Aunt May lost her cell-phone! And you're supposed to be covering one block over!
And how is that a "senior look"?
I'm planning to age super gracefully.
So much so that I'll need this bracelet for confused paramedics!
Hello? How-Downey Jr.? I was just robbed! Come quick!
Hey! You okay? Where'd the perp go??
He ran that way!

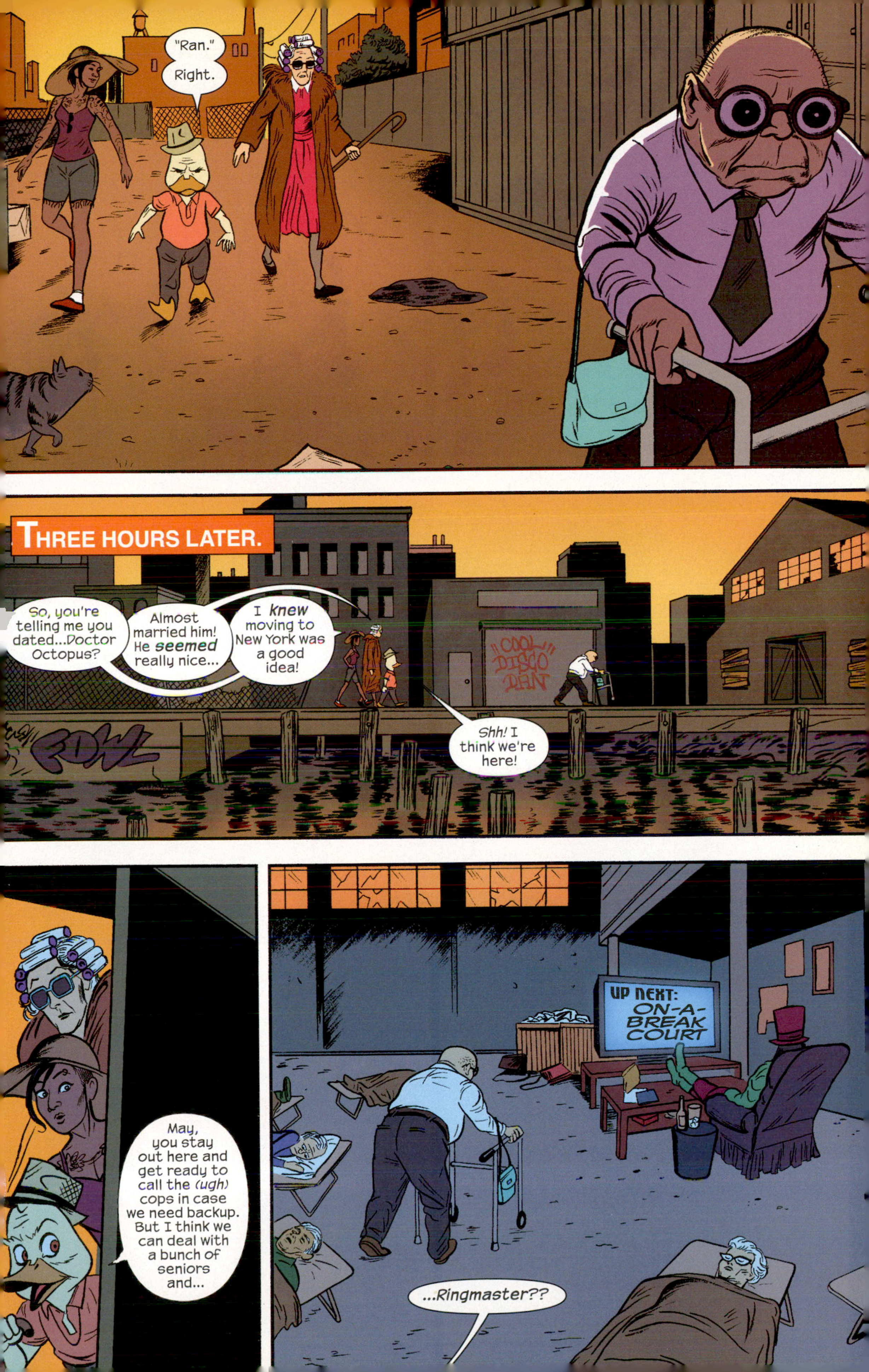
"Ran."
Right.
THREE HOURS LATER.
So, you're telling me you dated...Doctor Octopus?
Almost married him! He *seemed* really nice...
I *knew* moving to New York was a good idea!
COOL DISCO DAN
Shh! I think we're here!
UP NEXT: ON-A-BREAK COURT
May, you stay out here and get ready to call the *(ugh)* cops in case we need backup. But I think we can deal with a bunch of seniors and...
...Ringmaster??

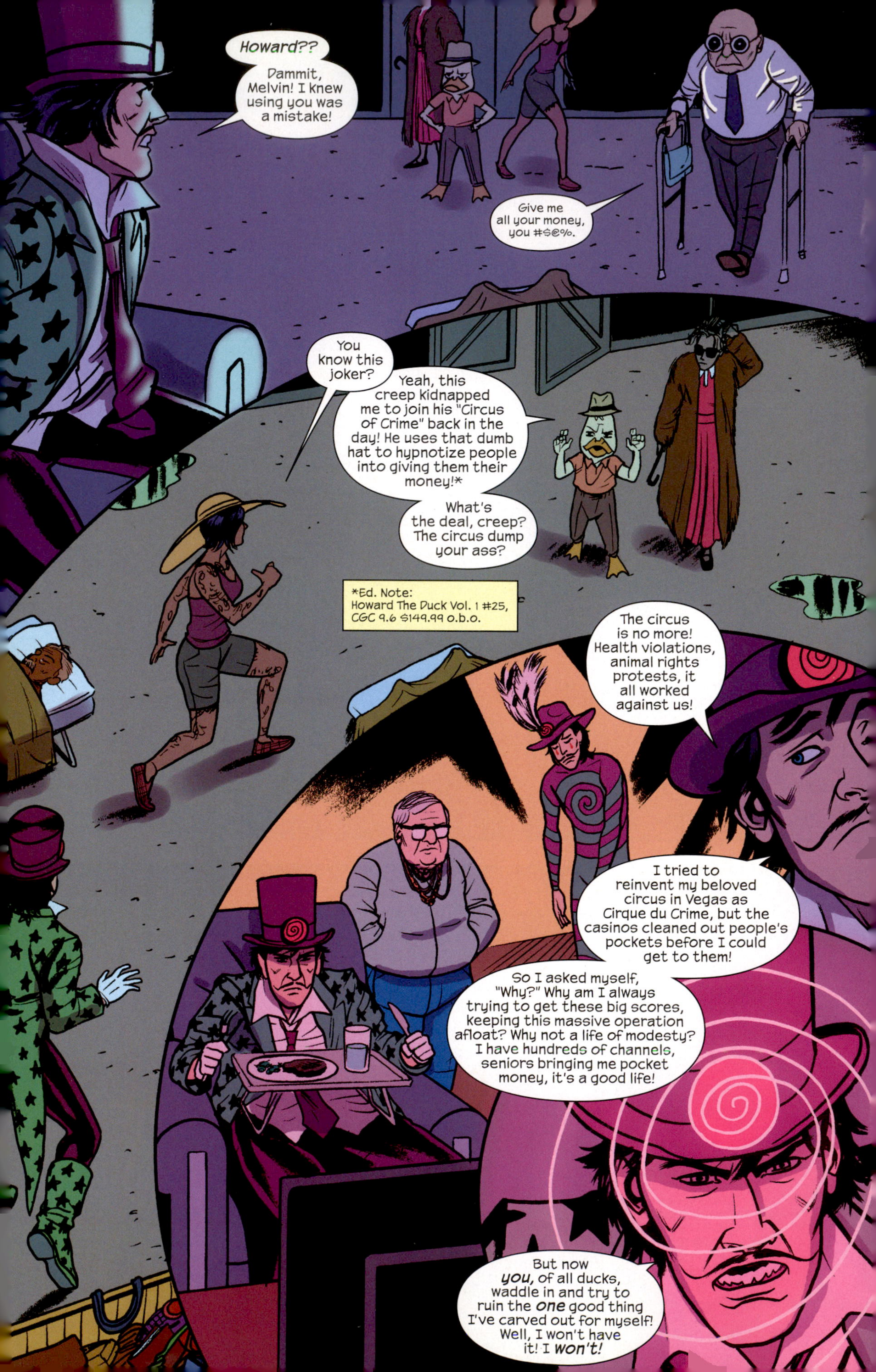
Howard??
Dammit, Melvin! I knew using you was a mistake!
Give me all your money, you #$@%.
You know this joker?
Yeah, this creep kidnapped me to join his "Circus of Crime" back in the day! He uses that dumb hat to hypnotize people into giving them their money!*
What's the deal, creep? The circus dump your ass?
*Ed. Note: Howard The Duck Vol. 1 #25, CGC 9.6 $149.99 o.b.o.
The circus is no more! Health violations, animal rights protests, it all worked against us!
I tried to reinvent my beloved circus in Vegas as Cirque du Crime, but the casinos cleaned out people's pockets before I could get to them!
So I asked myself, "Why?" Why am I always trying to get these big scores, keeping this massive operation afloat? Why not a life of modesty? I have hundreds of channels, seniors bringing me pocket money, it's a good life!
But now ***you,*** of all ducks, waddle in and try to ruin the ***one*** good thing I've carved out for myself! Well, I won't have it! I ***won't!***

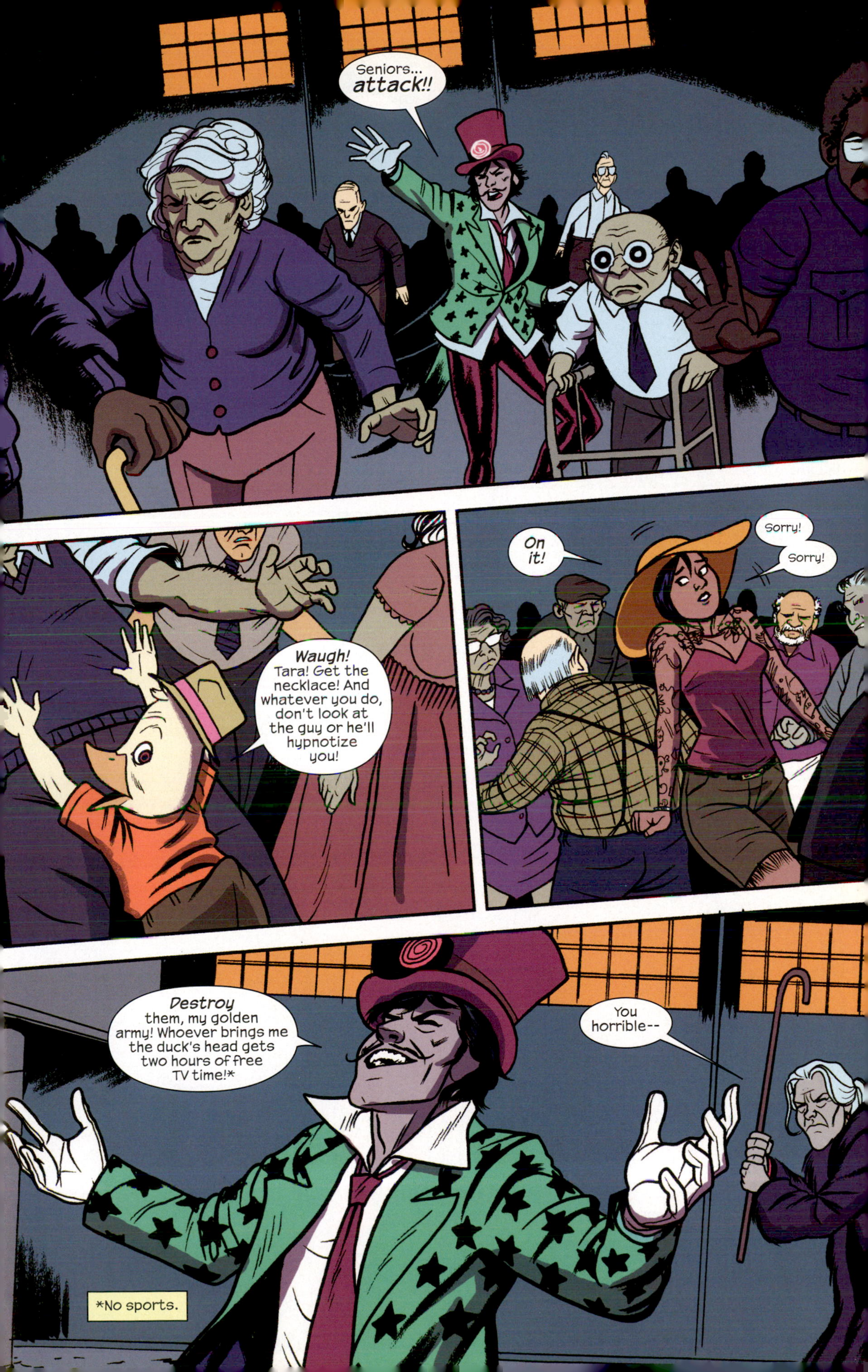
Seniors... *attack!!*
Waugh! Tara! Get the necklace! And whatever you do, don't look at the guy or he'll hypnotize you!
On it!
Sorry!
Sorry!
Destroy them, my golden army! Whoever brings me the duck's head gets two hours of free TV time!*
You horrible--
*No sports.

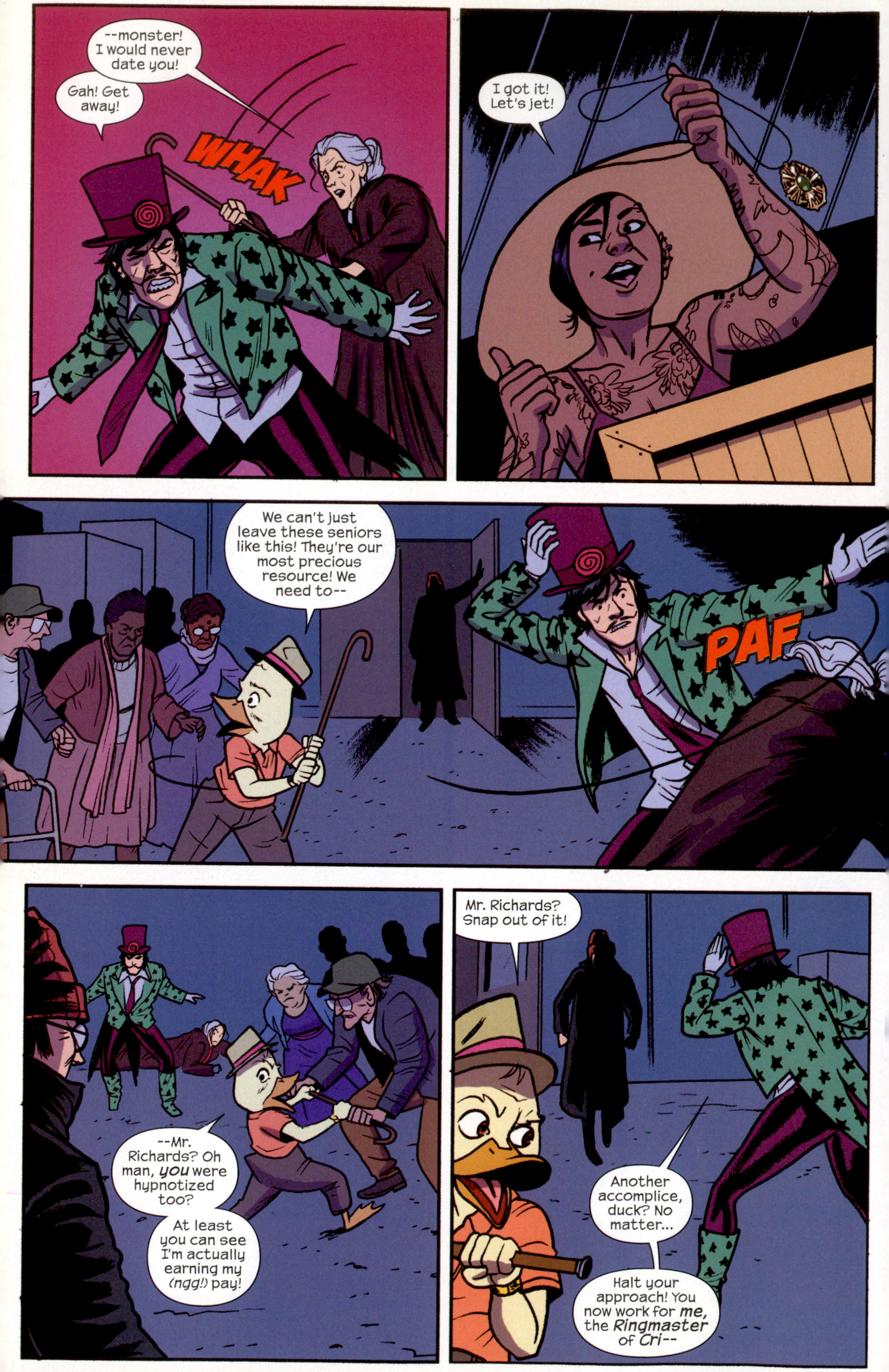

--monster! I would never date you!
Gah! Get away!
WHAK
I got it! Let's jet!
We can't just leave these seniors like this! They're our most precious resource! We need to--
PAF
--Mr. Richards? Oh man, *you* were hypnotized too?
At least you can see I'm actually earning my *(ngg!)* pay!
Mr. Richards? Snap out of it!
Another accomplice, duck? No matter...
Halt your approach! You now work for **me**, the ***Ringmaster*** of ***Cri***--

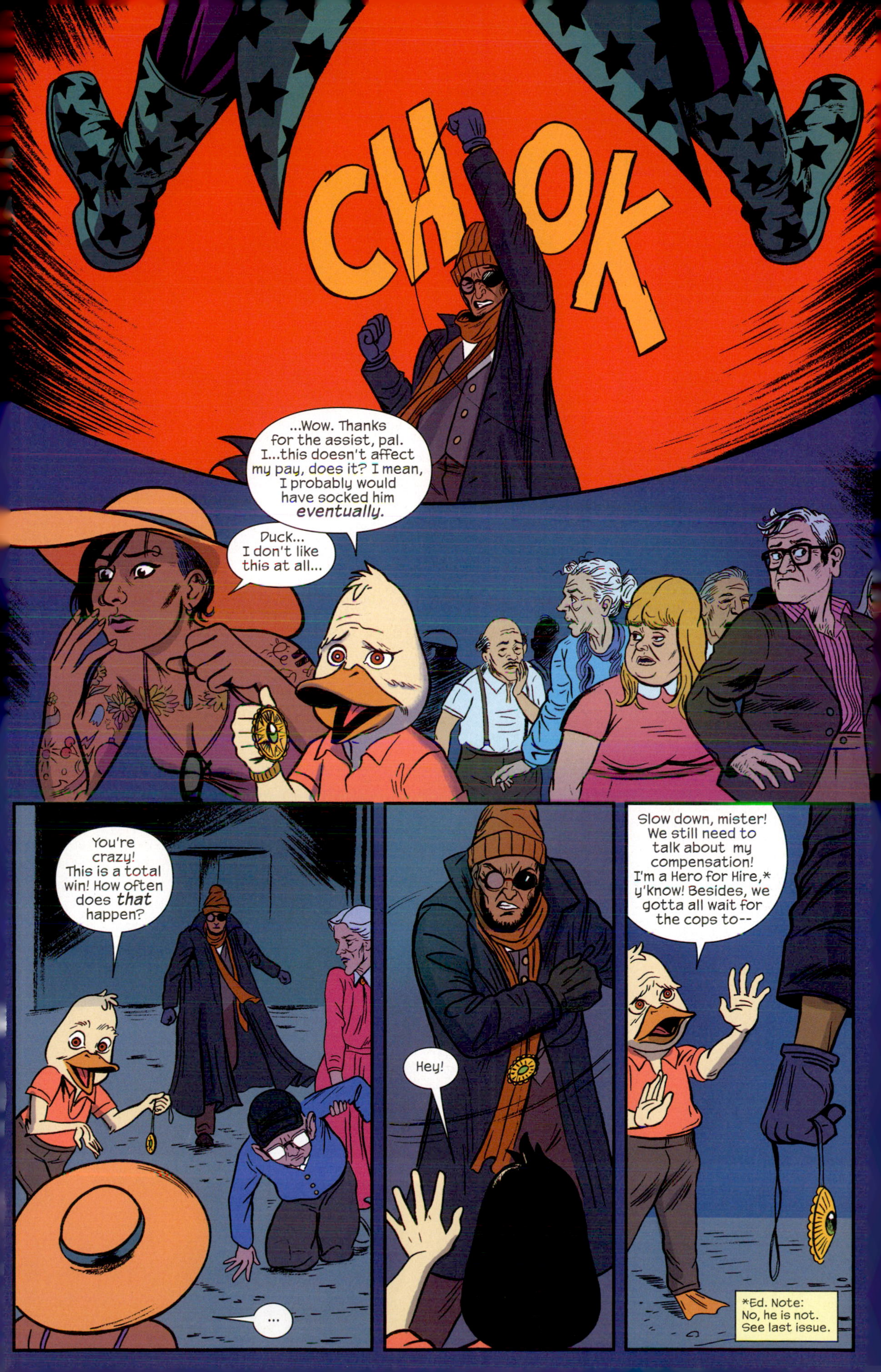
CHOOK
...Wow. Thanks for the assist, pal. I...this doesn't affect my pay, does it? I mean, I probably would have socked him *eventually*.
Duck... I don't like this at all...
You're crazy! This is a total win! How often does *that* happen?
...
Hey!
Slow down, mister! We still need to talk about my compensation! I'm a Hero for Hire,* y'know! Besides, we gotta all wait for the cops to--
*Ed. Note: No, he is not. See last issue.

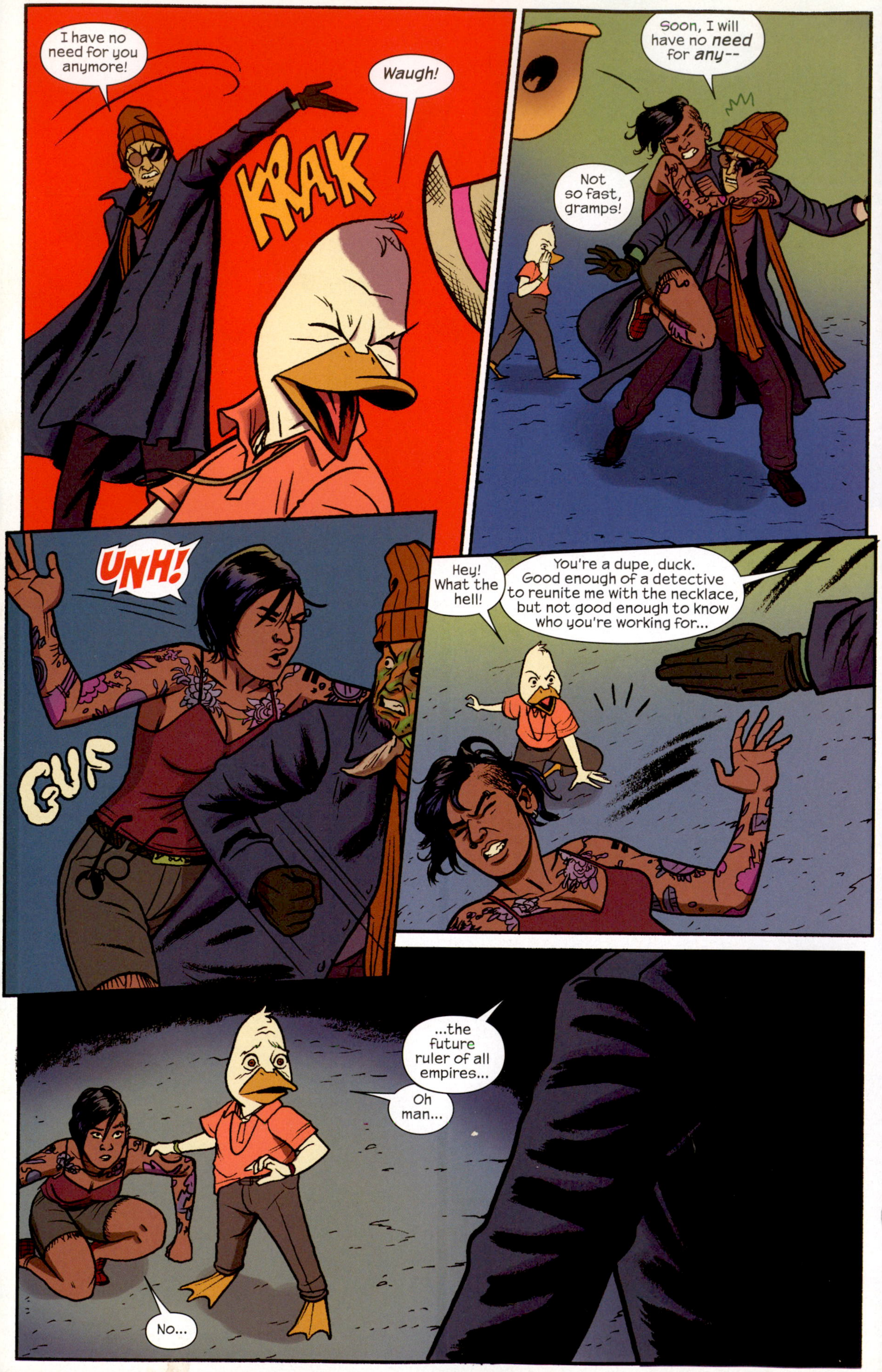
I have no need for you anymore!
KRAK
Waugh!
Soon, I will have no *need* for *any*--
Not so fast, gramps!
UNH!
GUF
Hey! What the hell!
You're a dupe, duck. Good enough of a detective to reunite me with the necklace, but not good enough to know who you're working for...
...the future ruler of all empires...
Oh man...
No...

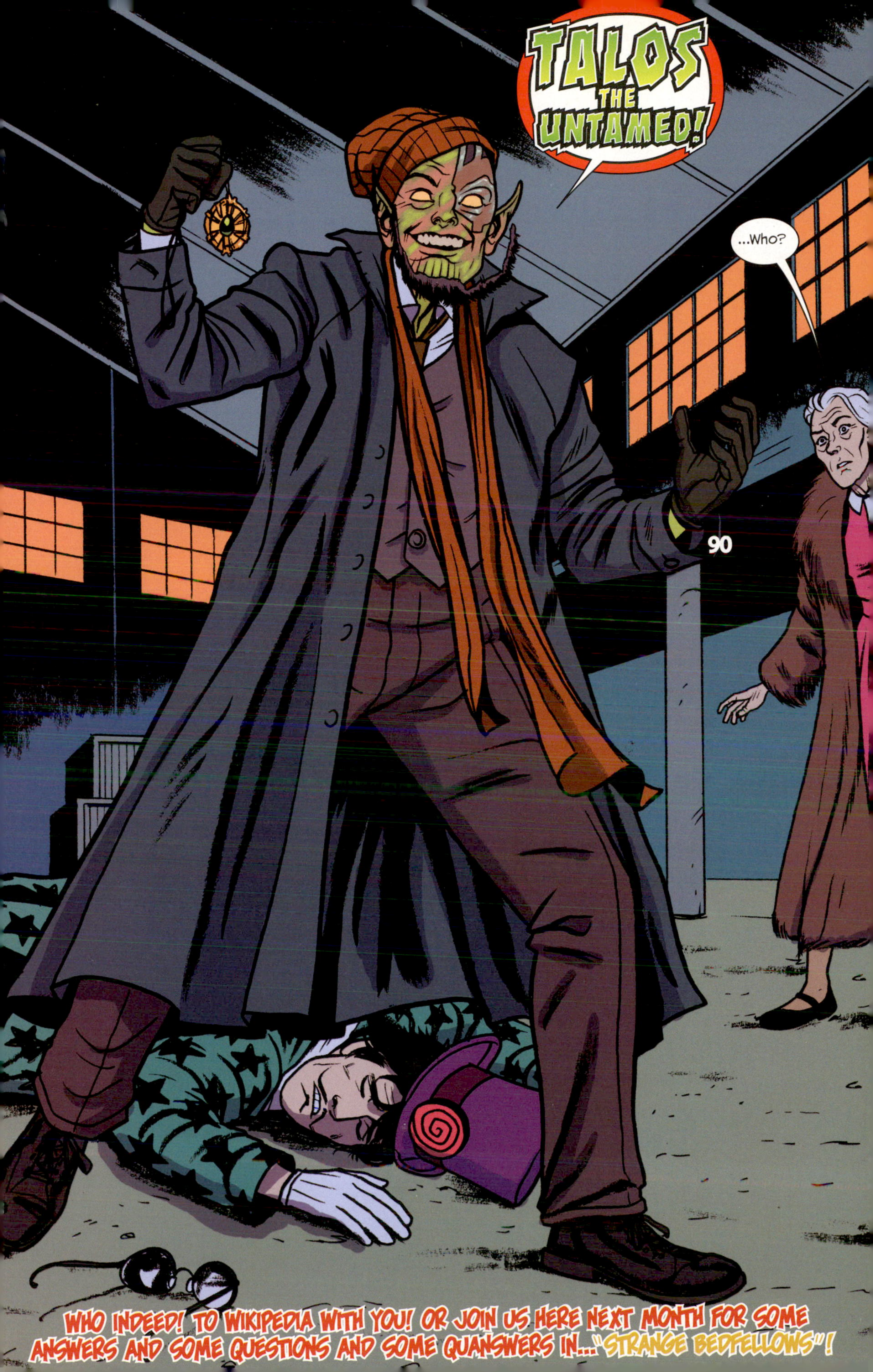
TALOS THE UNTAMED!
...Who?
WHO INDEED! TO WIKIPEDIA WITH YOU! OR JOIN US HERE NEXT MONTH FOR SOME ANSWERS AND SOME QUESTIONS AND SOME QUANSWERS IN..."STRANGE BEDFELLOWS"!

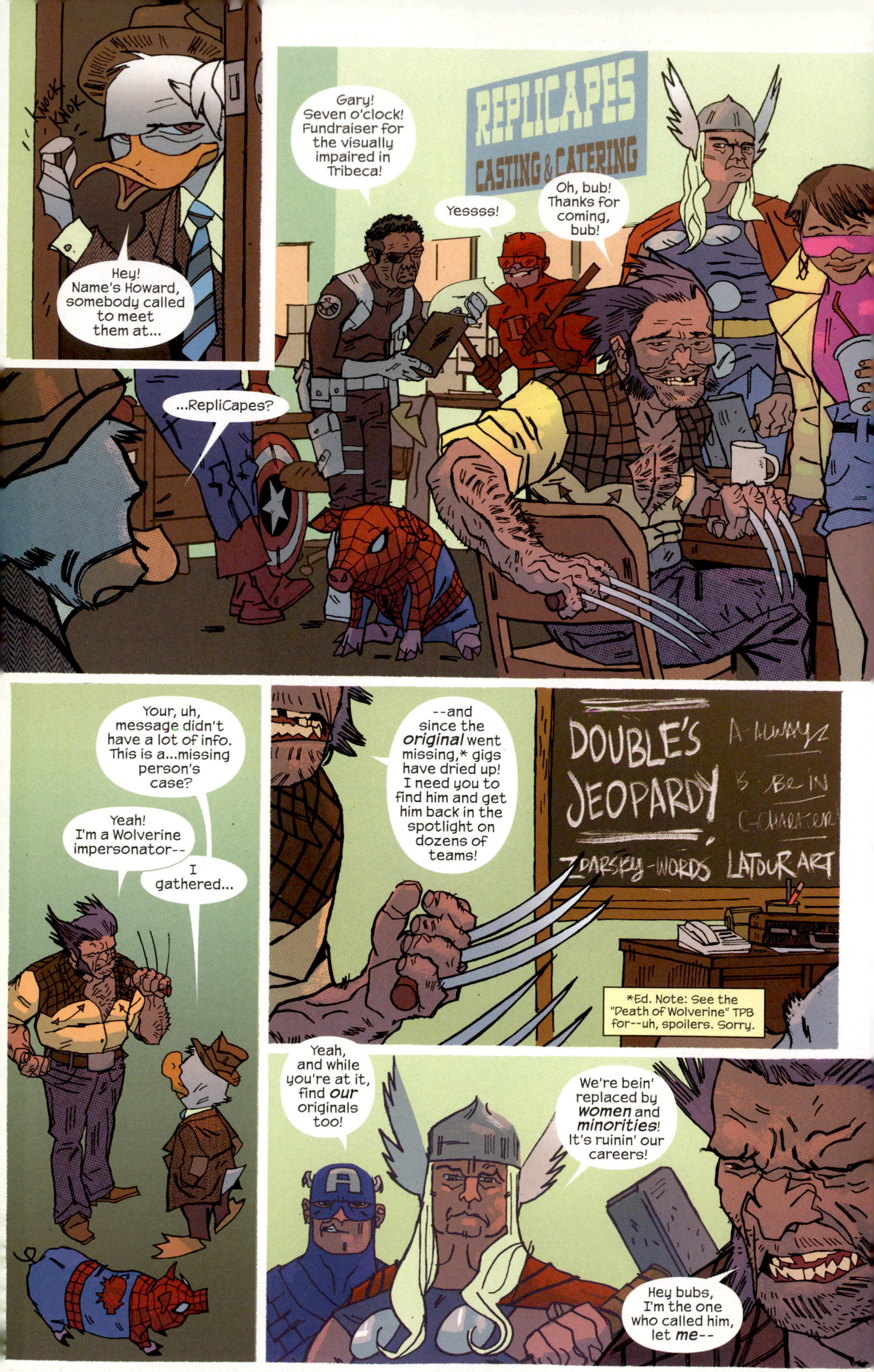
KNOCK KNOCK
Hey! Name's Howard, somebody called to meet them at...
REPLICAPES
CASTING & CATERING
Gary! Seven o'clock! Fundraiser for the visually impaired in Tribeca!
Yessss!
Oh, bub! Thanks for coming, bub!
...RepliCapes?
Your, uh, message didn't have a lot of info. This is a...missing person's case?
Yeah! I'm a Wolverine impersonator--
I gathered...
--and since the *original* went missing,* gigs have dried up! I need you to find him and get him back in the spotlight on dozens of teams!
DOUBLE'S JEOPARDY
ZDARSKY-WORDS LATOUR ART
*Ed. Note: See the "Death of Wolverine" TPB for--uh, spoilers. Sorry.
Yeah, and while you're at it, find *our* originals too!
We're bein' replaced by ***women*** and ***minorities***! It's ruinin' our careers!
Hey bubs, I'm the one who called him, let *me*--

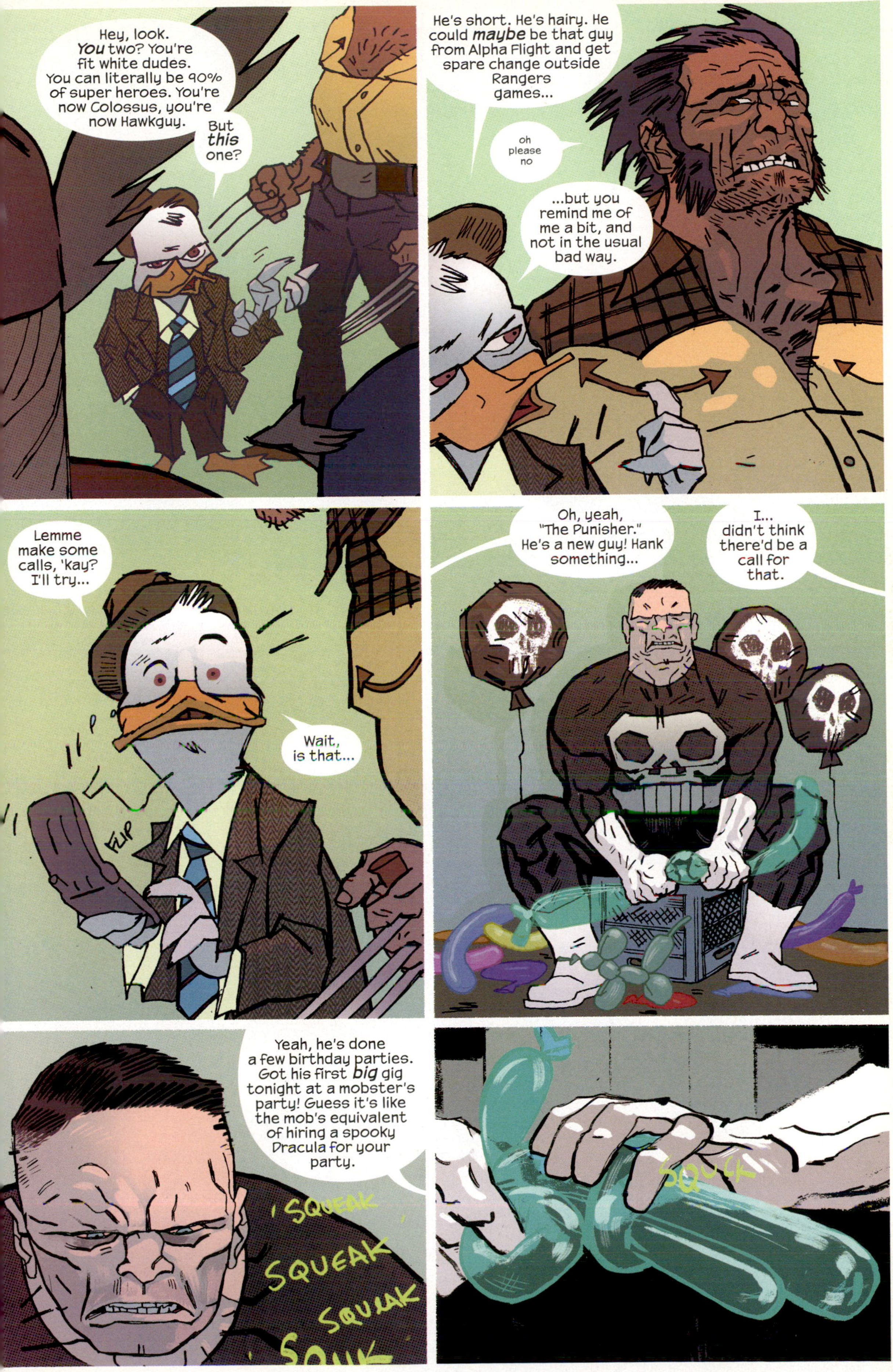

Hey, look. *You* two? You're fit white dudes. You can literally be 90% of super heroes. You're now Colossus, you're now Hawkguy.
But *this* one?
He's short. He's hairy. He could *maybe* be that guy from Alpha Flight and get spare change outside Rangers games...
oh please no
...but you remind me of me a bit, and not in the usual bad way.
Lemme make some calls, 'kay? I'll try...
FLIP
Wait, is that...
Oh, yeah, "The Punisher." He's a new guy! Hank something...
I... didn't think there'd be a call for that.
Yeah, he's done a few birthday parties. Got his first *big* gig tonight at a mobster's party! Guess it's like the mob's equivalent of hiring a spooky Dracula for your party.
SQUEAK
SQUEAK
SQUAK
SQUCK

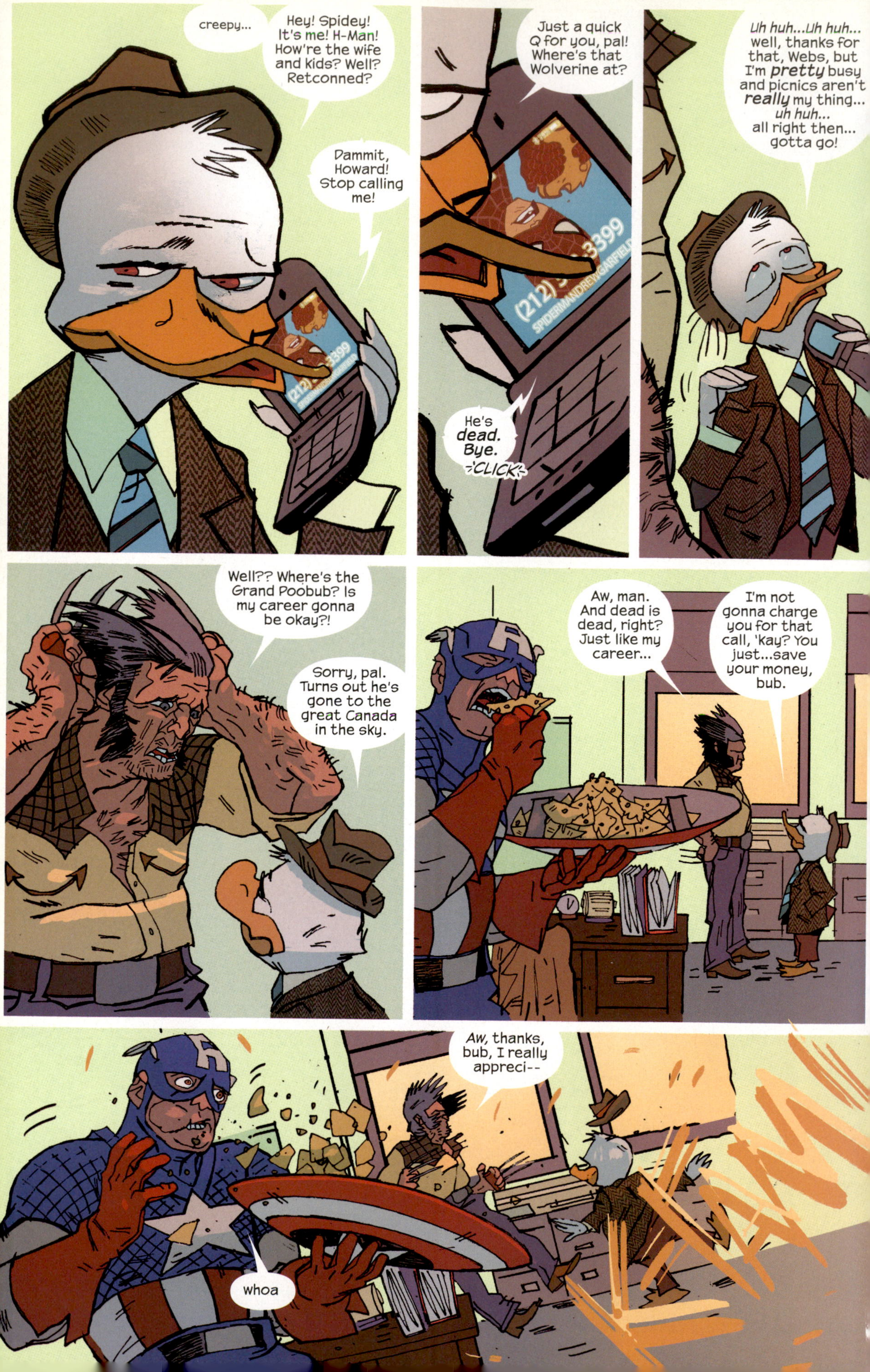
creepy...
Hey! Spidey! It's me! H-Man! How're the wife and kids? Well? Retconned?
Dammit, Howard! Stop calling me!
Just a quick Q for you, pal! Where's that Wolverine at?
He's dead. Bye.
CLICK
Uh huh...Uh huh... well, thanks for that, Webs, but I'm pretty busy and picnics aren't really my thing... uh huh... all right then... gotta go!
Well?? Where's the Grand Poobub? Is my career gonna be okay?!
Sorry, pal. Turns out he's gone to the great Canada in the sky.
Aw, man. And dead is dead, right? Just like my career...
I'm not gonna charge you for that call, 'kay? You just...save your money, bub.
Aw, thanks, bub, I really appreci--
whoa

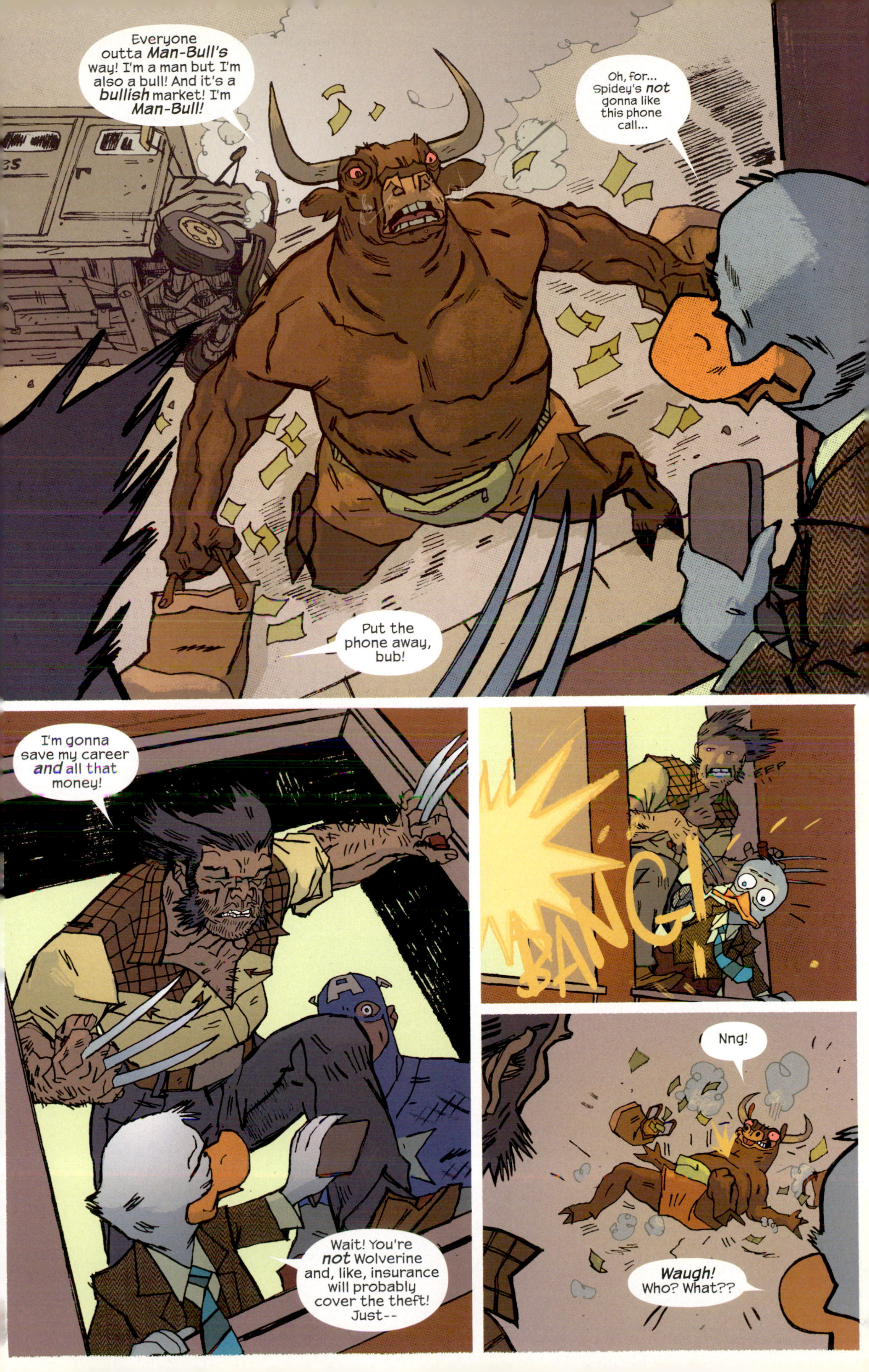
Everyone outta *Man-Bull's* way! I'm a man but I'm also a bull! And it's a **bullish** market! I'm *Man-Bull!*
Oh, for... Spidey's *not* gonna like this phone call...
Put the phone away, bub!
I'm gonna save my career *and* all that money!
Wait! You're *not* Wolverine and, like, insurance will probably cover the theft! Just--
BANG!
Nng!
Waugh! Who? What??

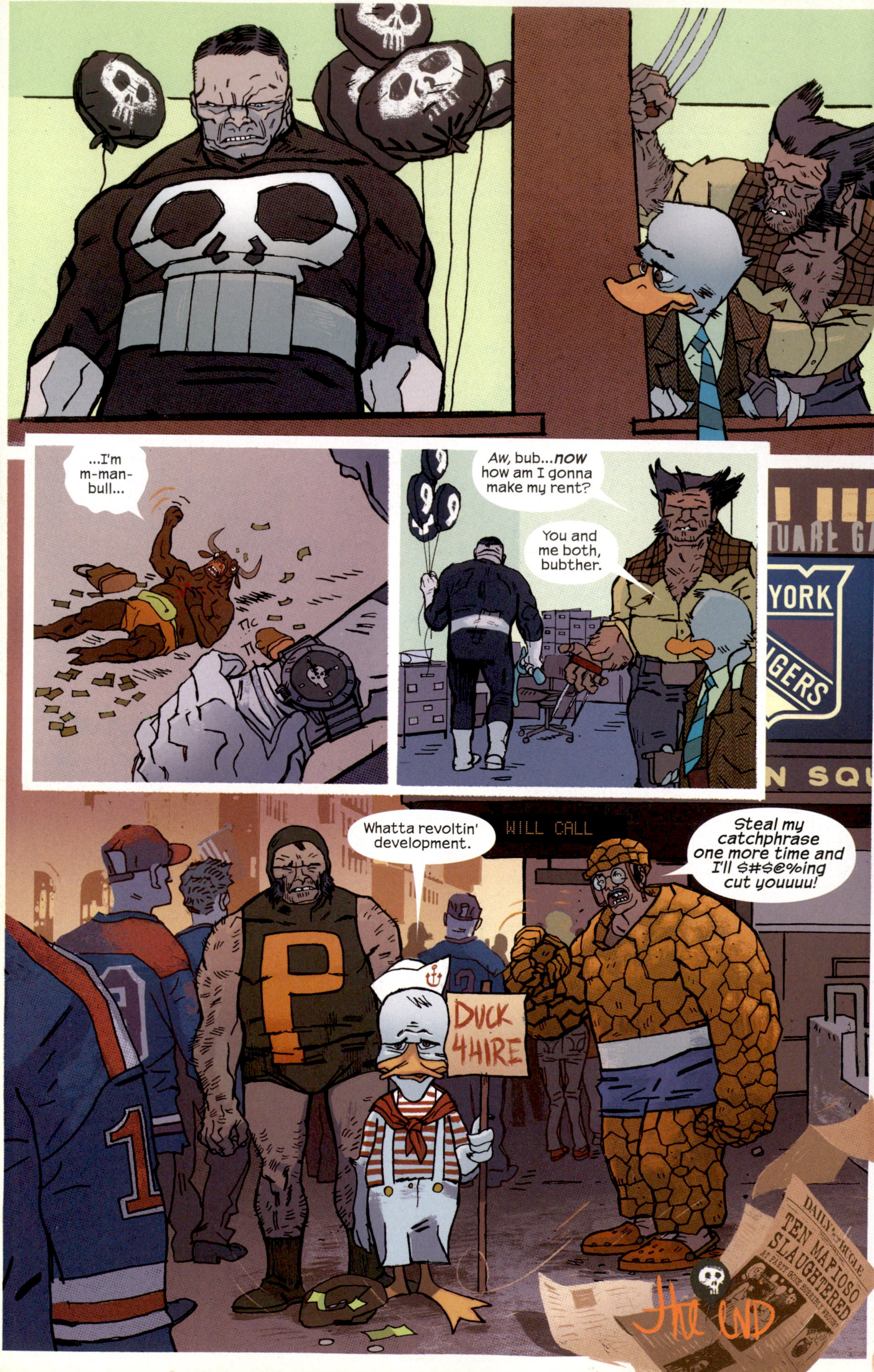
...I'm m-man-bull...
TIC
Aw, bub...now how am I gonna make my rent?
You and me both, bubther.
YORK
NGERS
WILL CALL
Whatta revoltin' development.
Steal my catchphrase one more time and I'll $#$@%ing cut youuuu!
DUCK 4HIRE
DAILY BUGLE
TEN MAFIOSO SLAUGHTERED
The End

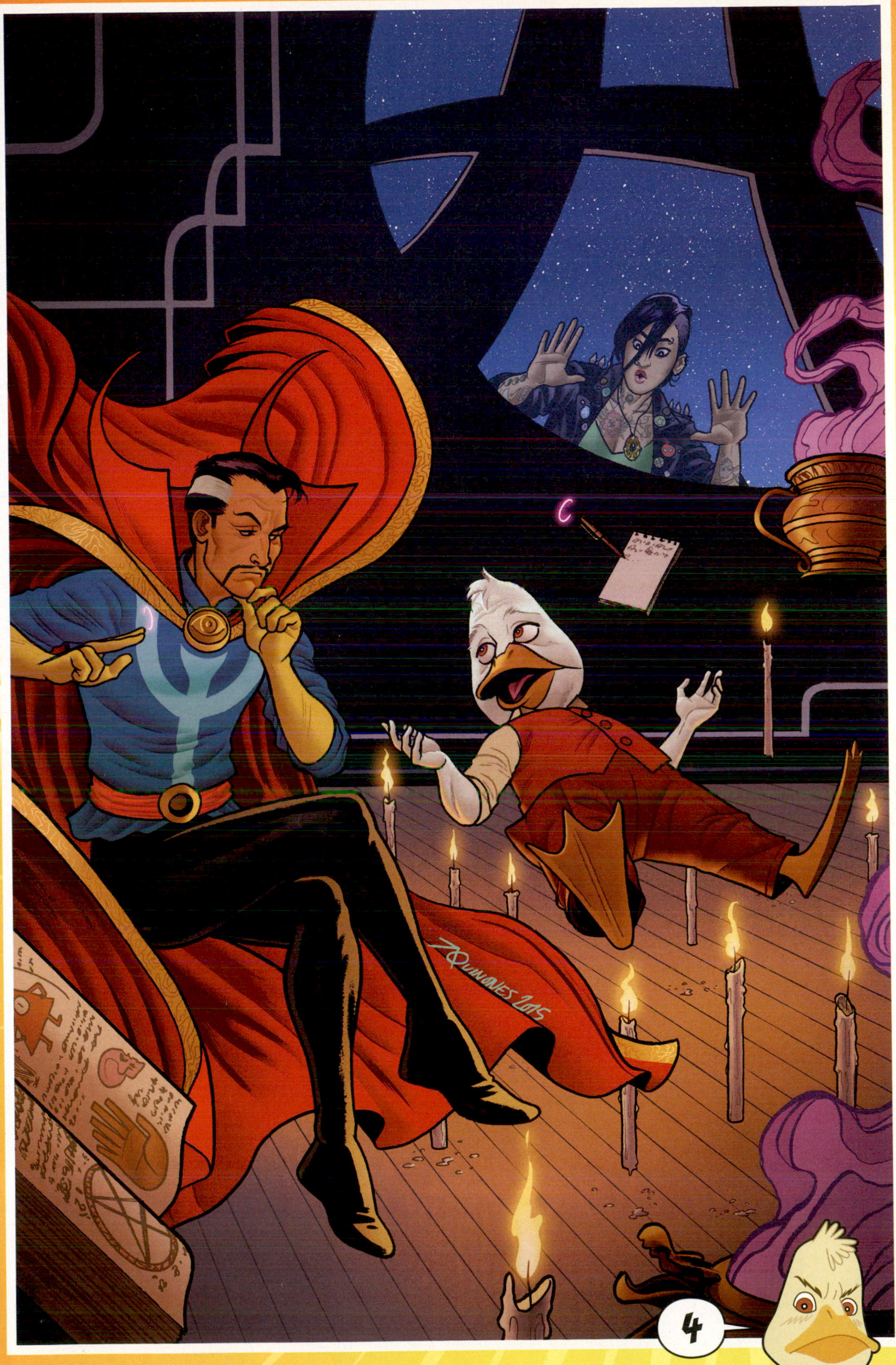

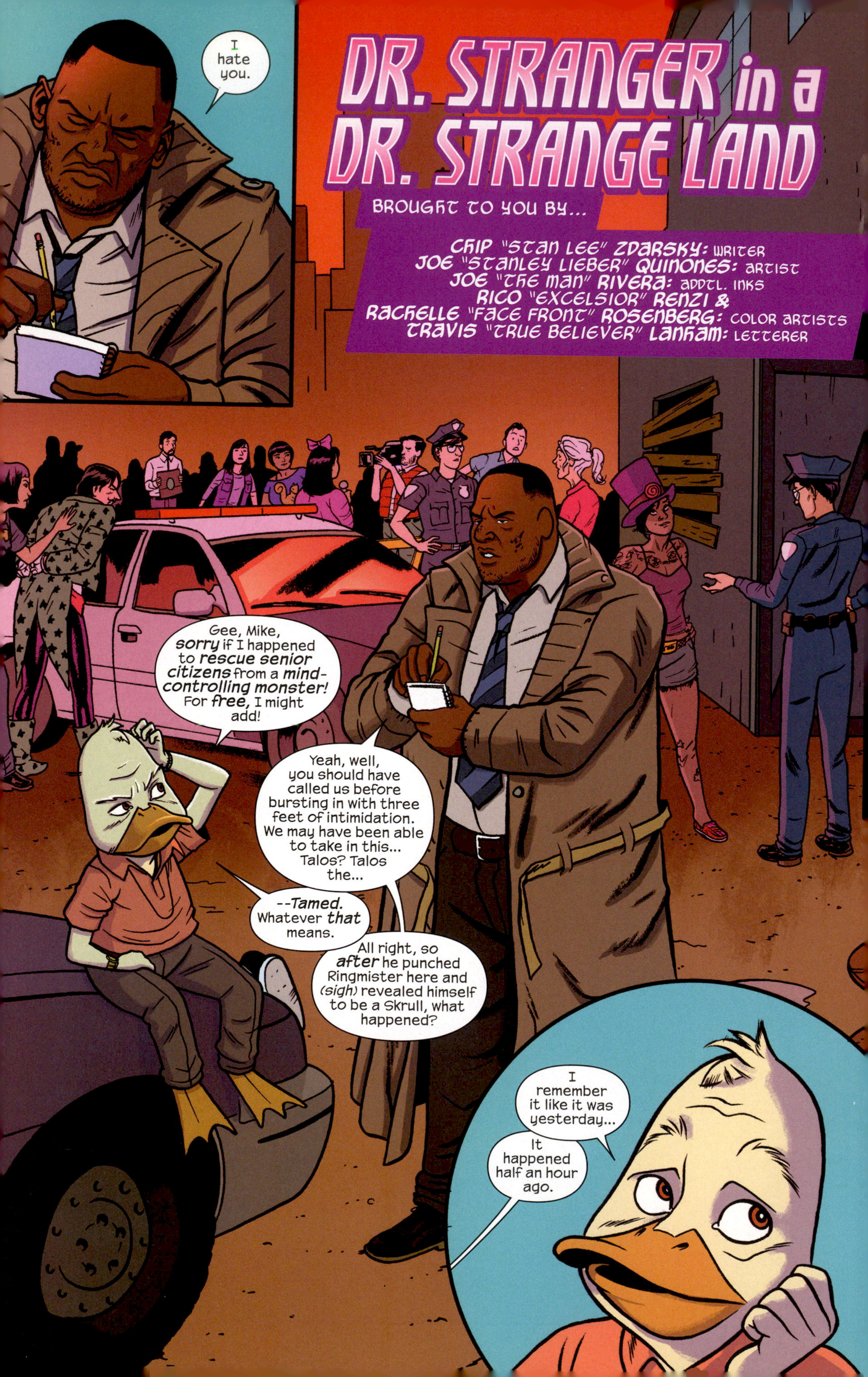

I hate you.
DR. STRANGER in a DR. STRANGE LAND
BROUGHT TO YOU BY...
CHIP "STAN LEE" ZDARSKY: WRITER
JOE "STANLEY LIEBER" QUINONES: ARTIST
JOE "THE MAN" RIVERA: ADDTL. INKS
RICO "EXCELSIOR" RENZI &
RACHELLE "FACE FRONT" ROSENBERG: COLOR ARTISTS
TRAVIS "TRUE BELIEVER" LANHAM: LETTERER
Gee, Mike, sorry if I happened to rescue senior citizens from a mind-controlling monster! For free, I might add!
Yeah, well, you should have called us before bursting in with three feet of intimidation. We may have been able to take in this... Talos? Talos the...
--Tamed. Whatever that means.
All right, so after he punched Ringmister here and (sigh) revealed himself to be a Skrull, what happened?
I remember it like it was yesterday...
It happened half an hour ago.

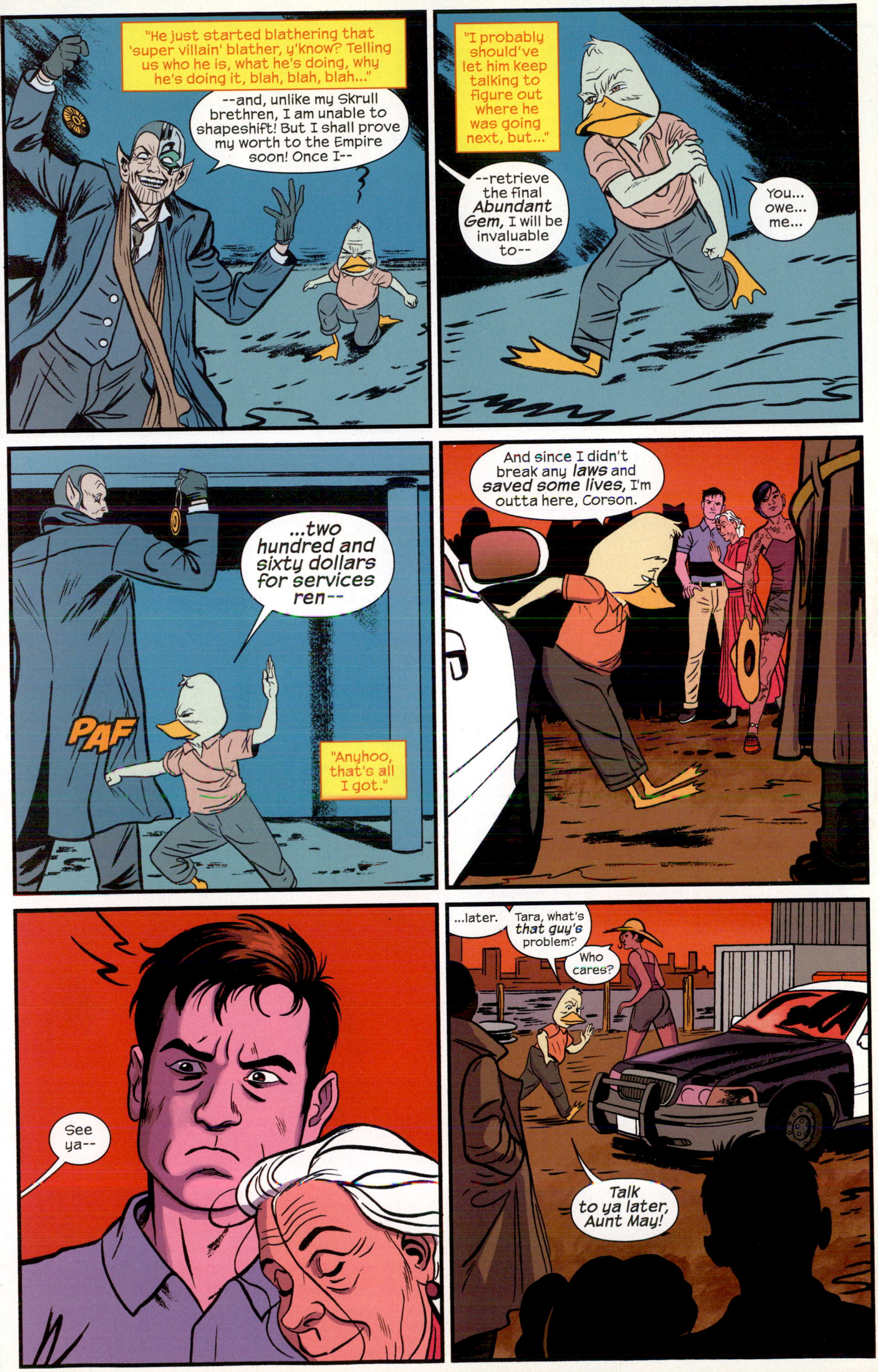

"He just started blathering that 'super villain' blather, y'know? Telling us who he is, what he's doing, why he's doing it, blah, blah, blah..."
--and, unlike my Skrull brethren, I am unable to shapeshift! But I shall prove my worth to the Empire soon! Once I--
?
"I probably should've let him keep talking to figure out where he was going next, but..."
--retrieve the final Abundant Gem, I will be invaluable to--
You... owe... me...
...two hundred and sixty dollars for services ren--
PAF
"Anyhoo, that's all I got."
And since I didn't break any laws and saved some lives, I'm outta here, Corson.
See ya--
...later.
Tara, what's that guy's problem?
Who cares?
Talk to ya later, Aunt May!

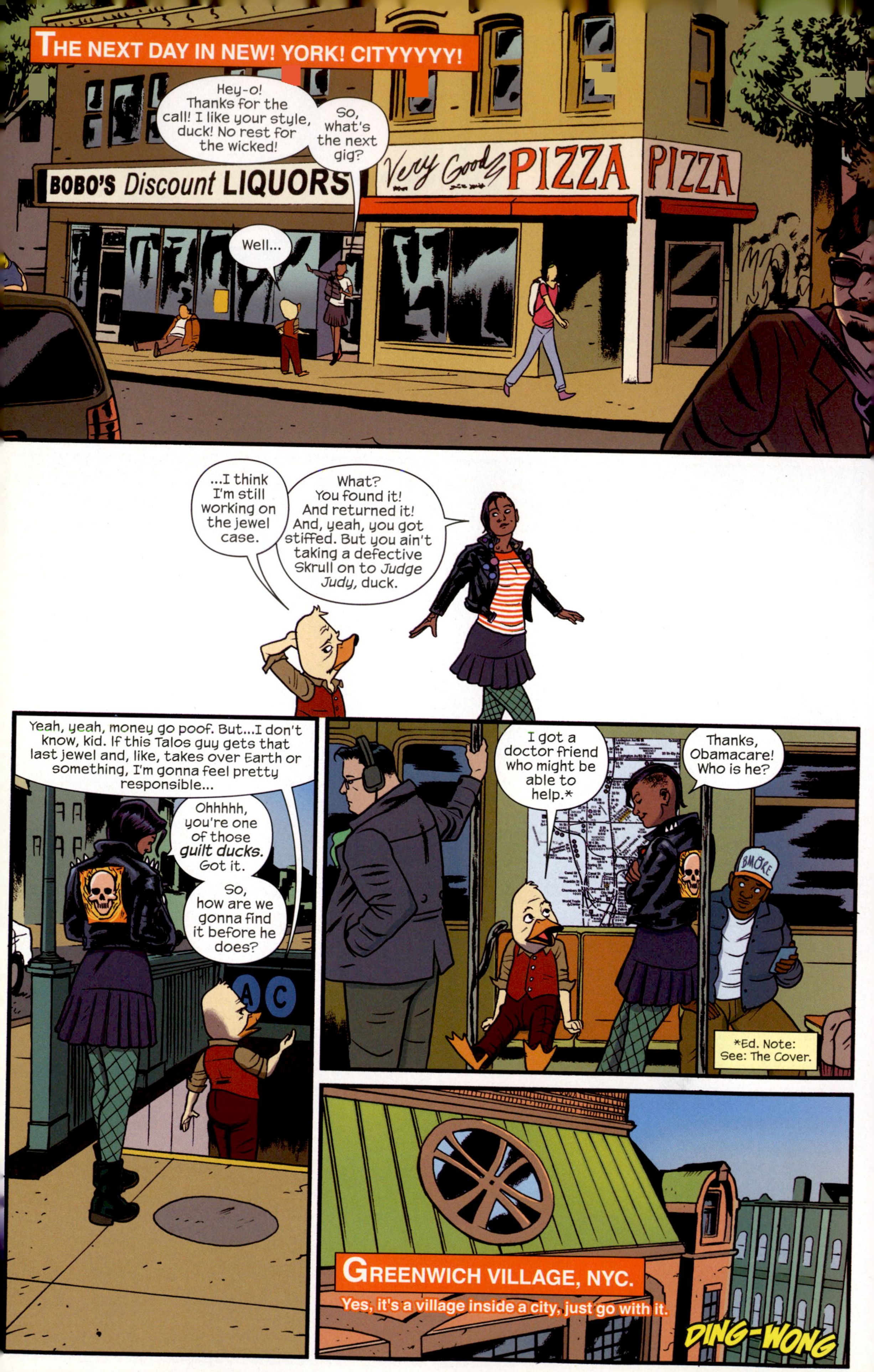

THE NEXT DAY IN NEW! YORK! CITYYYYY!
Hey-o! Thanks for the call! I like your style, duck! No rest for the wicked!
So, what's the next gig?
BOBO'S Discount LIQUORS
Very Good PIZZA
PIZZA
Well...
...I think I'm still working on the jewel case.
What? You found it! And returned it! And, yeah, you got stiffed. But you ain't taking a defective Skrull on to *Judge Judy*, duck.
Yeah, yeah, money go poof. But...I don't know, kid. If this Talos guy gets that last jewel and, like, takes over Earth or something, I'm gonna feel pretty responsible...
Ohhhhh, you're one of those **guilt ducks.** Got it.
So, how are we gonna find it before he does?
A C
I got a doctor friend who might be able to help.*
Thanks, Obamacare! Who is he?
*Ed. Note: See: The Cover.
GREENWICH VILLAGE, NYC.
Yes, it's a village inside a city, just go with it.
DING-WONG

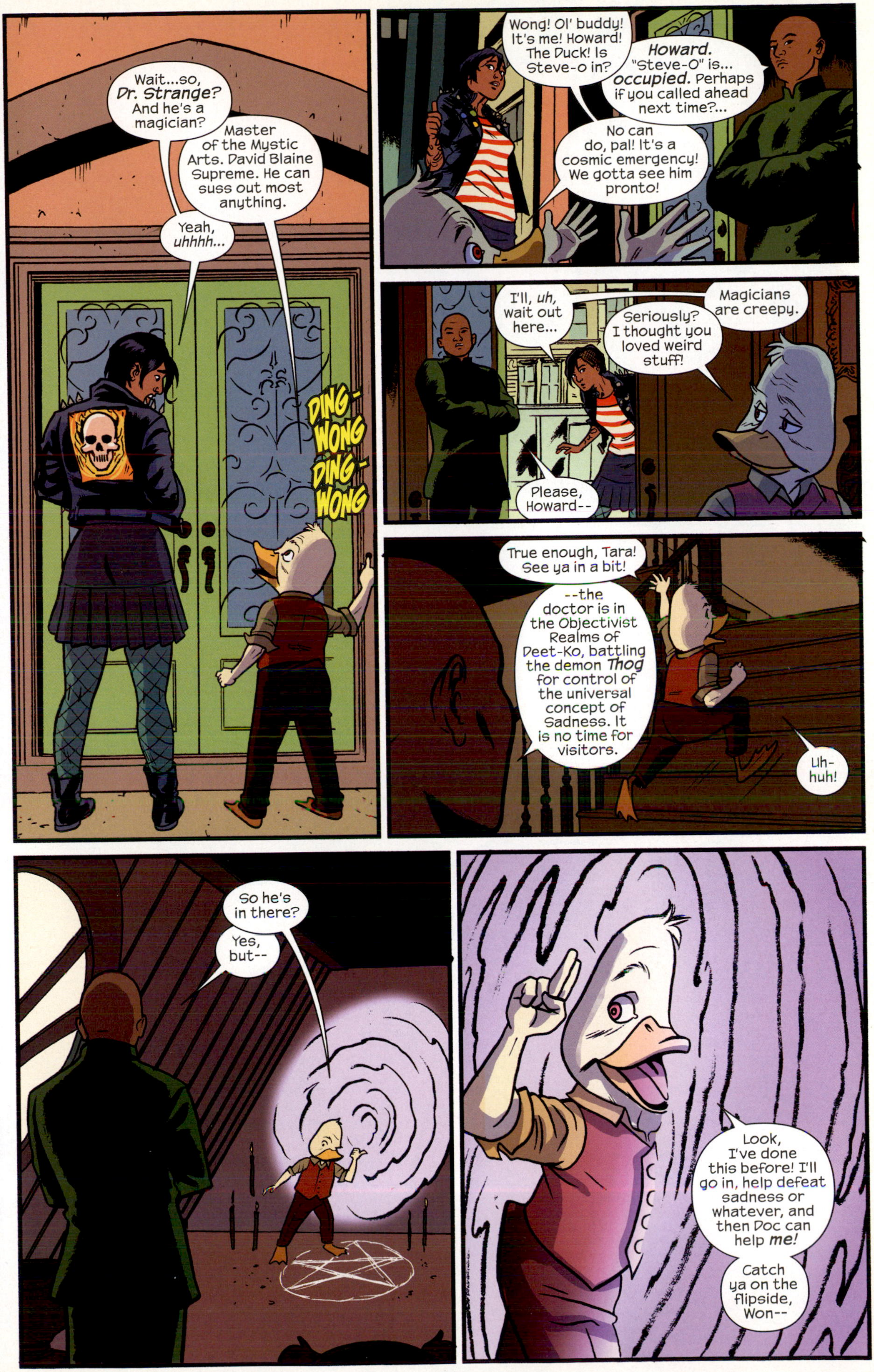

Wait...so, Dr. Strange? And he's a magician?
Master of the Mystic Arts. David Blaine Supreme. He can suss out most anything.
Yeah, uhhhh...
DING-WONG DING-WONG
Wong! Ol' buddy! It's me! Howard! The Duck! Is Steve-o in?
Howard. "Steve-O" is... occupied. Perhaps if you called ahead next time?...
No can do, pal! It's a cosmic emergency! We gotta see him pronto!
I'll, uh, wait out here...
Magicians are creepy.
Seriously? I thought you loved weird stuff!
Please, Howard--
True enough, Tara! See ya in a bit!
--the doctor is in the Objectivist Realms of Deet-Ko, battling the demon Thog for control of the universal concept of Sadness. It is no time for visitors.
Uh-huh!
So he's in there?
Yes, but--
Look, I've done this before! I'll go in, help defeat sadness or whatever, and then Doc can help me!
Catch ya on the flipside, Won--

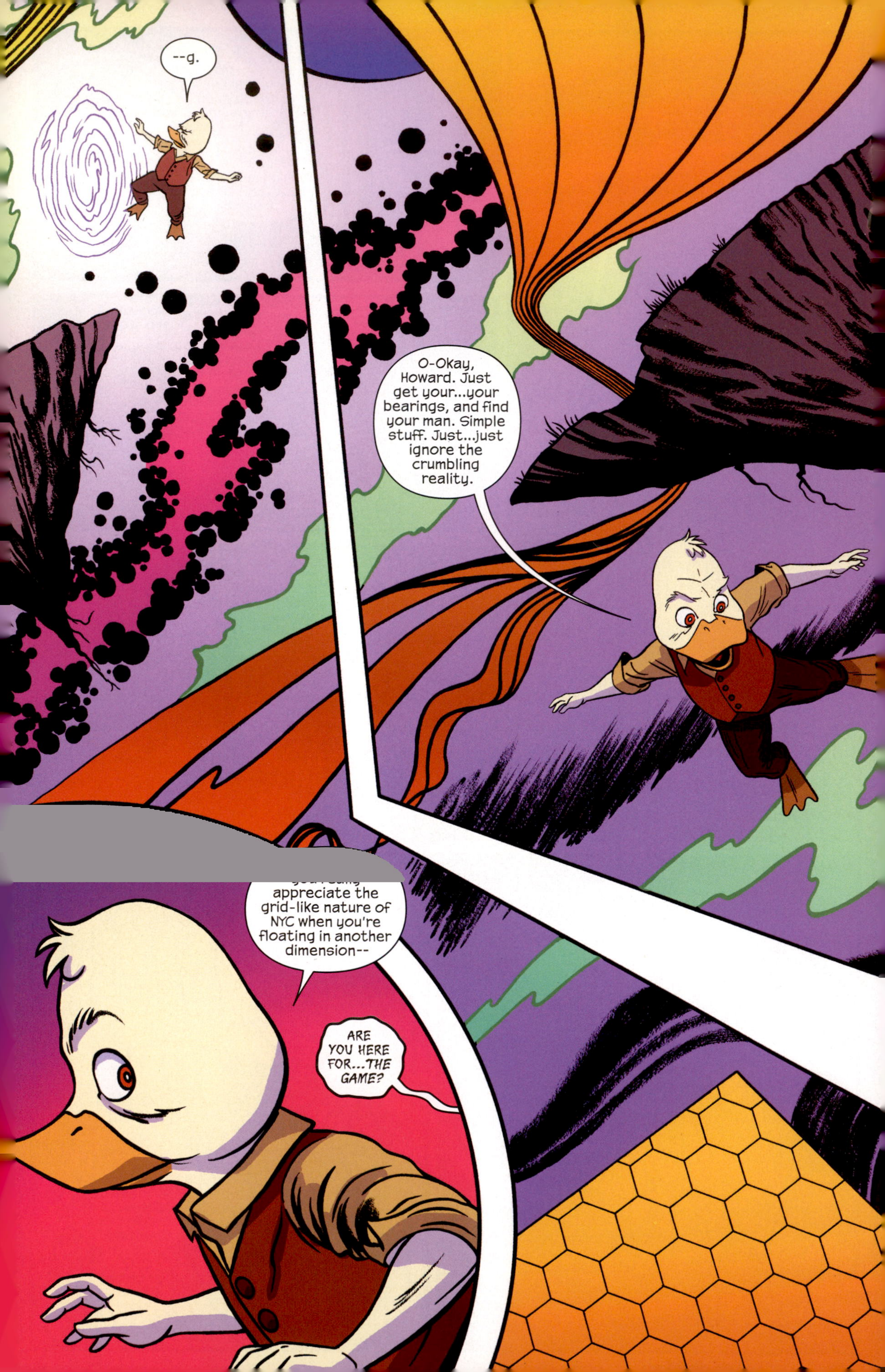
--g.
O-Okay, Howard. Just get your...your bearings, and find your man. Simple stuff. Just...just ignore the crumbling reality.
appreciate the grid-like nature of NYC when you're floating in another dimension--
ARE YOU HERE FOR...THE GAME?

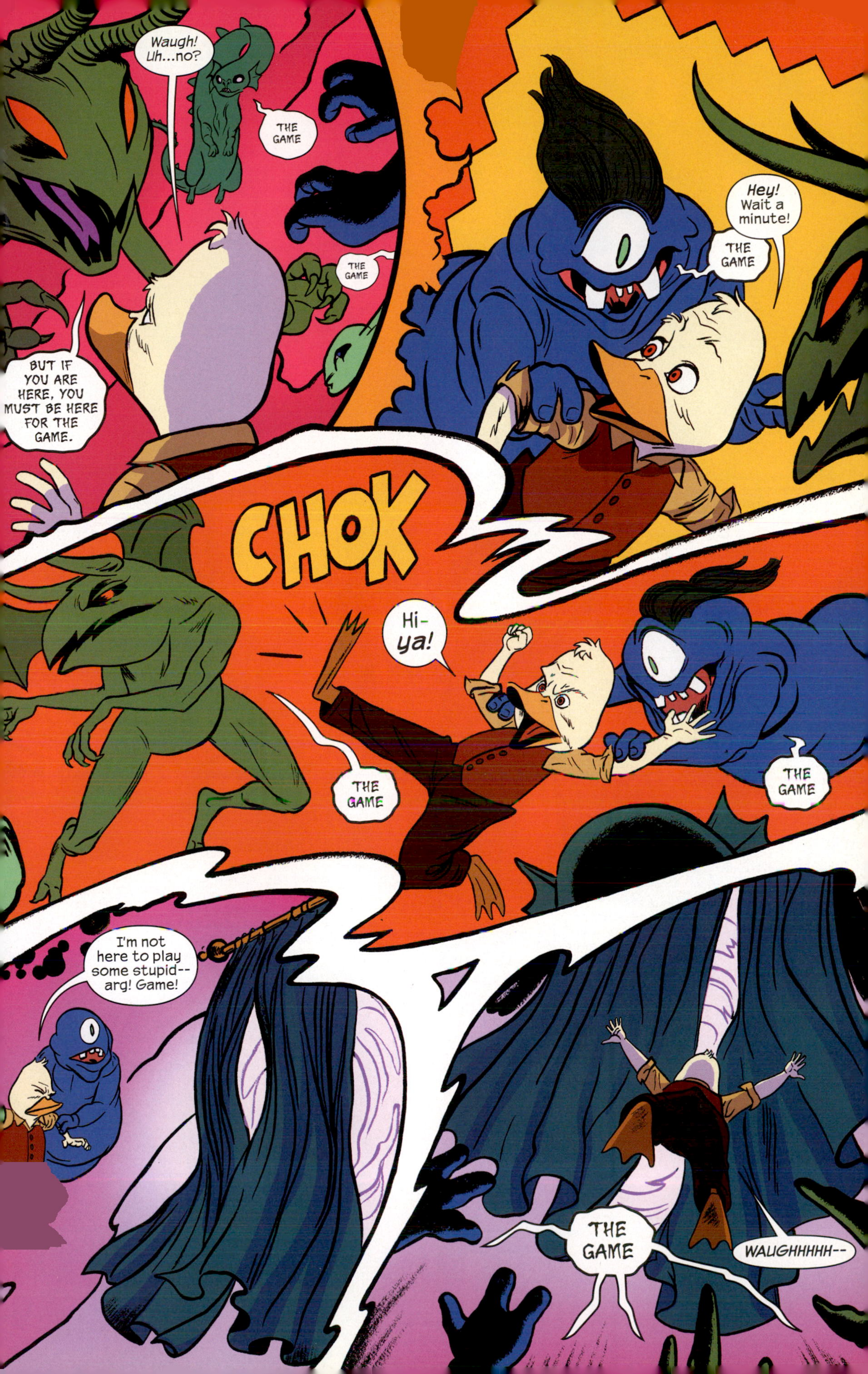
Waugh! Uh...no?
THE GAME
THE GAME
BUT IF YOU ARE HERE, YOU MUST BE HERE FOR THE GAME.
Hey! Wait a minute!
THE GAME
CHOK
Hi-ya!
THE GAME
THE GAME
I'm not here to play some stupid-- arg! Game!
THE GAME
WAUGHHHHH--

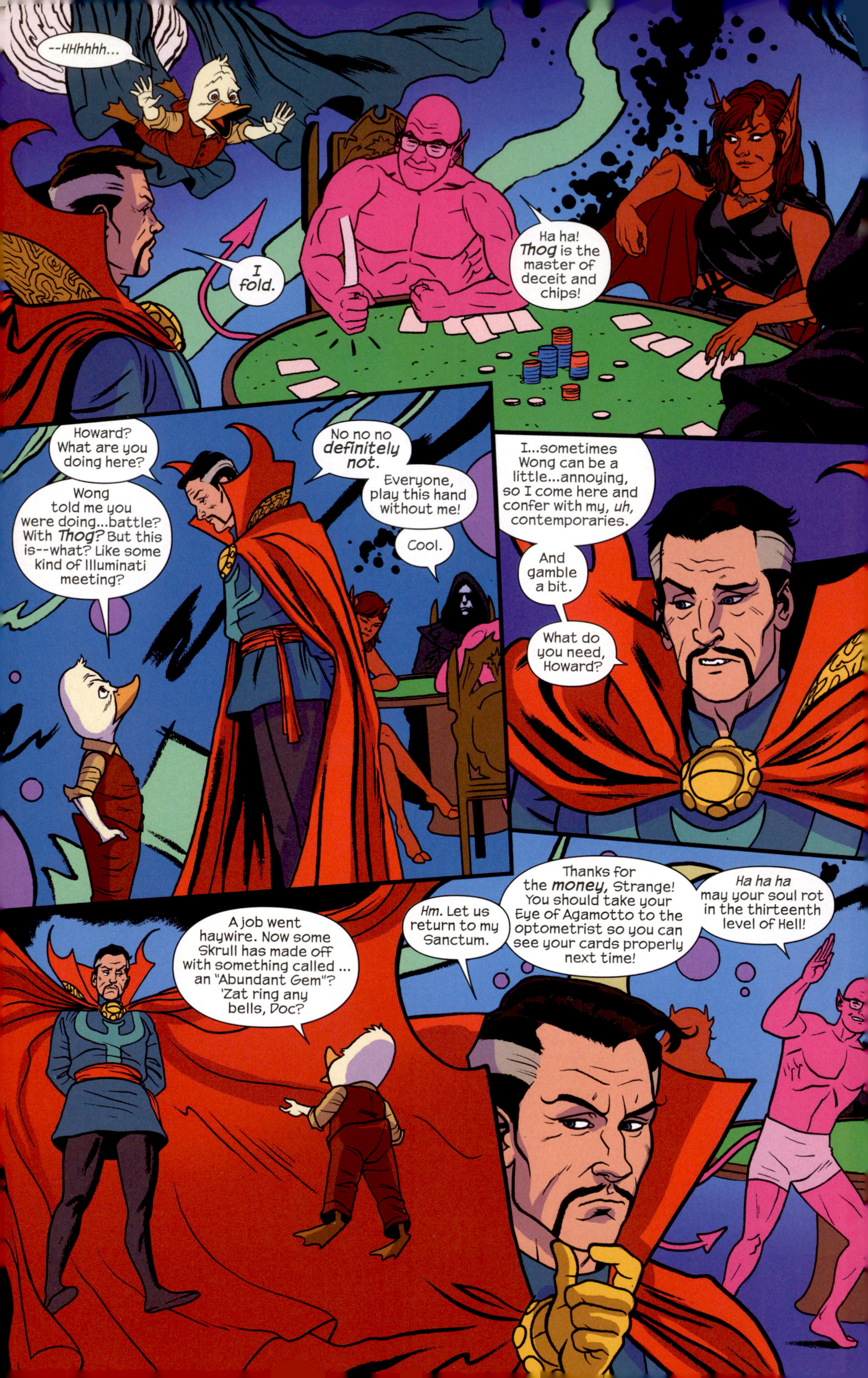
--HHhhhh...
I fold.
Ha ha! Thog is the master of deceit and chips!
Howard? What are you doing here?
Wong told me you were doing...battle? With Thog? But this is--what? Like some kind of Illuminati meeting?
No no no definitely not.
Everyone, play this hand without me!
Cool.
I...sometimes Wong can be a little...annoying, so I come here and confer with my, uh, contemporaries.
And gamble a bit.
What do you need, Howard?
A job went haywire. Now some Skrull has made off with something called ... an "Abundant Gem"? 'Zat ring any bells, Doc?
Hm. Let us return to my Sanctum.
Thanks for the money, Strange! You should take your Eye of Agamotto to the optometrist so you can see your cards properly next time!
Ha ha ha may your soul rot in the thirteenth level of Hell!

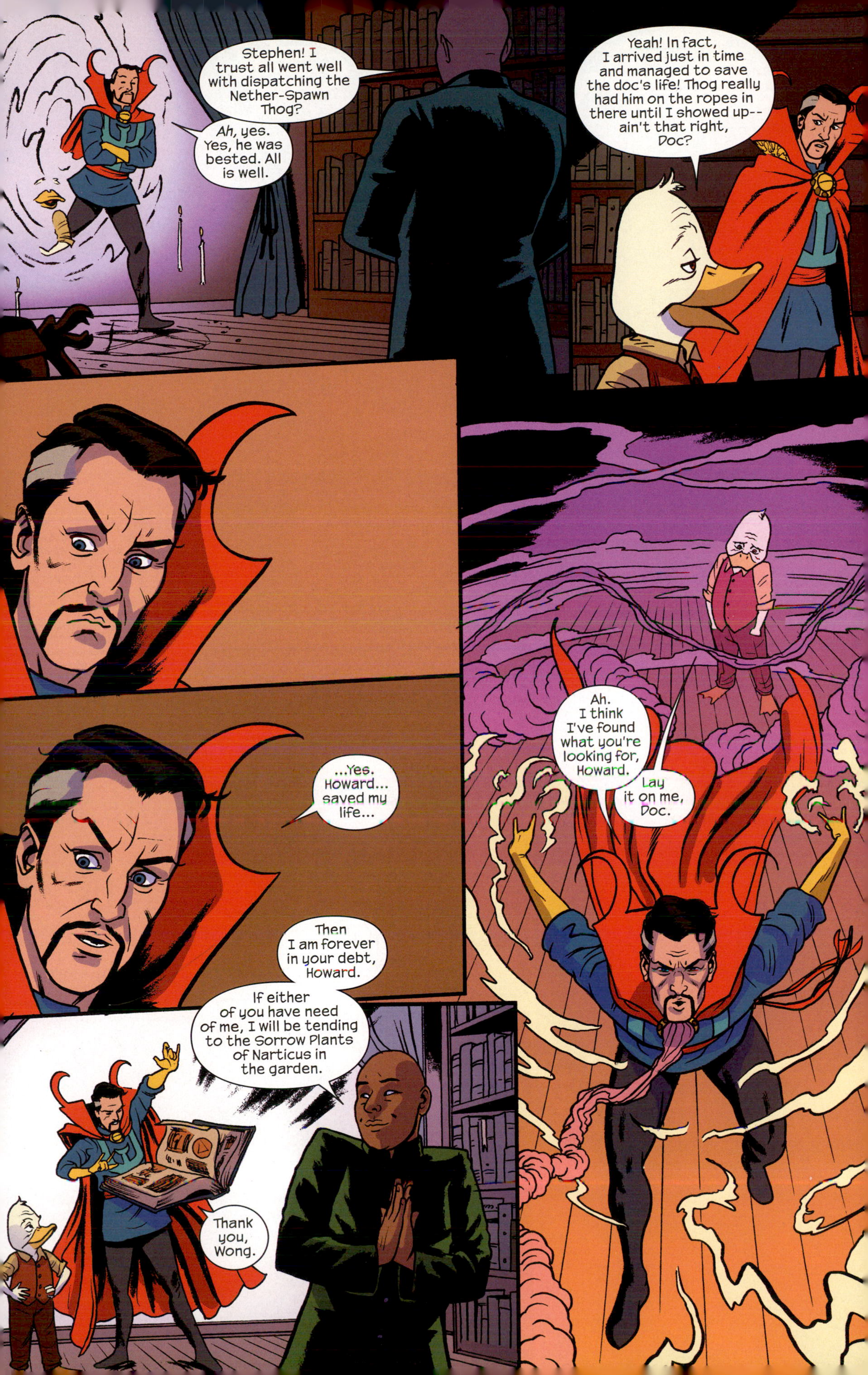
Stephen! I trust all went well with dispatching the Nether-Spawn Thog?
Ah, yes. Yes, he was bested. All is well.
Yeah! In fact, I arrived just in time and managed to save the doc's life! Thog really had him on the ropes in there until I showed up-- ain't that right, Doc?
...Yes. Howard... saved my life...
Then I am forever in your debt, Howard.
If either of you have need of me, I will be tending to the Sorrow Plants of Narticus in the garden.
Thank you, Wong.
Ah. I think I've found what you're looking for, Howard.
Lay it on me, Doc.

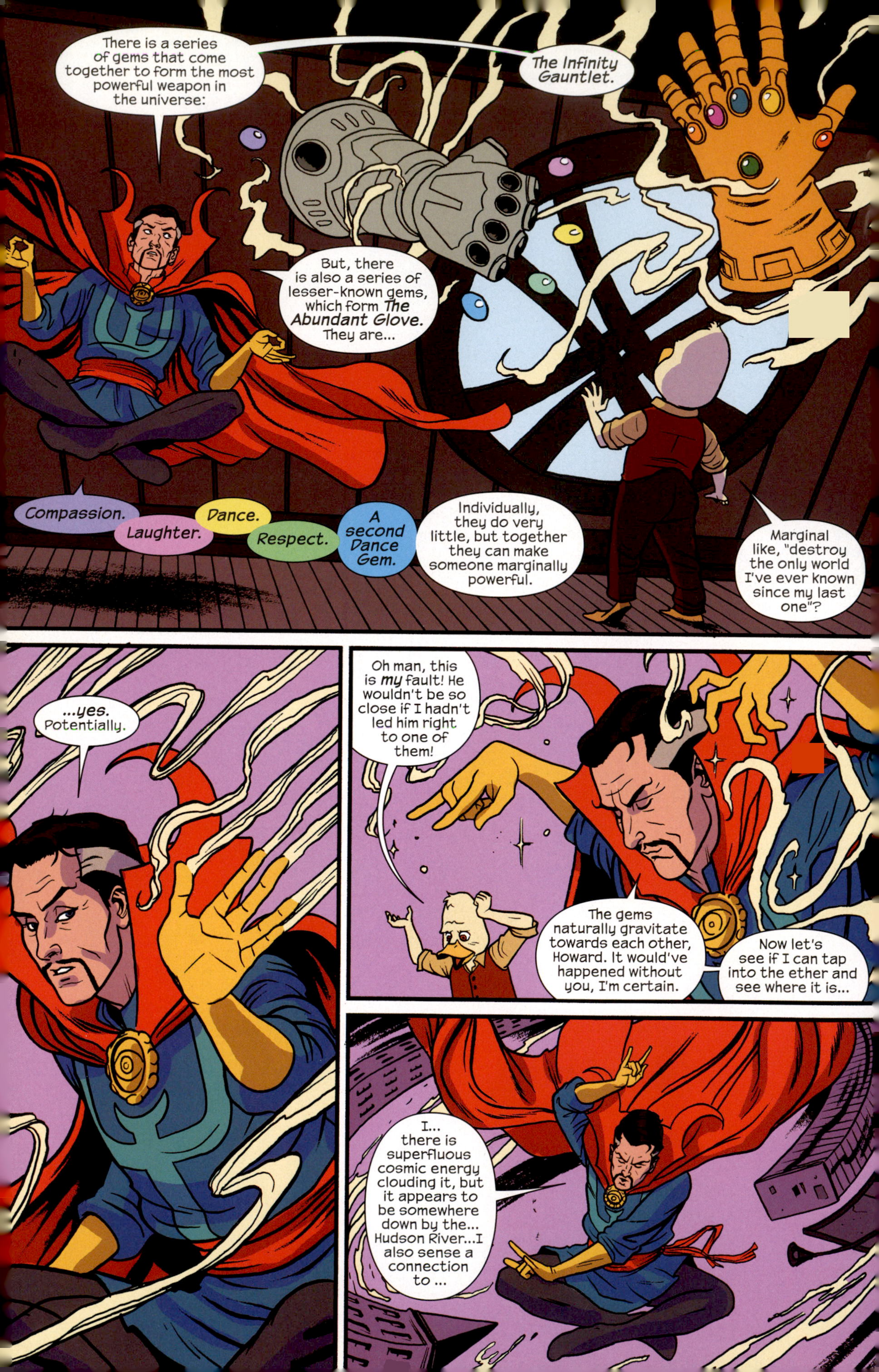
There is a series of gems that come together to form the most powerful weapon in the universe:
The Infinity Gauntlet.
But, there is also a series of lesser-known gems, which form *The Abundant Glove.* They are...
Compassion.
Laughter.
Dance.
Respect.
A second Dance Gem.
Individually, they do very little, but together they can make someone marginally powerful.
Marginal like, "destroy the only world I've ever known since my last one"?
...yes. Potentially.
Oh man, this is *my* fault! He wouldn't be so close if I hadn't led him right to one of them!
The gems naturally gravitate towards each other, Howard. It would've happened without you, I'm certain.
Now let's see if I can tap into the ether and see where it is...
I... there is superfluous cosmic energy clouding it, but it appears to be somewhere down by the... Hudson River...I also sense a connection to ...

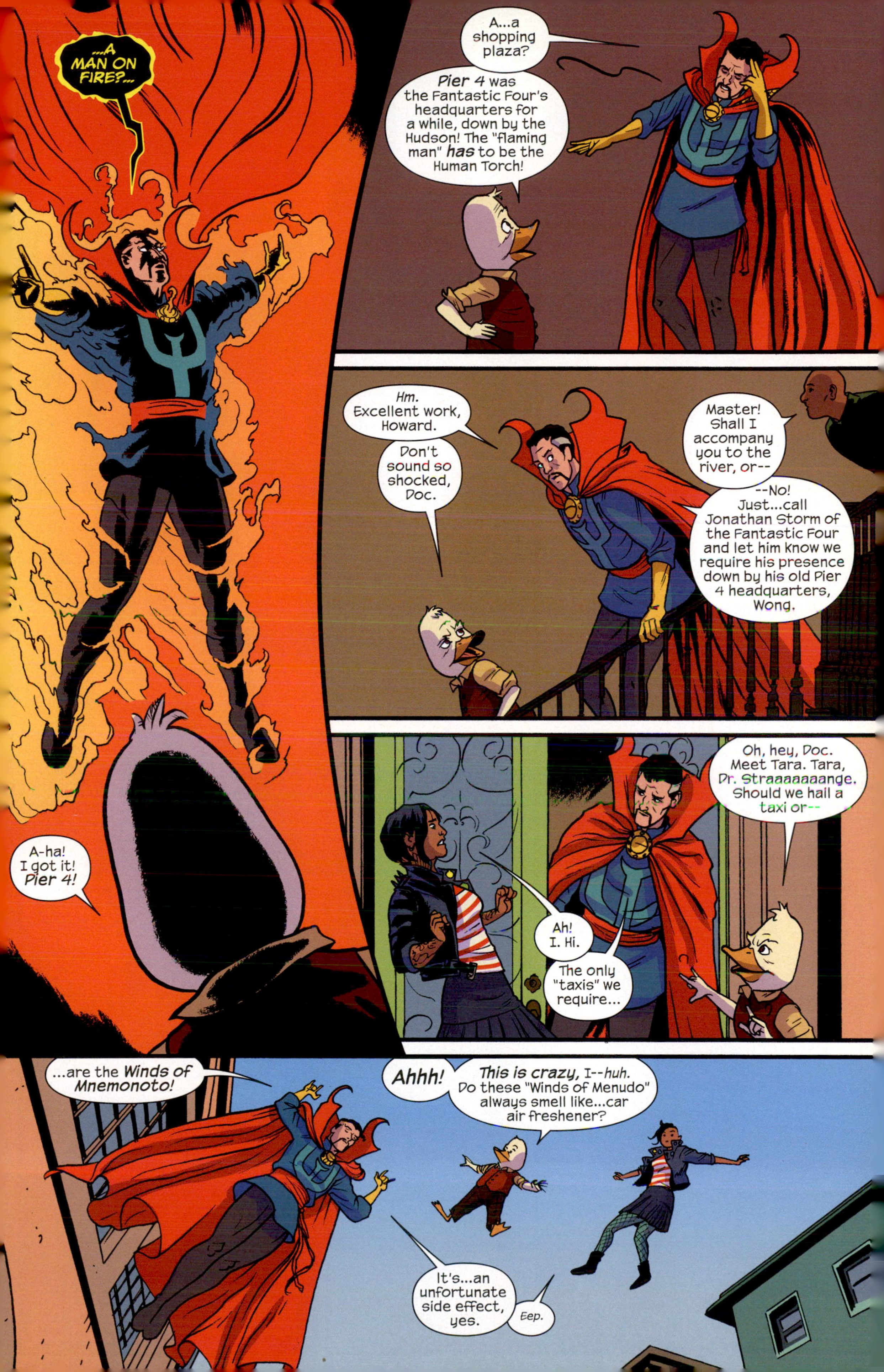

...A MAN ON FIRE?...
A-ha! I got it! Pier 4!
A...a shopping plaza?
Pier 4 was the Fantastic Four's headquarters for a while, down by the Hudson! The "flaming man" has to be the Human Torch!
Hm. Excellent work, Howard.
Don't sound so shocked, Doc.
Master! Shall I accompany you to the river, or--
--No! Just...call Jonathan Storm of the Fantastic Four and let him know we require his presence down by his old Pier 4 headquarters, Wong.
Oh, hey, Doc. Meet Tara. Tara, Dr. Straaaaaaaange. Should we hail a taxi or--
Ah! I. Hi.
The only "taxis" we require...
...are the Winds of Mnemonoto!
Ahhh!
This is crazy, I--huh. Do these "Winds of Menudo" always smell like...car air freshener?
It's...an unfortunate side effect, yes.
Eep.

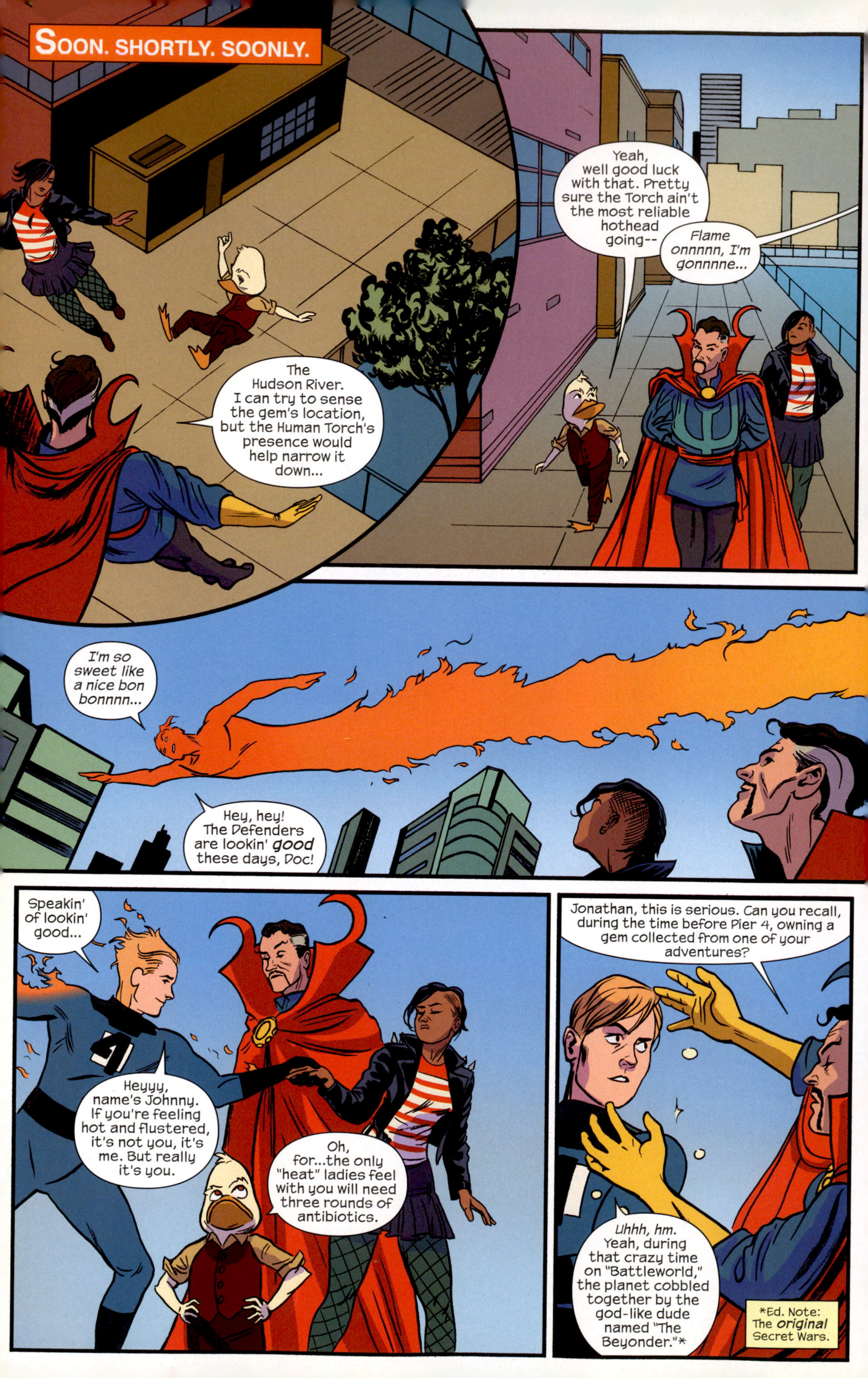
SOON. SHORTLY. SOONLY.
The Hudson River. I can try to sense the gem's location, but the Human Torch's presence would help narrow it down...
Yeah, well good luck with that. Pretty sure the Torch ain't the most reliable hothead going--
Flame onnnnn, I'm gonnnne...
I'm so sweet like a nice bon bonnnn...
Hey, hey! The Defenders are lookin' good these days, Doc!
Speakin' of lookin' good...
Heyyy, name's Johnny. If you're feeling hot and flustered, it's not you, it's me. But really it's you.
Oh, for...the only "heat" ladies feel with you will need three rounds of antibiotics.
Jonathan, this is serious. Can you recall, during the time before Pier 4, owning a gem collected from one of your adventures?
Uhhh, hm. Yeah, during that crazy time on "Battleworld," the planet cobbled together by the god-like dude named "The Beyonder."*
*Ed. Note: The original Secret Wars.

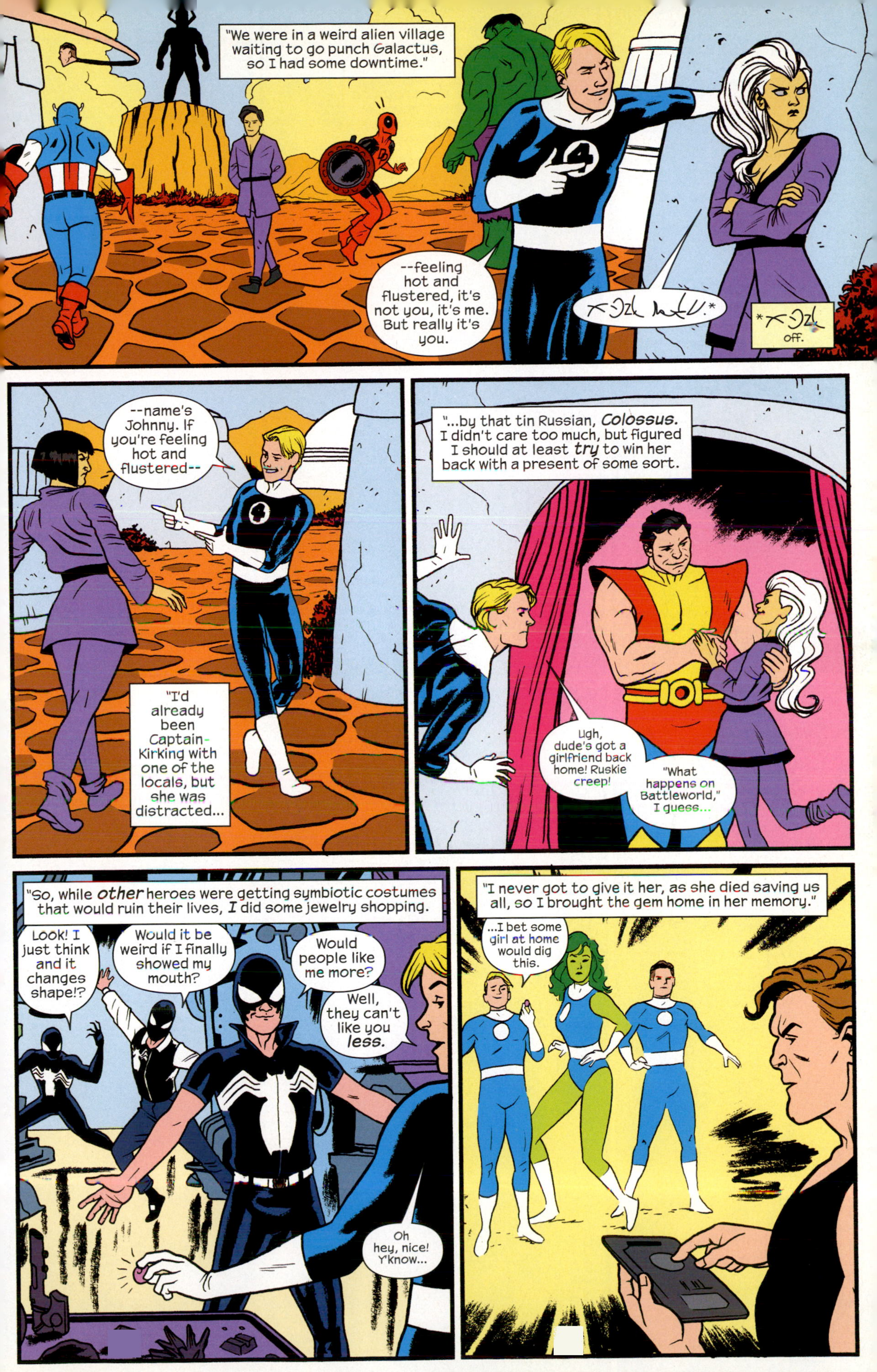
"We were in a weird alien village waiting to go punch Galactus, so I had some downtime."
--feeling hot and flustered, it's not you, it's me. But really it's you.
*
*
off.
--name's Johnny. If you're feeling hot and flustered--
"I'd already been Captain-Kirking with one of the locals, but she was distracted...
"...by that tin Russian, Colossus. I didn't care too much, but figured I should at least try to win her back with a present of some sort.
Ugh, dude's got a girlfriend back home! Ruskie creep!
"What happens on Battleworld," I guess...
"So, while other heroes were getting symbiotic costumes that would ruin their lives, I did some jewelry shopping.
Look! I just think and it changes shape!?
Would it be weird if I finally showed my mouth?
Would people like me more?
Well, they can't like you less.
Oh hey, nice! Y'know...
"I never got to give it her, as she died saving us all, so I brought the gem home in her memory."
...I bet some girl at home would dig this.

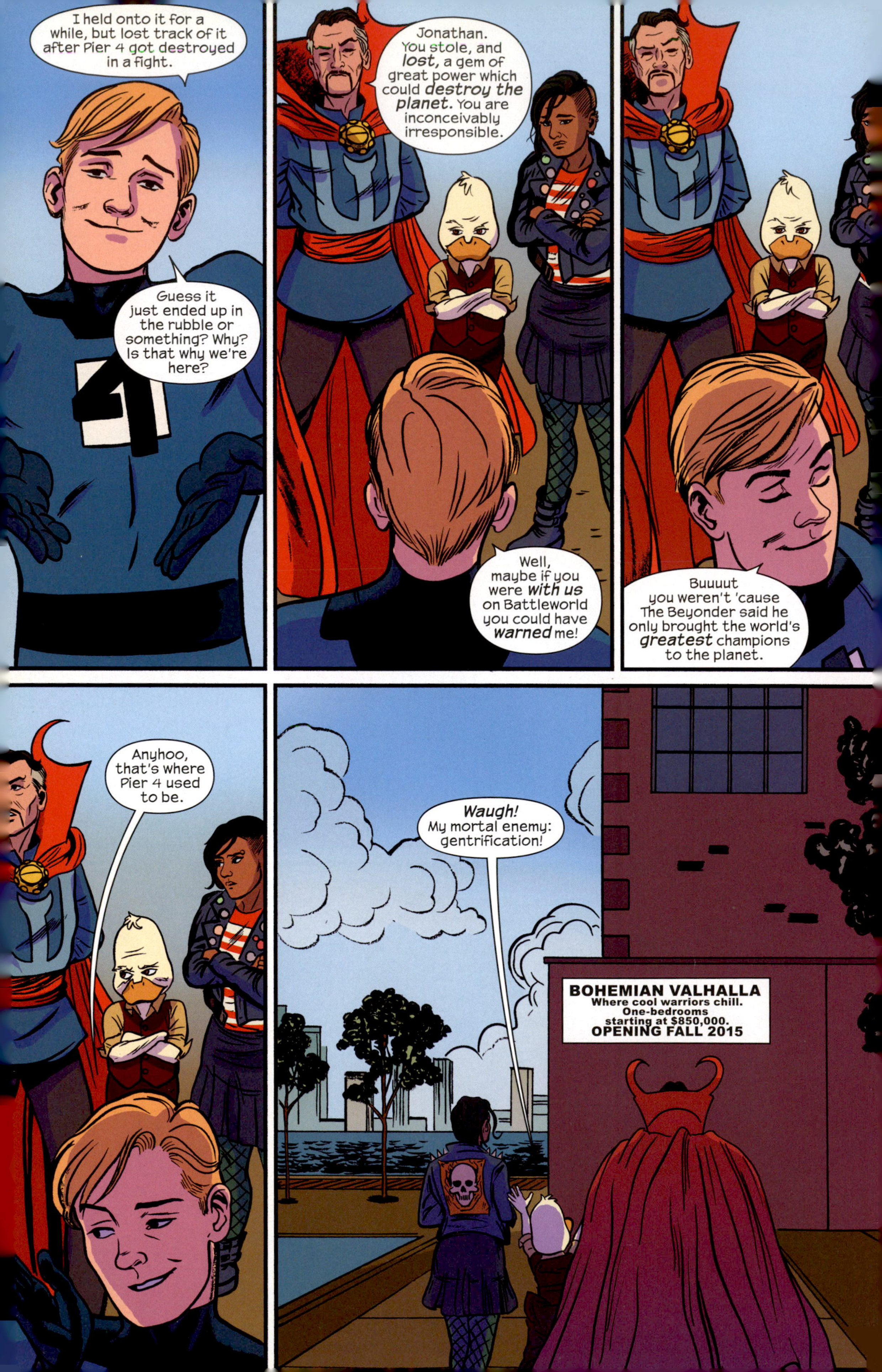

I held onto it for a while, but lost track of it after Pier 4 got destroyed in a fight.
Guess it just ended up in the rubble or something? Why? Is that why we're here?
Jonathan. You stole, and *lost,* a gem of great power which could *destroy the planet.* You are inconceivably irresponsible.
Well, maybe if you were *with us* on Battleworld you could have *warned* me!
Buuuut you weren't 'cause The Beyonder said he only brought the world's *greatest* champions to the planet.
Anyhoo, that's where Pier 4 used to be.
Waugh! My mortal enemy: gentrification!
BOHEMIAN VALHALLA
Where cool warriors chill.
One-bedrooms starting at $850,000.
OPENING FALL 2015

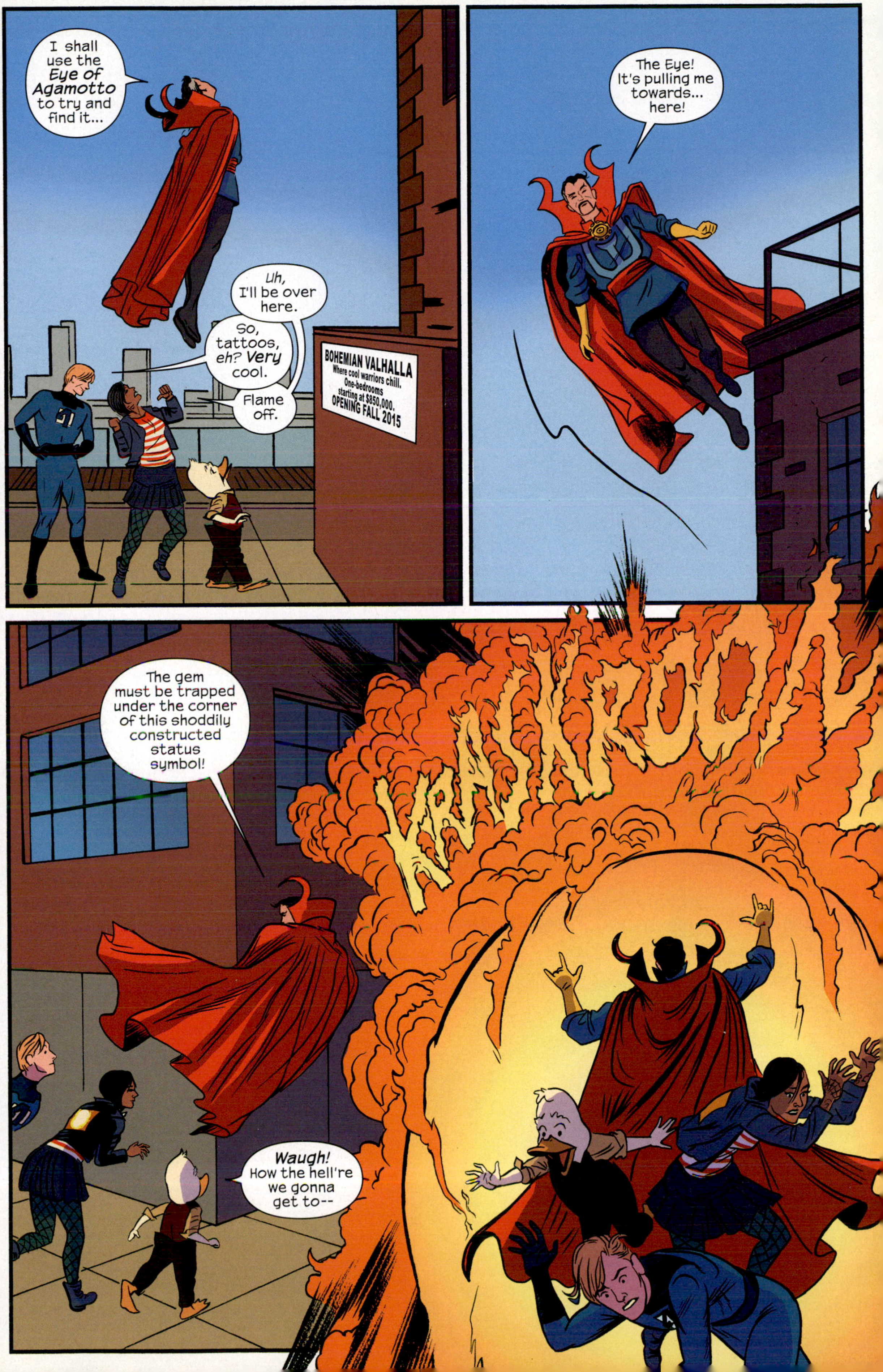
I shall use the *Eye of Agamotto* to try and find it...
Uh, I'll be over here.
So, tattoos, eh? *Very* cool.
Flame off.
BOHEMIAN VALHALLA
Where cool warriors chill.
One-bedrooms starting at $850,000.
OPENING FALL 2015
The Eye! It's pulling me towards... here!
The gem must be trapped under the corner of this shoddily constructed status symbol!
Waugh! How the hell're we gonna get to--
KRASKROOM

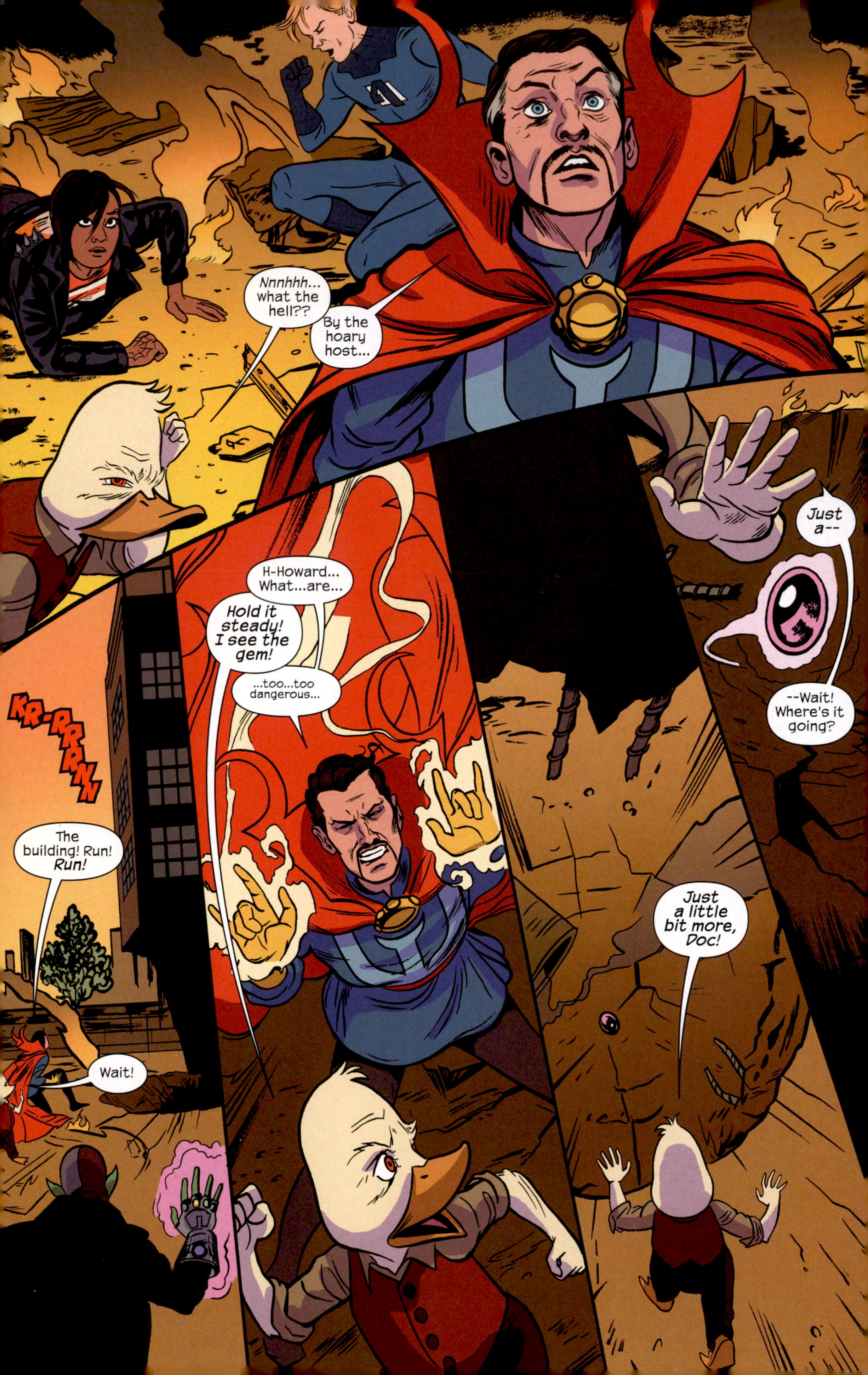
Nnnhhh... what the hell??
By the hoary host...
H-Howard... What...are...
...too...too dangerous...
Hold it steady! I see the gem!
Just a--
--Wait! Where's it going?
Just a little bit more, Doc!
KR-RRRNN
The building! Run! Run!
Wait!

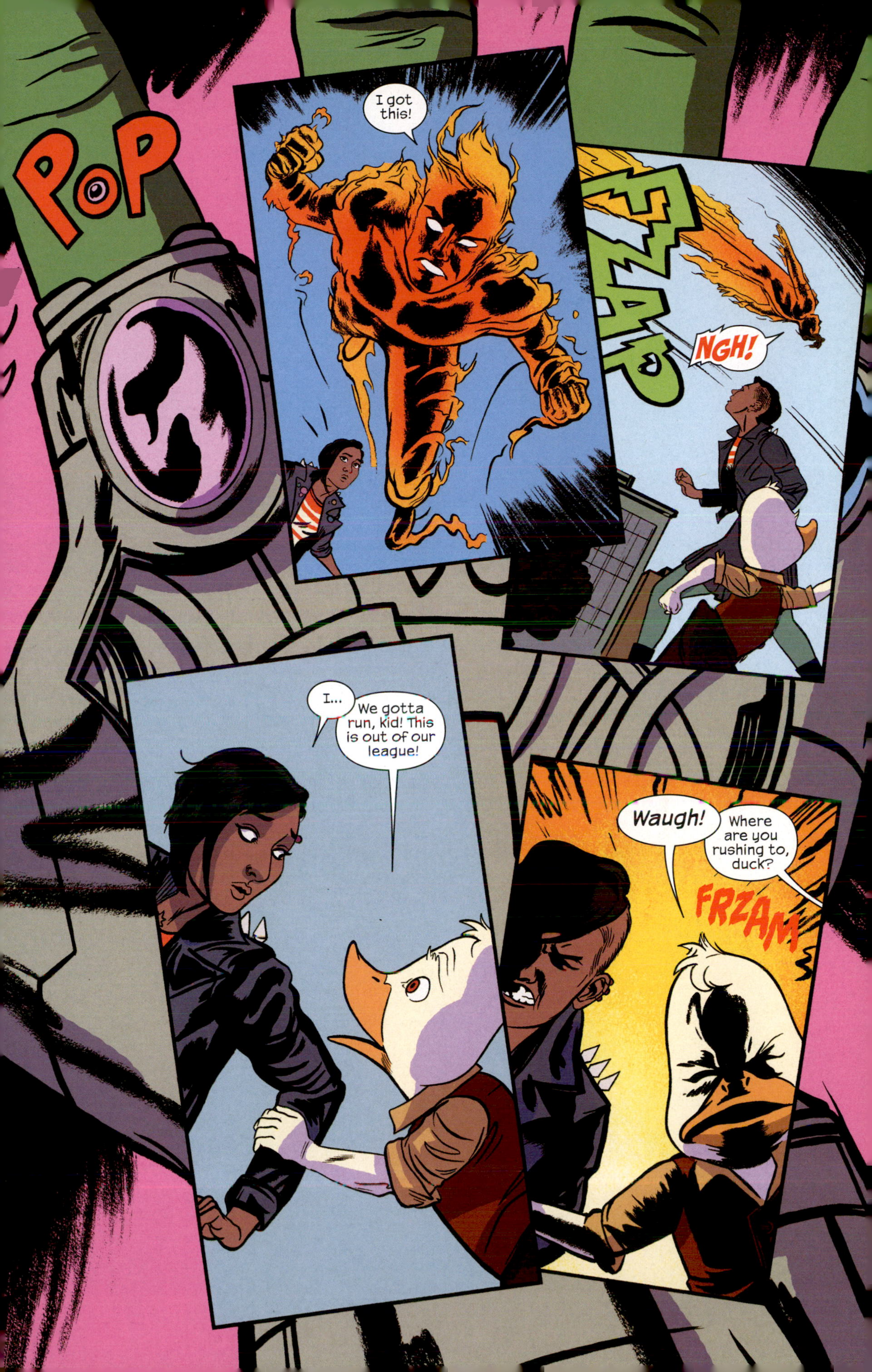
POP
I got this!
FZAP
NGH!
I...
We gotta run, kid! This is out of our league!
Waugh!
Where are you rushing to, duck?
FRZAM

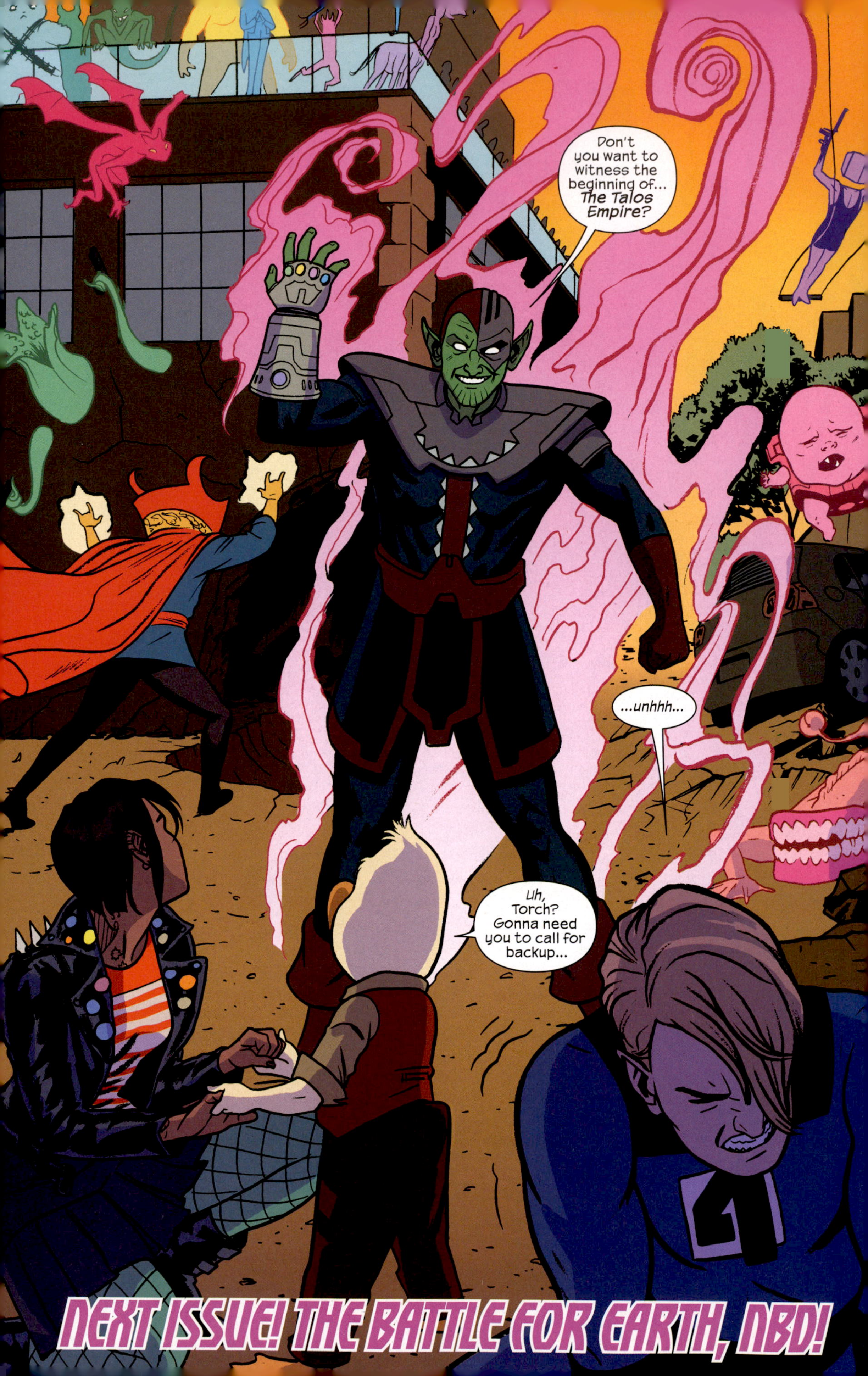
Don't you want to witness the beginning of... The Talos Empire?
...unhhh...
Uh, Torch? Gonna need you to call for backup...
NEXT ISSUE! THE BATTLE FOR EARTH, NBD!

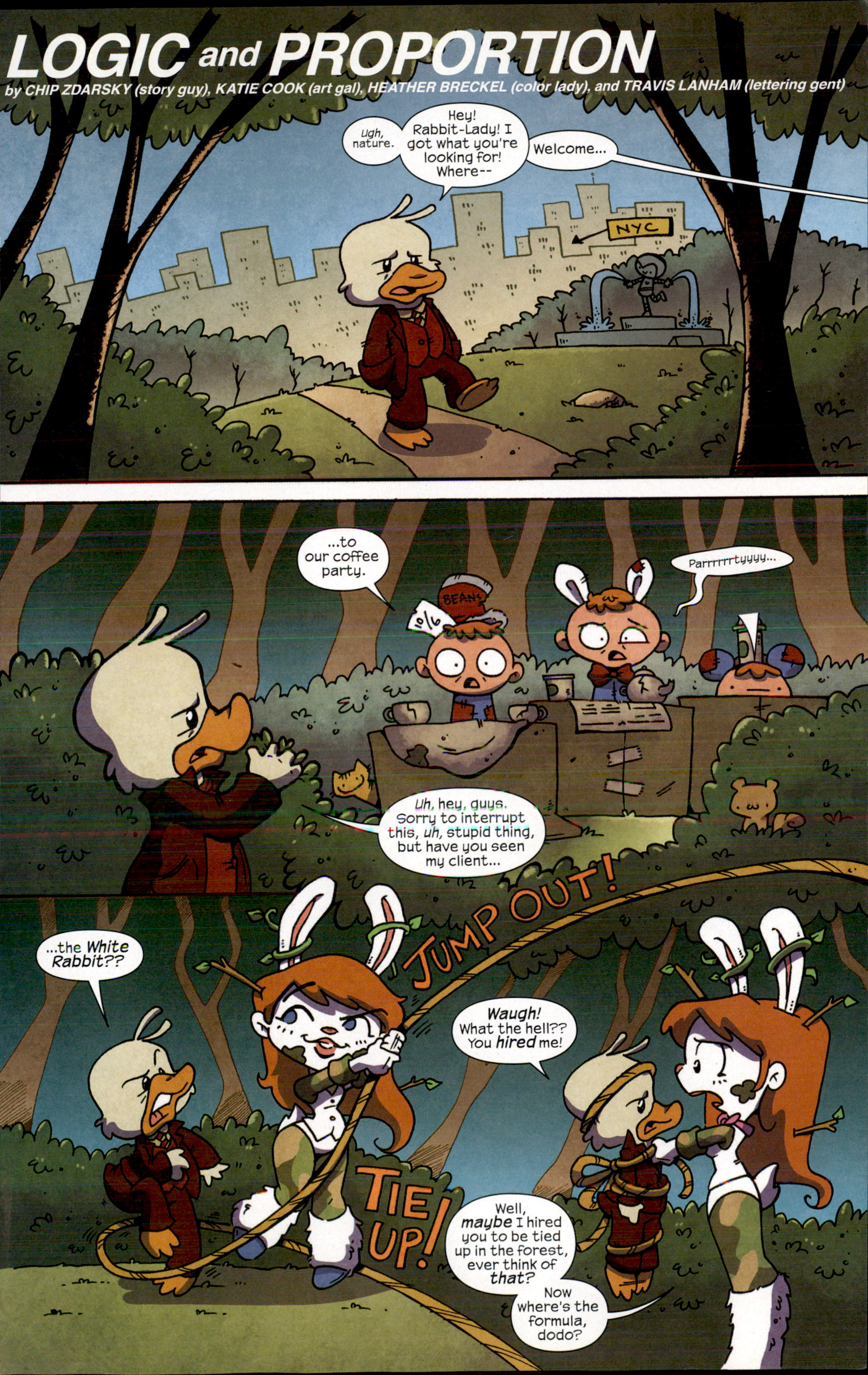
LOGIC and PROPORTION
by CHIP ZDARSKY (story guy), KATIE COOK (art gal), HEATHER BRECKEL (color lady), and TRAVIS LANHAM (lettering gent)
Ugh, nature.
Hey! Rabbit-Lady! I got what you're looking for! Where--
Welcome...
NYC
...to our coffee party.
BEANS
10/6
Parrrrrrtyyyy...
Uh, hey, guys. Sorry to interrupt this, uh, stupid thing, but have you seen my client...
...the White Rabbit??
JUMP OUT!
Waugh! What the hell?? You hired me!
TIE UP!
Well, maybe I hired you to be tied up in the forest, ever think of that?
Now where's the formula, dodo?

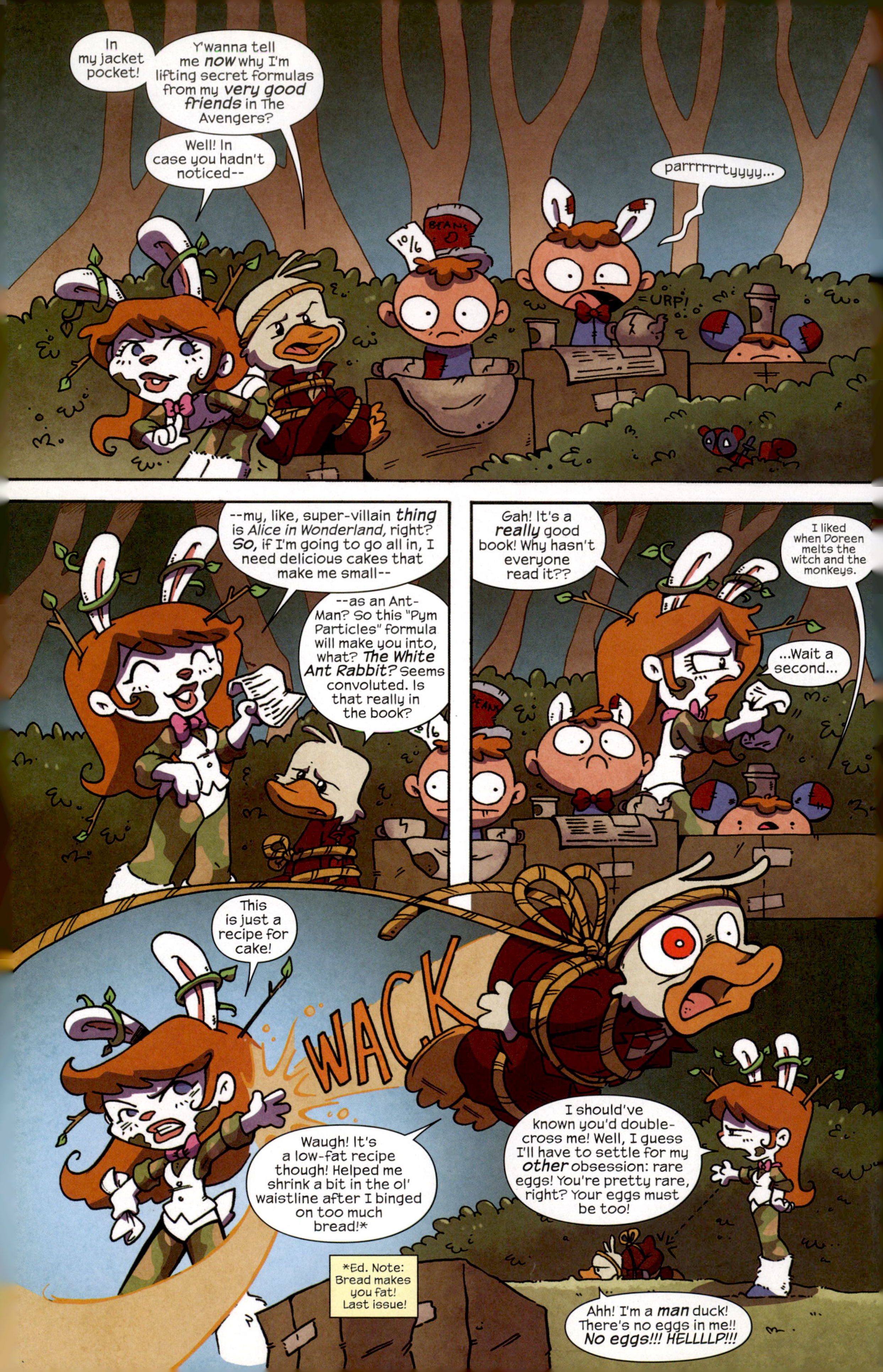
In my jacket pocket!
Y'wanna tell me NOW why I'm lifting secret formulas from my very good friends in The Avengers?
Well! In case you hadn't noticed--
parrrrrrtyyyy...
=URP!
--my, like, super-villain thing is Alice in Wonderland, right? So, if I'm going to go all in, I need delicious cakes that make me small--
--as an Ant-Man? So this "Pym Particles" formula will make you into, what? The White Ant Rabbit? Seems convoluted. Is that really in the book?
Gah! It's a really good book! Why hasn't everyone read it??
I liked when Doreen melts the witch and the monkeys.
...Wait a second...
This is just a recipe for cake!
WACK
Waugh! It's a low-fat recipe though! Helped me shrink a bit in the ol' waistline after I binged on too much bread!*
*Ed. Note: Bread makes you fat! Last issue!
I should've known you'd double-cross me! Well, I guess I'll have to settle for my other obsession: rare eggs! You're pretty rare, right? Your eggs must be too!
Ahh! I'm a man duck! There's no eggs in me!! No eggs!!! HELLLLP!!!

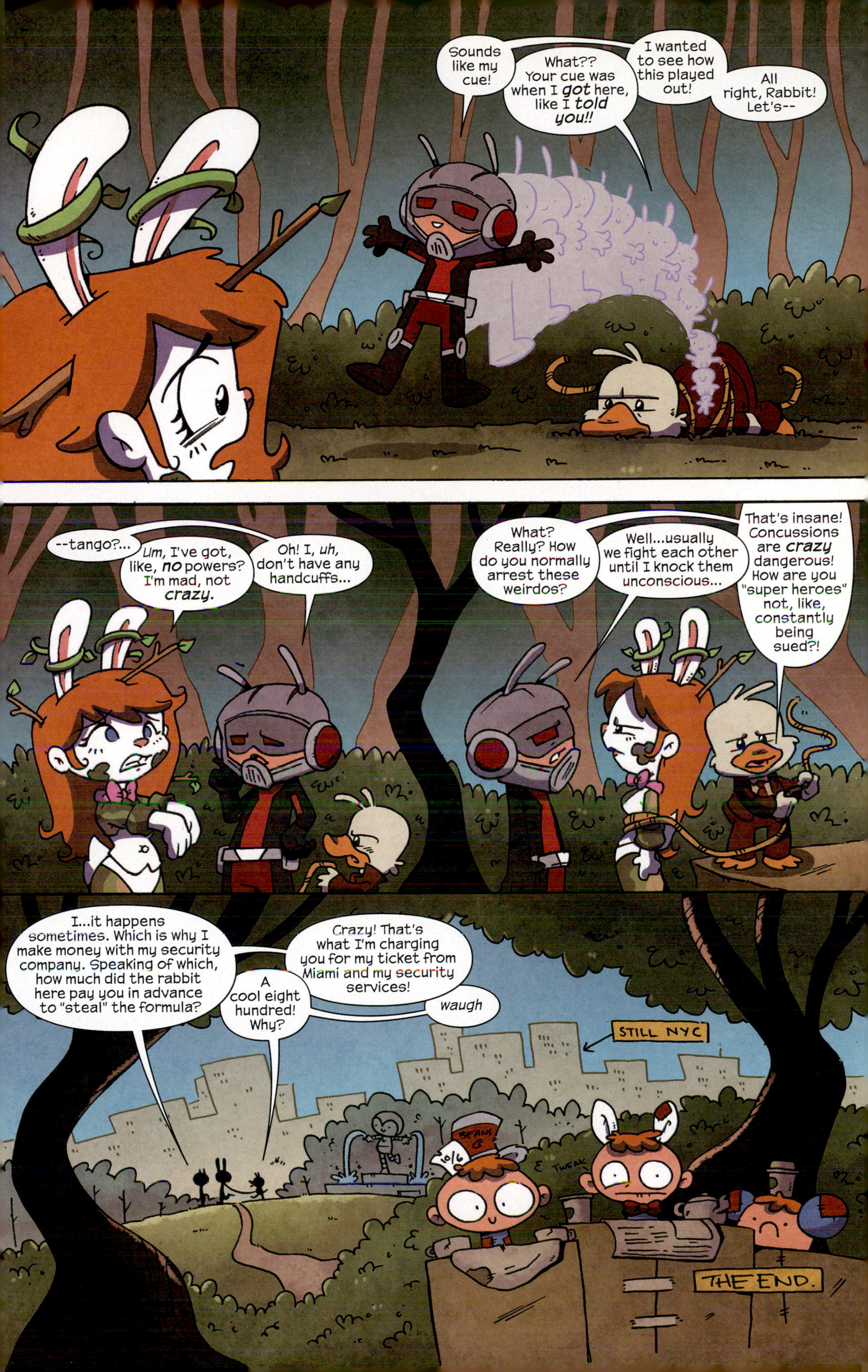
Sounds like my cue!
What?? Your cue was when I got here, like I told you!!
I wanted to see how this played out!
All right, Rabbit! Let's--
--tango?...
Um, I've got, like, no powers? I'm mad, not crazy.
Oh! I, uh, don't have any handcuffs...
What? Really? How do you normally arrest these weirdos?
Well...usually we fight each other until I knock them unconscious...
That's insane! Concussions are crazy dangerous! How are you "super heroes" not, like, constantly being sued?!
I...it happens sometimes. Which is why I make money with my security company. Speaking of which, how much did the rabbit here pay you in advance to "steal" the formula?
A cool eight hundred! Why?
Crazy! That's what I'm charging you for my ticket from Miami and my security services!
waugh
STILL NYC
TWEAK
THE END.

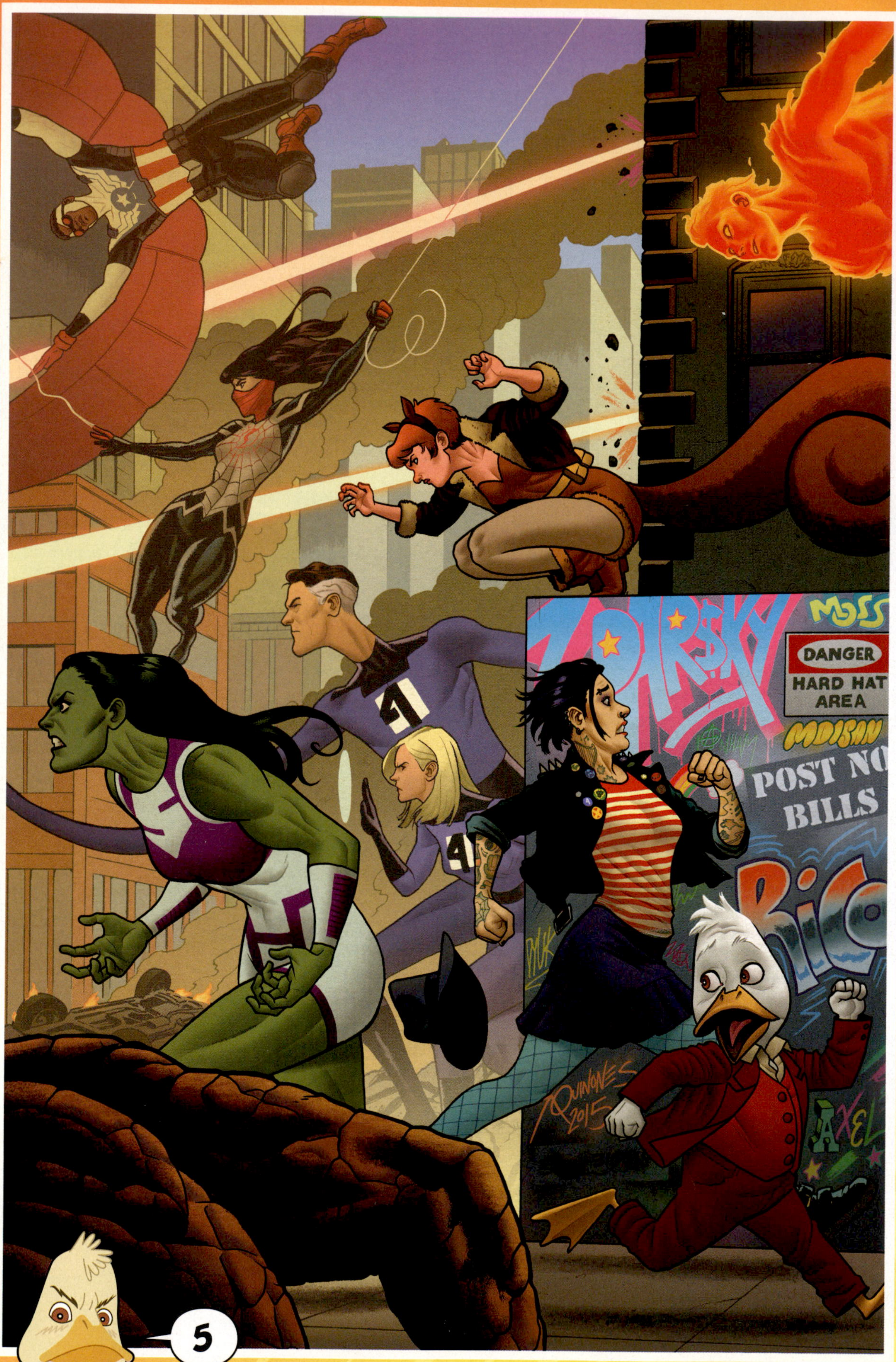
DANGER
HARD HAT AREA
POST NO
BILLS
QUINONES 2015

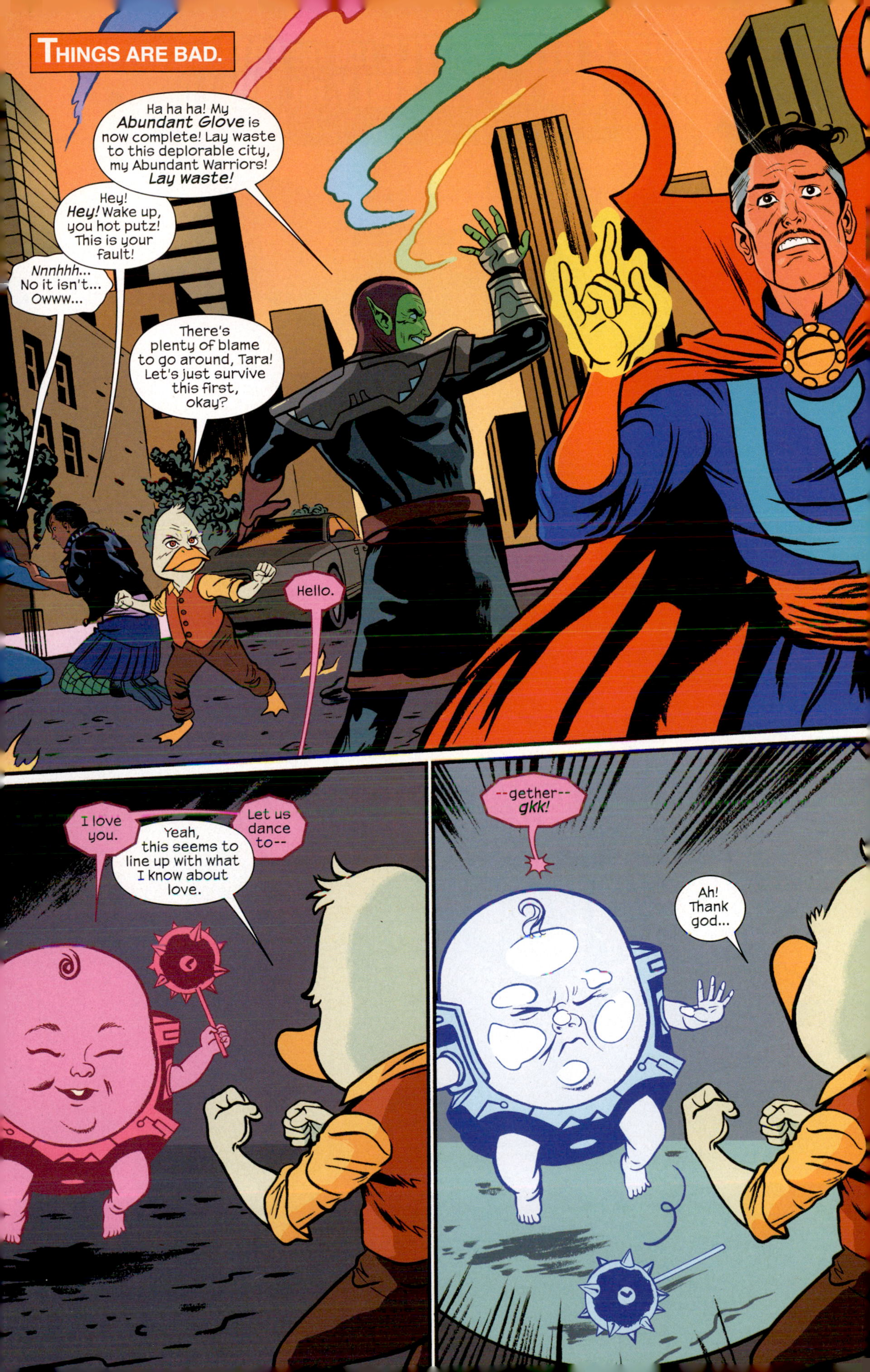
THINGS ARE BAD.
Ha ha ha! My *Abundant Glove* is now complete! Lay waste to this deplorable city, my Abundant Warriors! *Lay waste!*
Hey! *Hey!* Wake up, you hot putz! This is your fault!
Nnnhhh... No it isn't... Owww...
There's plenty of blame to go around, Tara! Let's just survive this first, okay?
Hello.
I love you.
Let us dance to--
Yeah, this seems to line up with what I know about love.
--gether-- *gkk!*
Ah! Thank god...

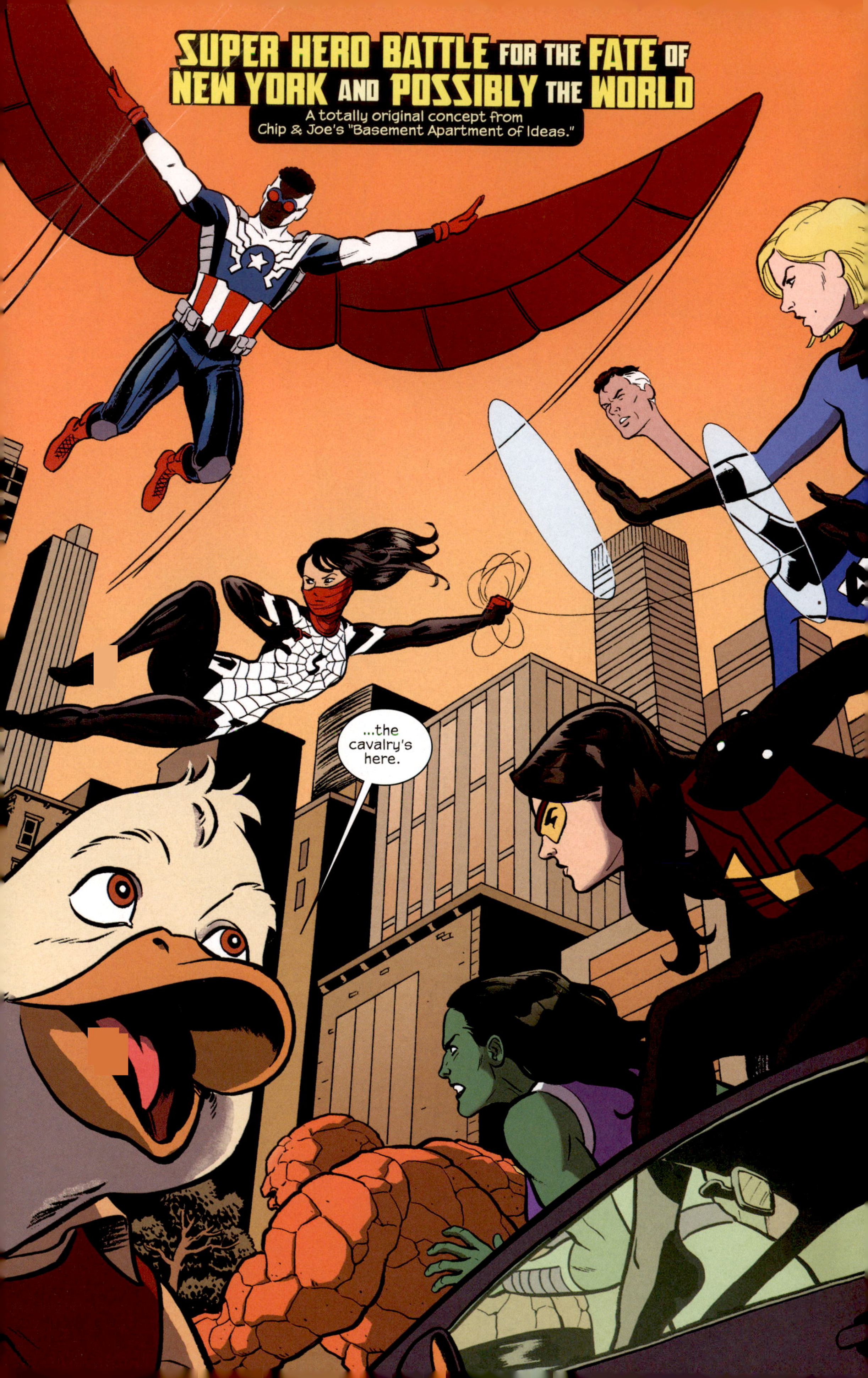
SUPER HERO BATTLE FOR THE FATE OF NEW YORK AND POSSIBLY THE WORLD
A totally original concept from Chip & Joe's "Basement Apartment of Ideas."
...the cavalry's here.

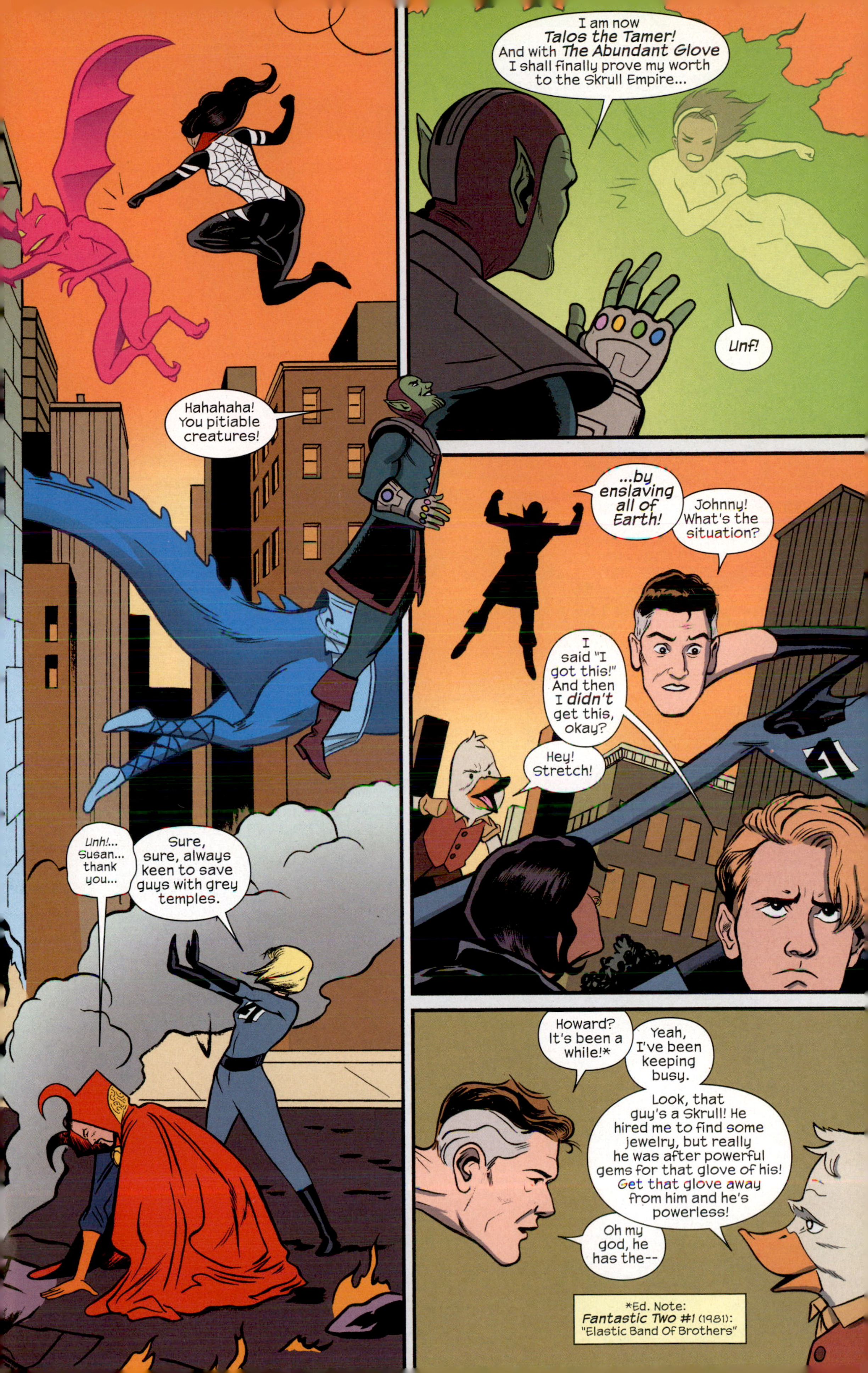
Hahahaha! You pitiable creatures!
Unh!... Susan... thank you...
Sure, sure, always keen to save guys with grey temples.
I am now Talos the Tamer! And with The Abundant Glove I shall finally prove my worth to the Skrull Empire...
Unf!
...by enslaving all of Earth!
Johnny! What's the situation?
I said "I got this!" And then I didn't get this, okay?
Hey! Stretch!
Howard? It's been a while!*
Yeah, I've been keeping busy.
Look, that guy's a Skrull! He hired me to find some jewelry, but really he was after powerful gems for that glove of his! Get that glove away from him and he's powerless!
Oh my god, he has the--
*Ed. Note: Fantastic Two #1 (1981): "Elastic Band Of Brothers"

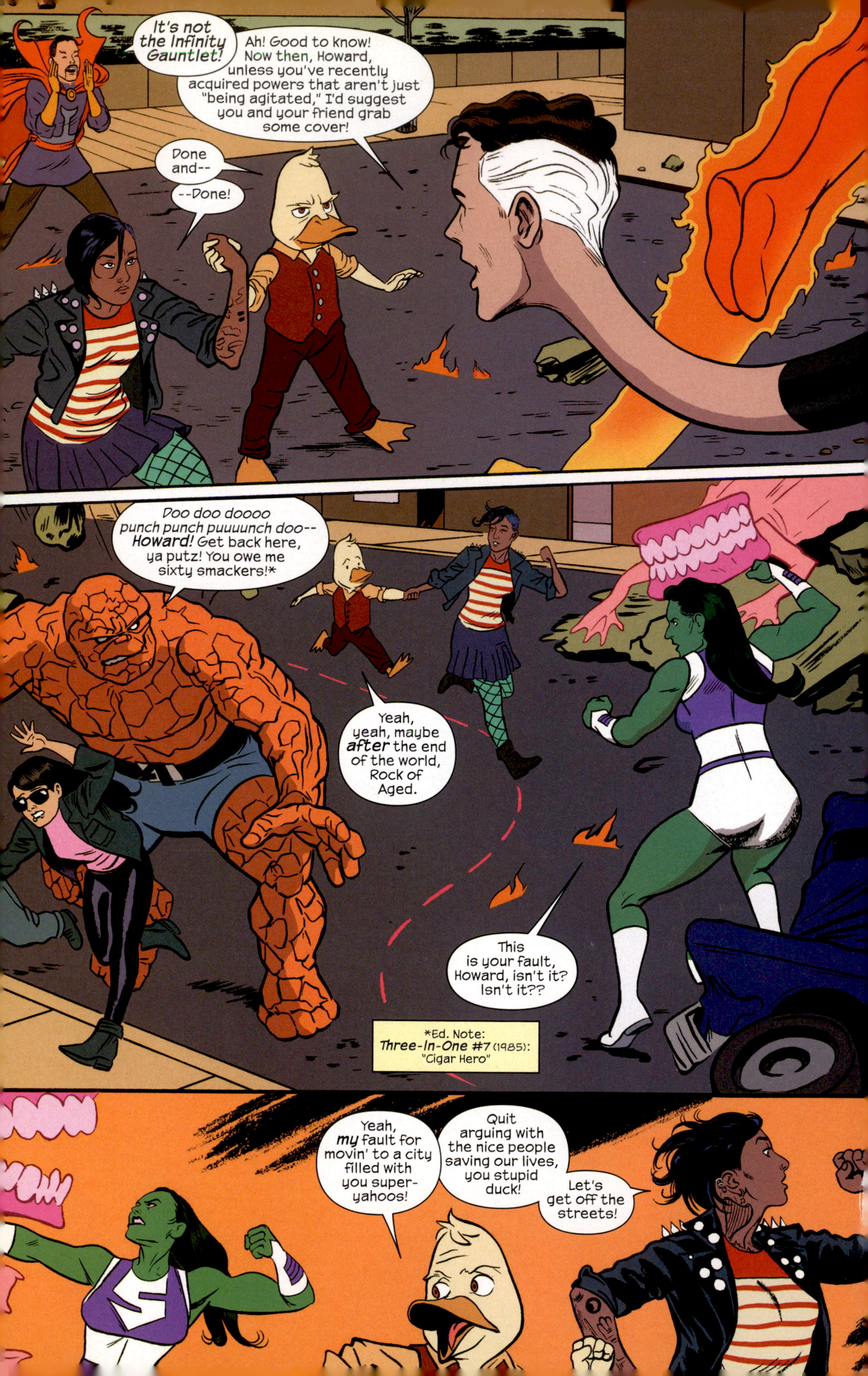
It's not the Infinity Gauntlet!
Ah! Good to know! Now then, Howard, unless you've recently acquired powers that aren't just "being agitated," I'd suggest you and your friend grab some cover!
Done and--
--Done!
Doo doo doooo punch punch puuuunch doo-- Howard! Get back here, ya putz! You owe me sixty smackers!*
Yeah, yeah, maybe after the end of the world, Rock of Aged.
This is your fault, Howard, isn't it? Isn't it??
*Ed. Note: Three-In-One #7 (1985): "Cigar Hero"
Yeah, my fault for movin' to a city filled with you super-yahoos!
Quit arguing with the nice people saving our lives, you stupid duck!
Let's get off the streets!

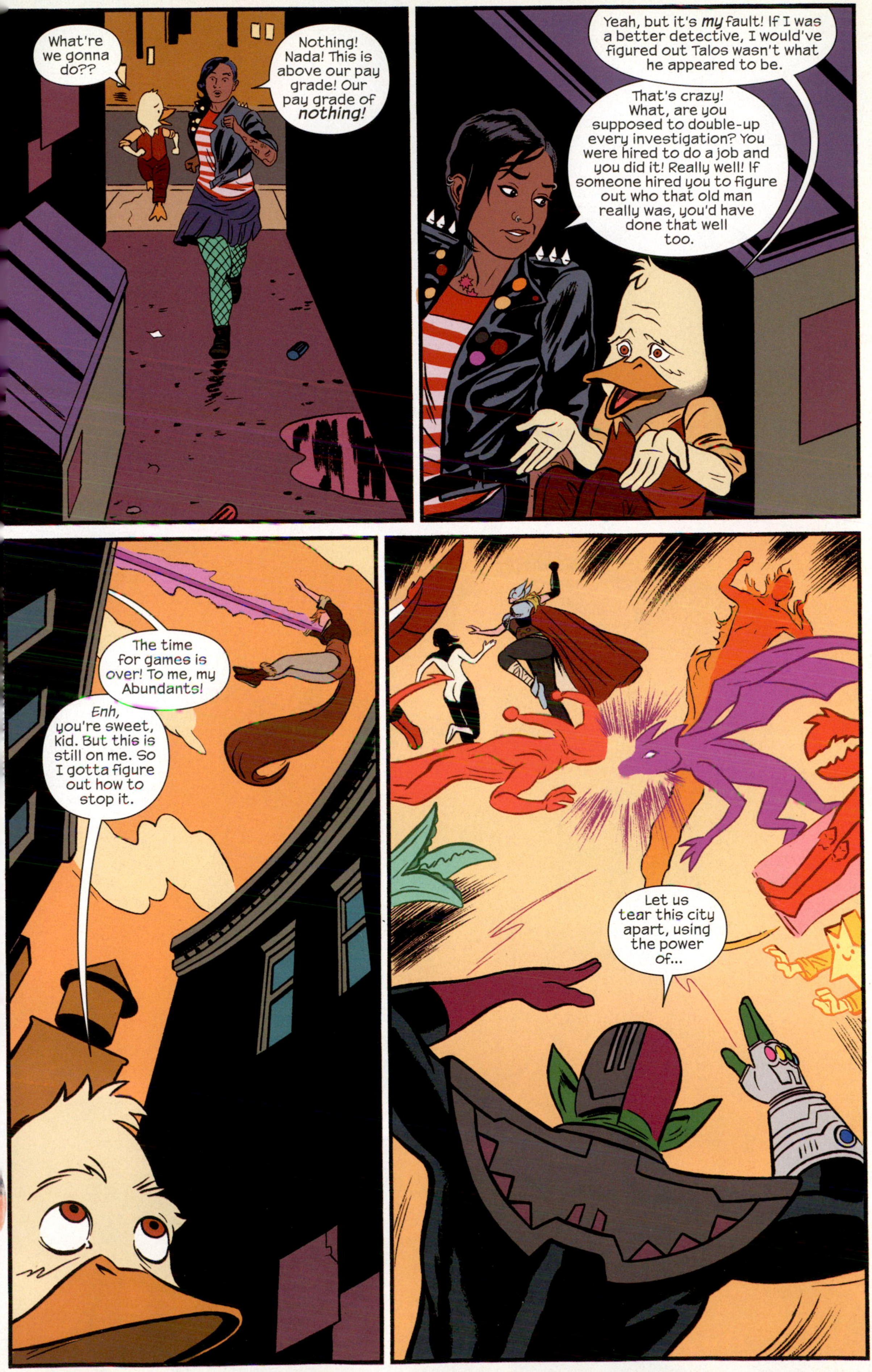
What're we gonna do??
Nothing! Nada! This is above our pay grade! Our pay grade of *nothing!*
Yeah, but it's *my* fault! If I was a better detective, I would've figured out Talos wasn't what he appeared to be.
That's crazy! What, are you supposed to double-up every investigation? You were hired to do a job and you did it! Really well! If someone hired you to figure out who that old man really was, you'd have done that well too.
The time for games is over! To me, my Abundants!
Enh, you're sweet, kid. But this is still on me. So I gotta figure out how to stop it.
Let us tear this city apart, using the power of...

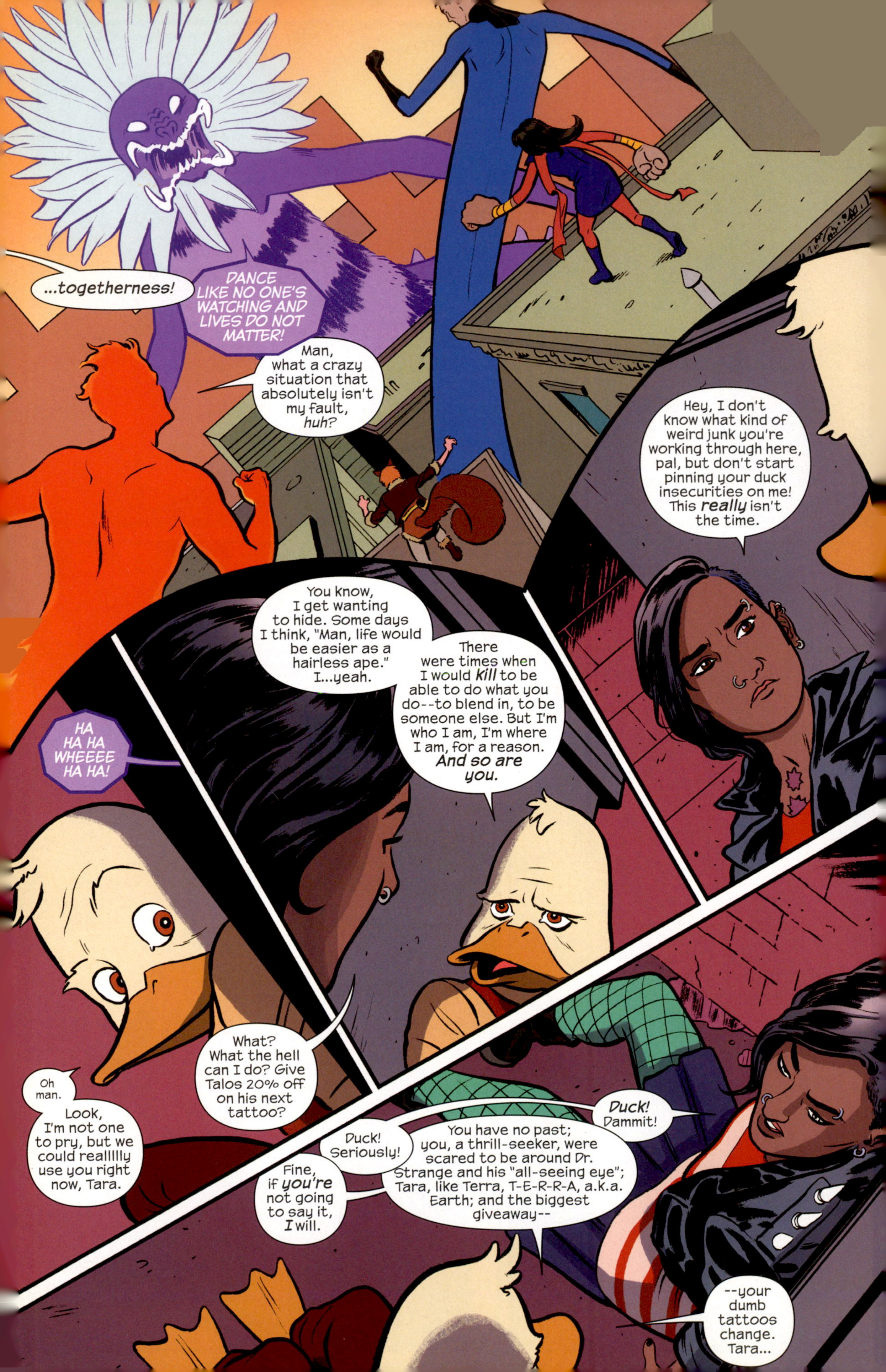
...togetherness!
DANCE LIKE NO ONE'S WATCHING AND LIVES DO NOT MATTER!
Man, what a crazy situation that absolutely isn't my fault, huh?
Hey, I don't know what kind of weird junk you're working through here, pal, but don't start pinning your duck insecurities on me! This really isn't the time.
You know, I get wanting to hide. Some days I think, "Man, life would be easier as a hairless ape." I...yeah.
There were times when I would kill to be able to do what you do--to blend in, to be someone else. But I'm who I am, I'm where I am, for a reason. And so are you.
HA HA HA WHEEEE HA HA!
What? What the hell can I do? Give Talos 20% off on his next tattoo?
Oh man.
Look, I'm not one to pry, but we could reallllly use you right now, Tara.
Duck! Dammit!
Duck! Seriously!
You have no past; you, a thrill-seeker, were scared to be around Dr. Strange and his "all-seeing eye"; Tara, like Terra, T-E-R-R-A, a.k.a. Earth; and the biggest giveaway--
Fine, if you're not going to say it, I will.
--your dumb tattoos change. Tara...

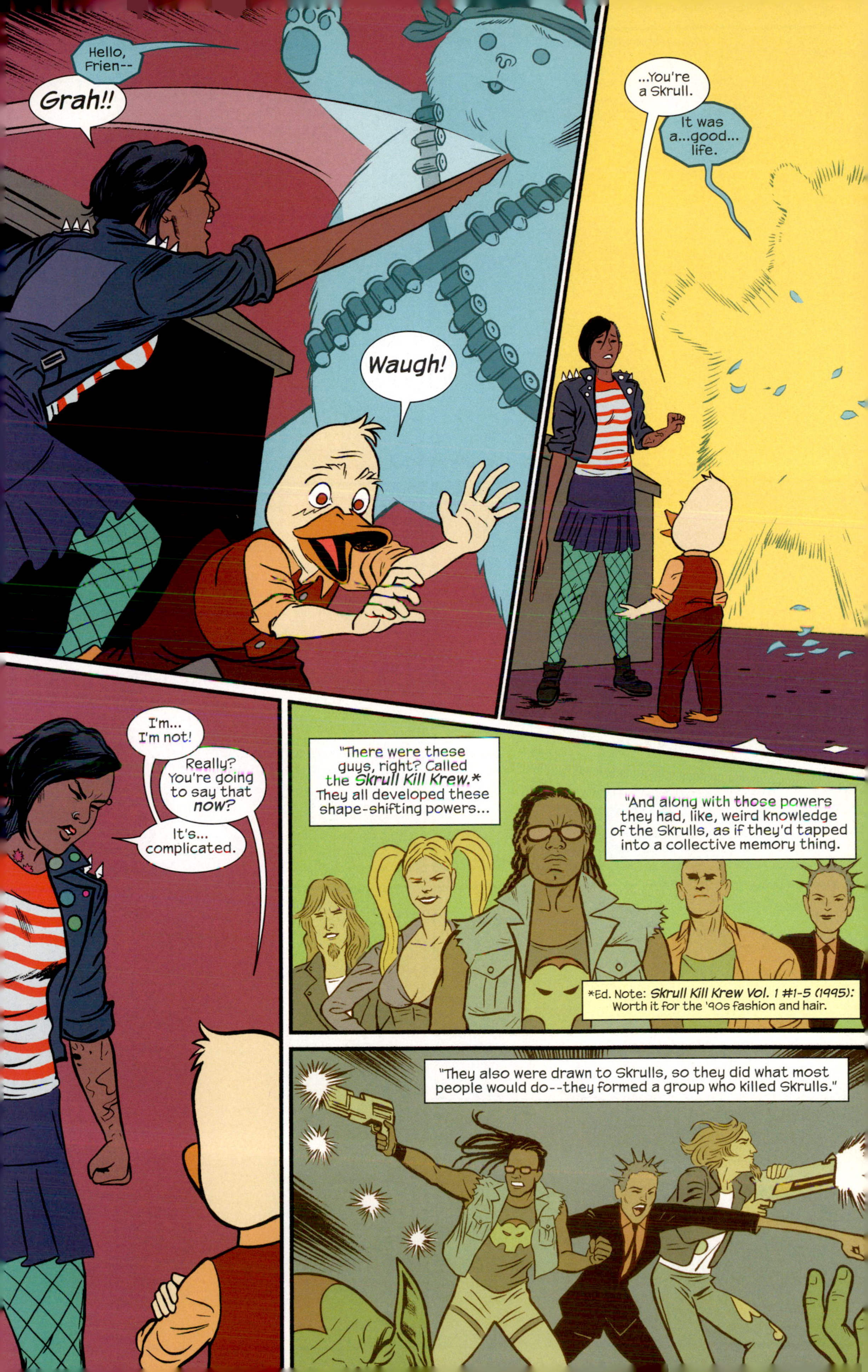
Hello, Frien--
Grah!!
Waugh!
...You're a Skrull.
It was a...good... life.
I'm... I'm not!
Really? You're going to say that *now?*
It's... complicated.
"There were these guys, right? Called the *Skrull Kill Krew.** They all developed these shape-shifting powers...
"And along with those powers they had, like, weird knowledge of the Skrulls, as if they'd tapped into a collective memory thing.
*Ed. Note: *Skrull Kill Krew Vol. 1 #1-5 (1995):* Worth it for the '90s fashion and hair.
"They also were drawn to Skrulls, so they did what most people would do--they formed a group who killed Skrulls."

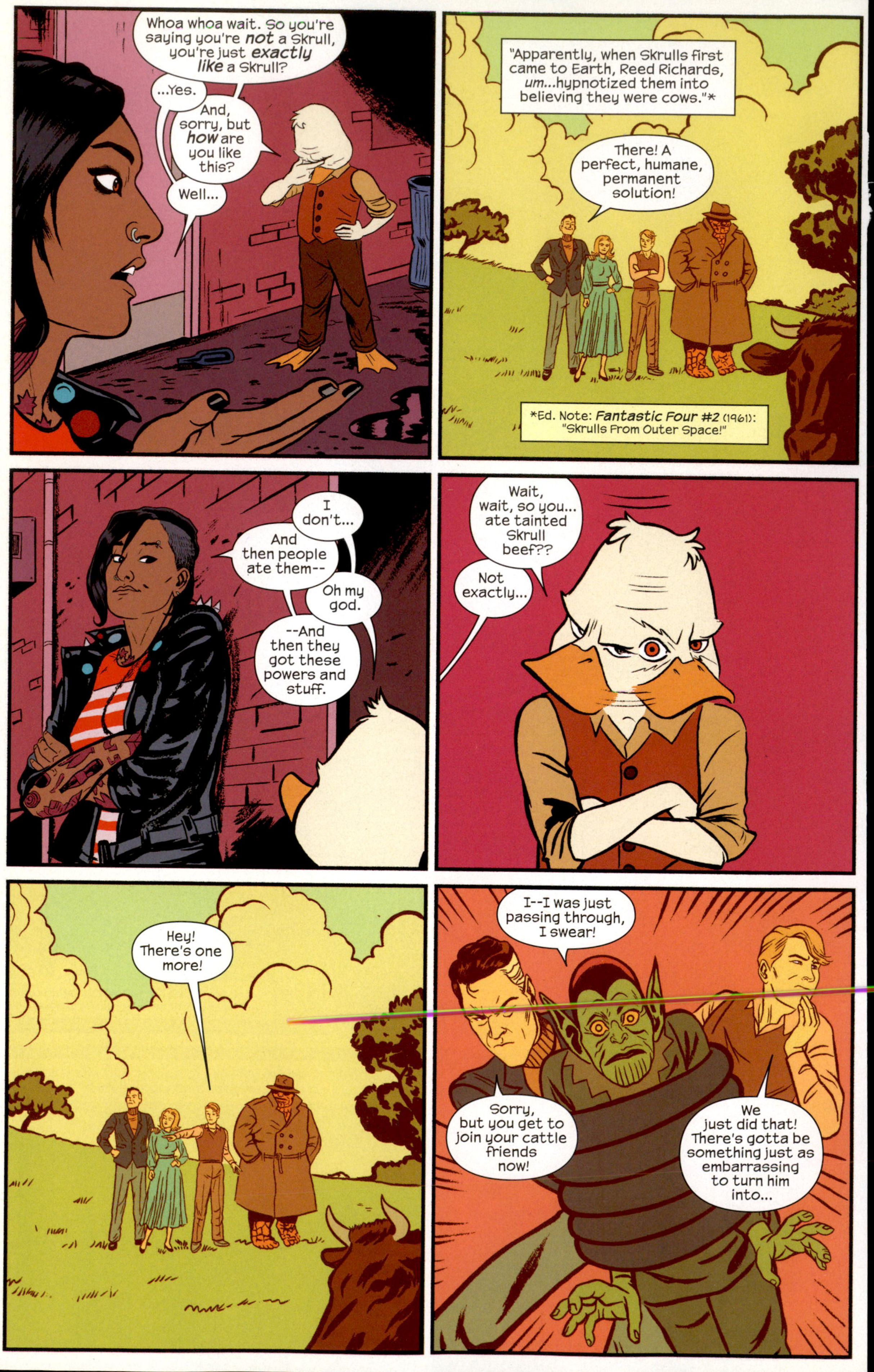

Whoa whoa wait. So you're saying you're *not* a Skrull, you're just *exactly like* a Skrull?
...Yes.
And, sorry, but *how* are you like this?
Well...
"Apparently, when Skrulls first came to Earth, Reed Richards, *um*...hypnotized them into believing they were cows."*
There! A perfect, humane, permanent solution!
*Ed. Note: *Fantastic Four #2* (1961): "Skrulls From Outer Space!"
I don't...
And then people ate them--
Oh my god.
--And then they got these powers and stuff.
Wait, wait, so you... ate tainted Skrull beef??
Not exactly...
Hey! There's one more!
I--I was just passing through, I swear!
Sorry, but you get to join your cattle friends now!
We just did that! There's gotta be something just as embarrassing to turn him into...

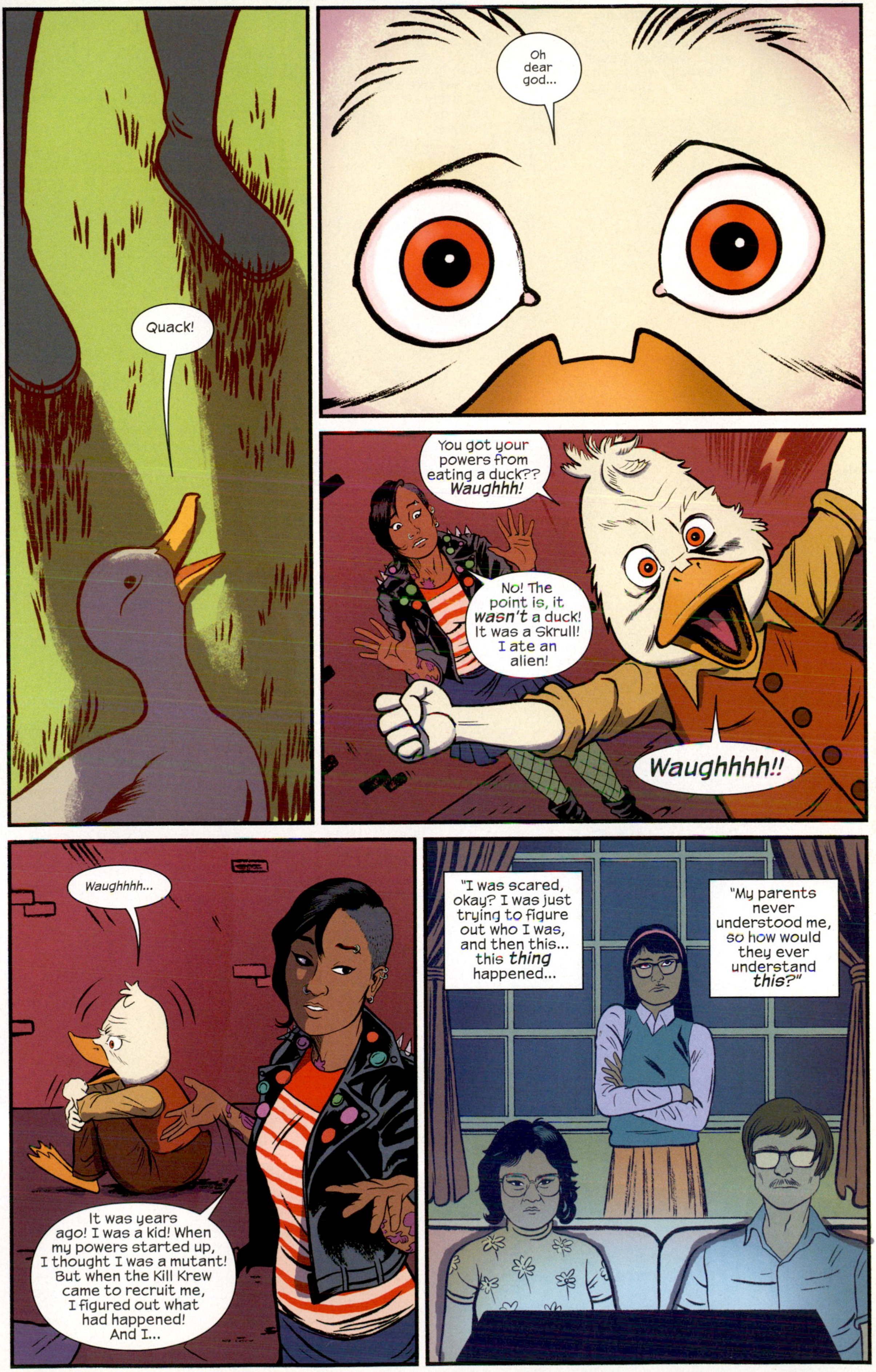
Quack!
Oh dear god...
You got your powers from eating a duck?? Waughhh!
No! The point is, it wasn't a duck! It was a Skrull! I ate an alien!
Waughhhh!!
Waughhhh...
It was years ago! I was a kid! When my powers started up, I thought I was a mutant! But when the Kill Krew came to recruit me, I figured out what had happened! And I...
"I was scared, okay? I was just trying to figure out who I was, and then this... this thing happened...
"My parents never understood me, so how would they ever understand this?"

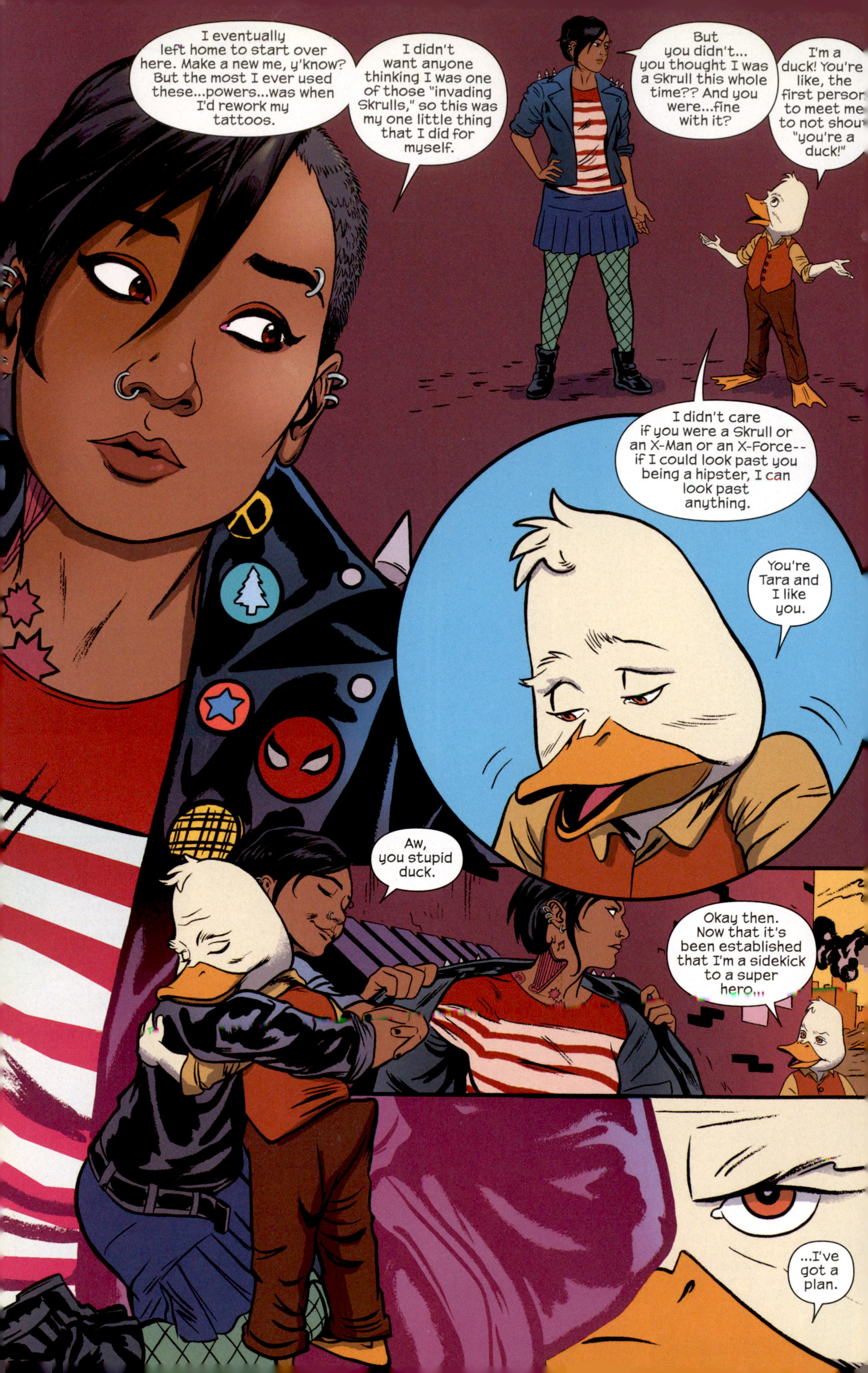
I eventually left home to start over here. Make a new me, y'know? But the most I ever used these...powers...was when I'd rework my tattoos.
I didn't want anyone thinking I was one of those "invading Skrulls," so this was my one little thing that I did for myself.
But you didn't... you thought I was a Skrull this whole time?? And you were...fine with it?
I'm a duck! You're like, the first person to meet me to not shout "you're a duck!"
I didn't care if you were a Skrull or an X-Man or an X-Force-- if I could look past you being a hipster, I can look past anything.
You're Tara and I like you.
Aw, you stupid duck.
Okay then. Now that it's been established that I'm a sidekick to a super hero...
...I've got a plan.

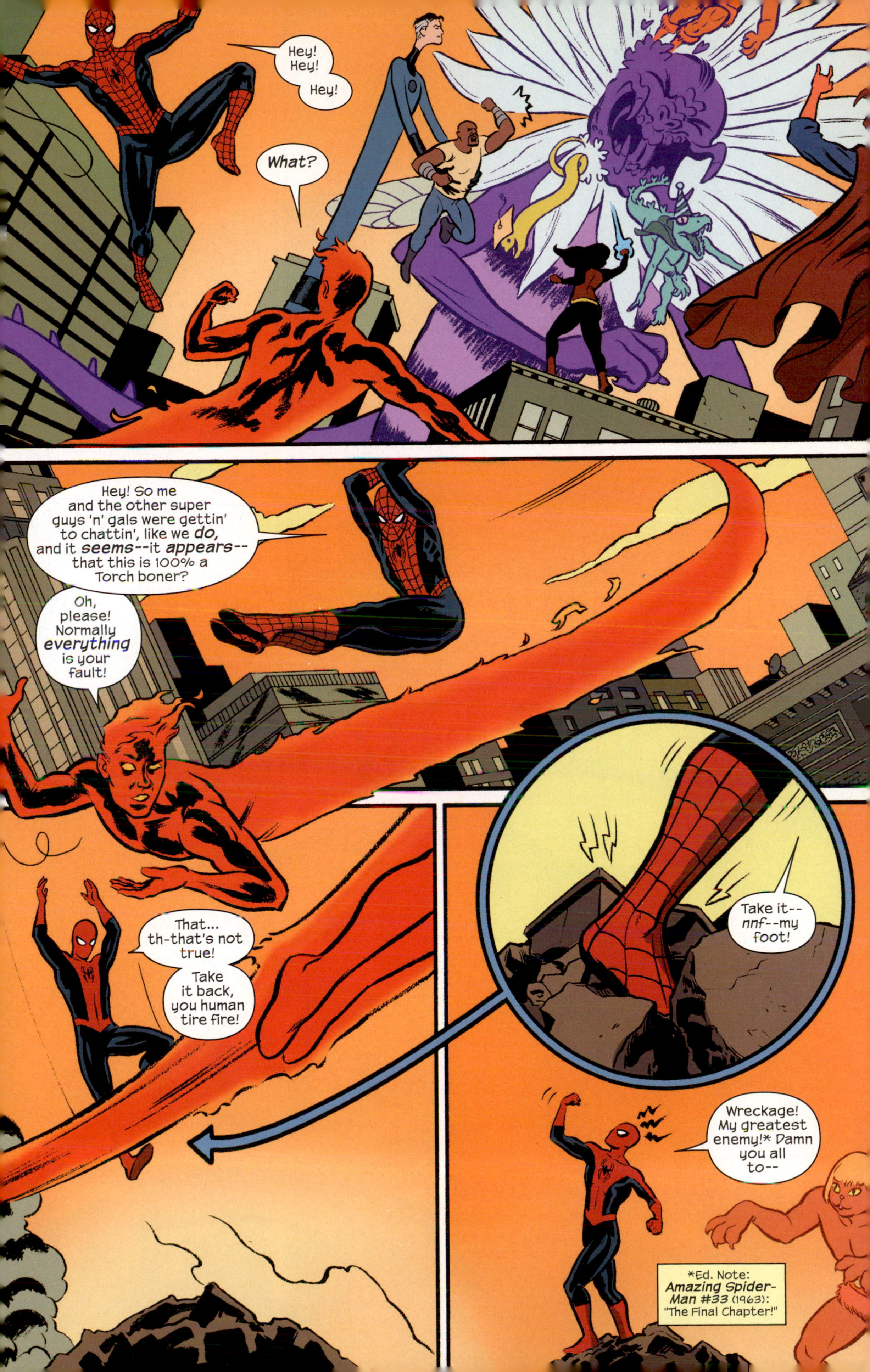
Hey!
Hey!
Hey!
What?
Hey! So me and the other super guys 'n' gals were gettin' to chattin', like we *do*, and it *seems*--it *appears*--that this is 100% a Torch boner?
Oh, please! Normally *everything* is your fault!
That... th-that's not true!
Take it back, you human tire fire!
Take it-- *nnf*--my foot!
Wreckage! My greatest enemy!* Damn you all to--
*Ed. Note: *Amazing Spider-Man #33* (1963): "The Final Chapter!"

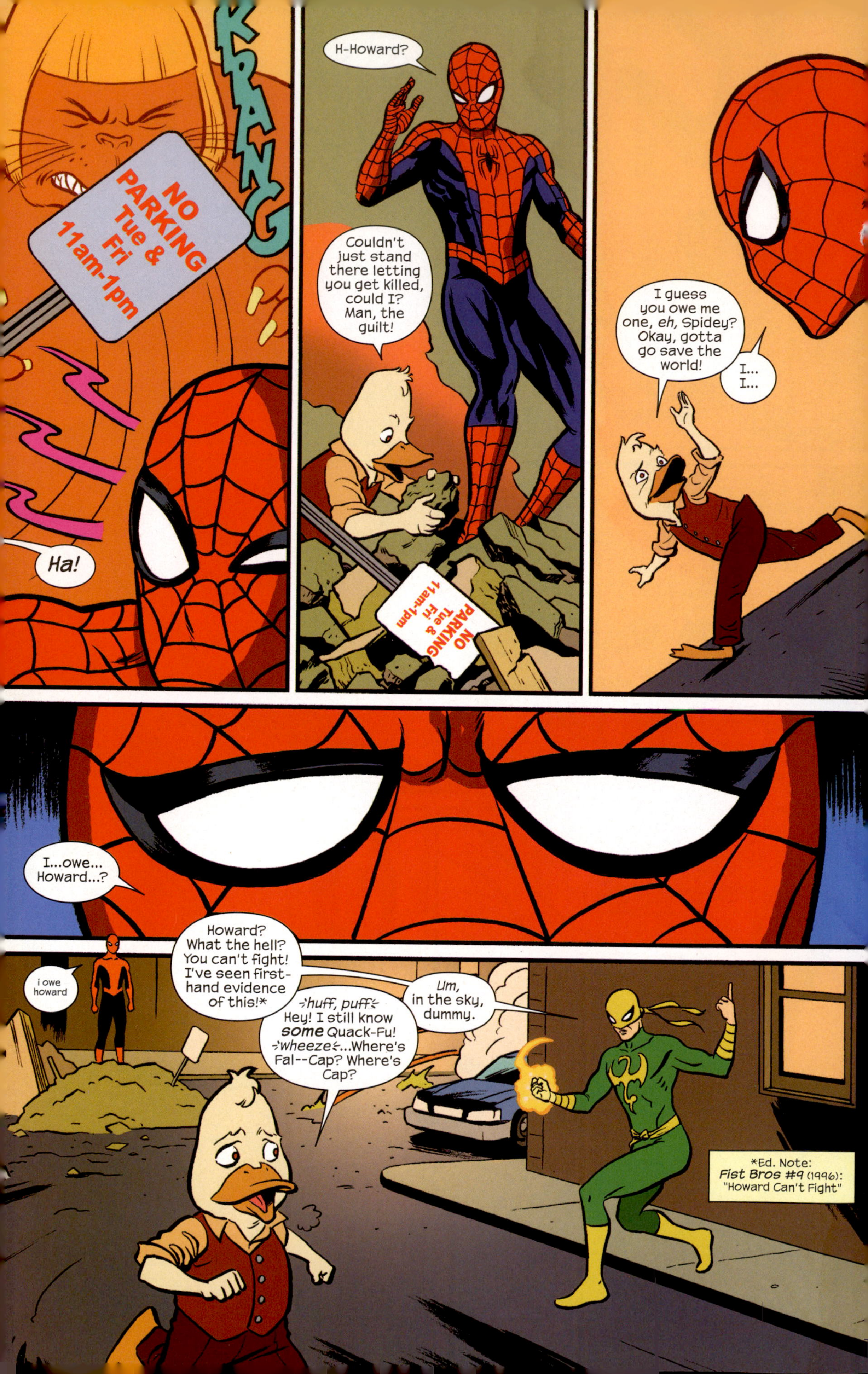
KRANG
NO PARKING Tue & Fri 11am-1pm
Ha!
H-Howard?
Couldn't just stand there letting you get killed, could I? Man, the guilt!
NO PARKING Tue & Fri 11am-1pm
I guess you owe me one, eh, Spidey? Okay, gotta go save the world!
I... I...
I...owe... Howard...?
i owe howard
Howard? What the hell? You can't fight! I've seen first-hand evidence of this!*
huff, puff Hey! I still know some Quack-Fu! *wheeze*...Where's Fal--Cap? Where's Cap?
Um, in the sky, dummy.
*Ed. Note: Fist Bros #9 (1996): "Howard Can't Fight"

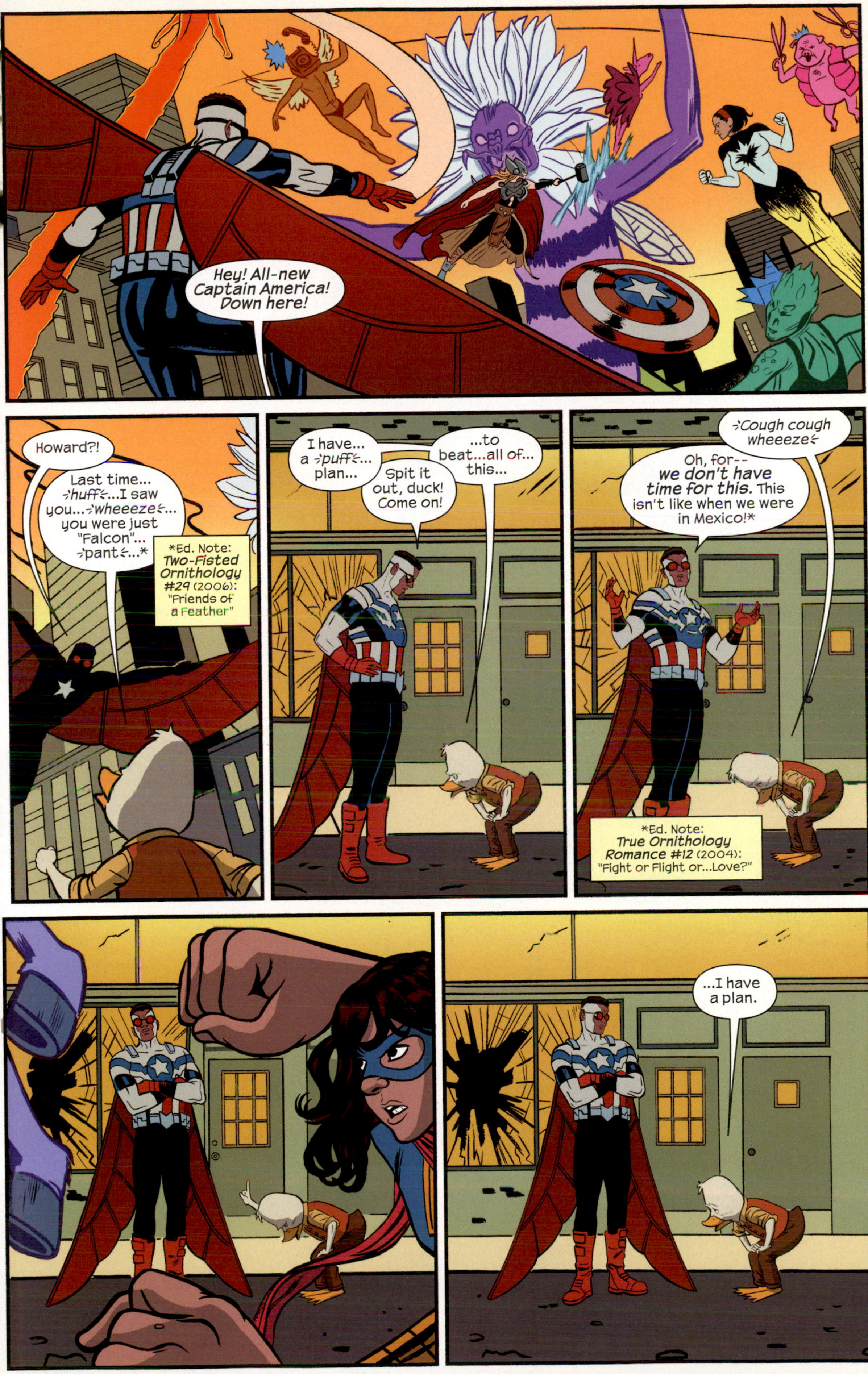
Hey! All-new Captain America! Down here!
Howard?!
Last time... ~huff~...I saw you...~wheeeze~... you were just "Falcon"... ~pant~...*
*Ed. Note: Two-Fisted Ornithology #29 (2006): "Friends of a Feather"
I have... a ~puff~... plan...
Spit it out, duck! Come on!
...to beat...all of... this...
~Cough cough wheeeze~
Oh, for-- we don't have time for this. This isn't like when we were in Mexico!*
*Ed. Note: True Ornithology Romance #12 (2004): "Fight or Flight or...Love?"
...I have a plan.

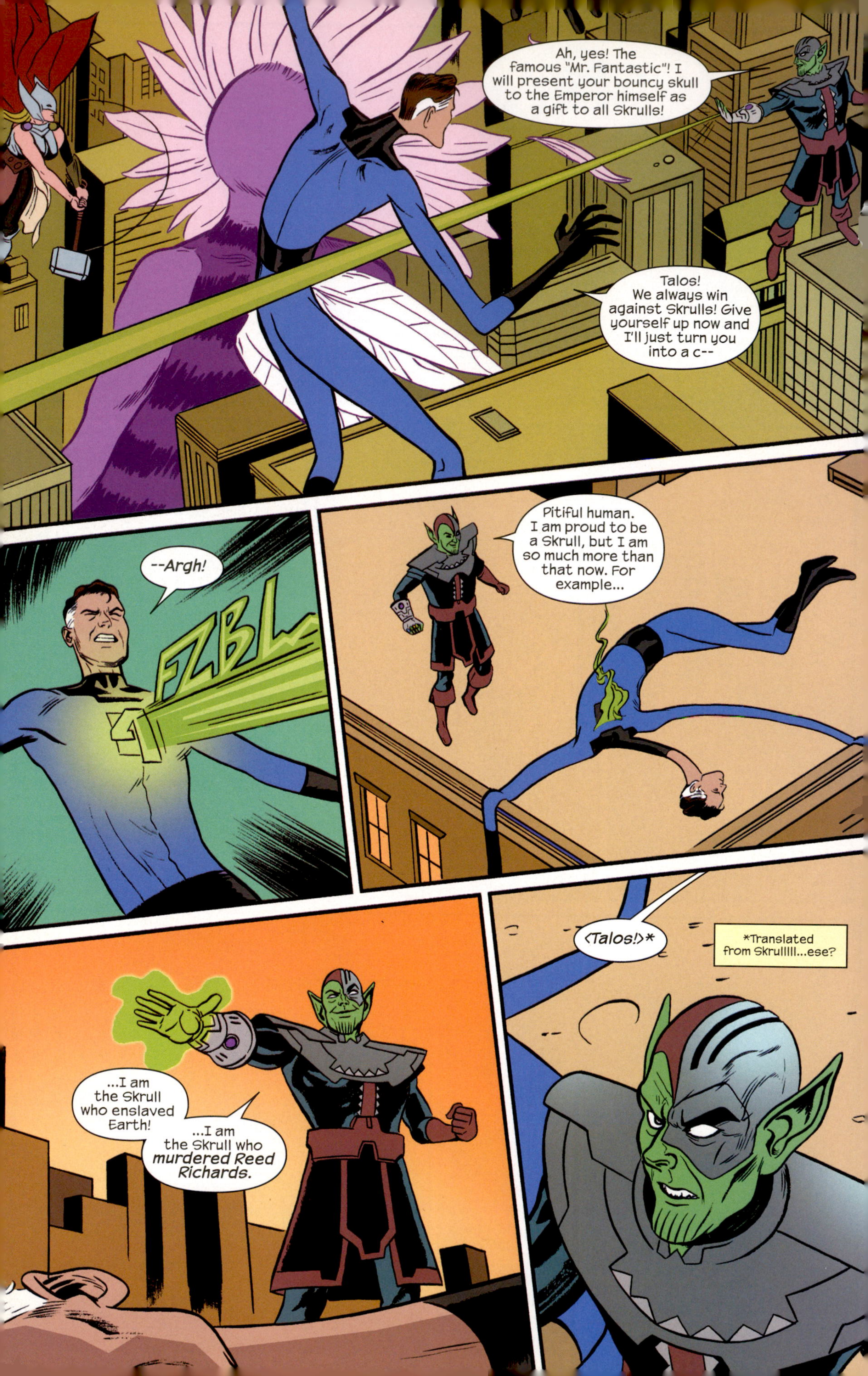
Ah, yes! The famous "Mr. Fantastic"! I will present your bouncy skull to the Emperor himself as a gift to all Skrulls!
Talos! We always win against Skrulls! Give yourself up now and I'll just turn you into a c--
--Argh!
FZBL
Pitiful human. I am proud to be a Skrull, but I am so much more than that now. For example...
...I am the Skrull who enslaved Earth!
...I am the Skrull who murdered Reed Richards.
<Talos!>*
*Translated from Skrullllll...ese?

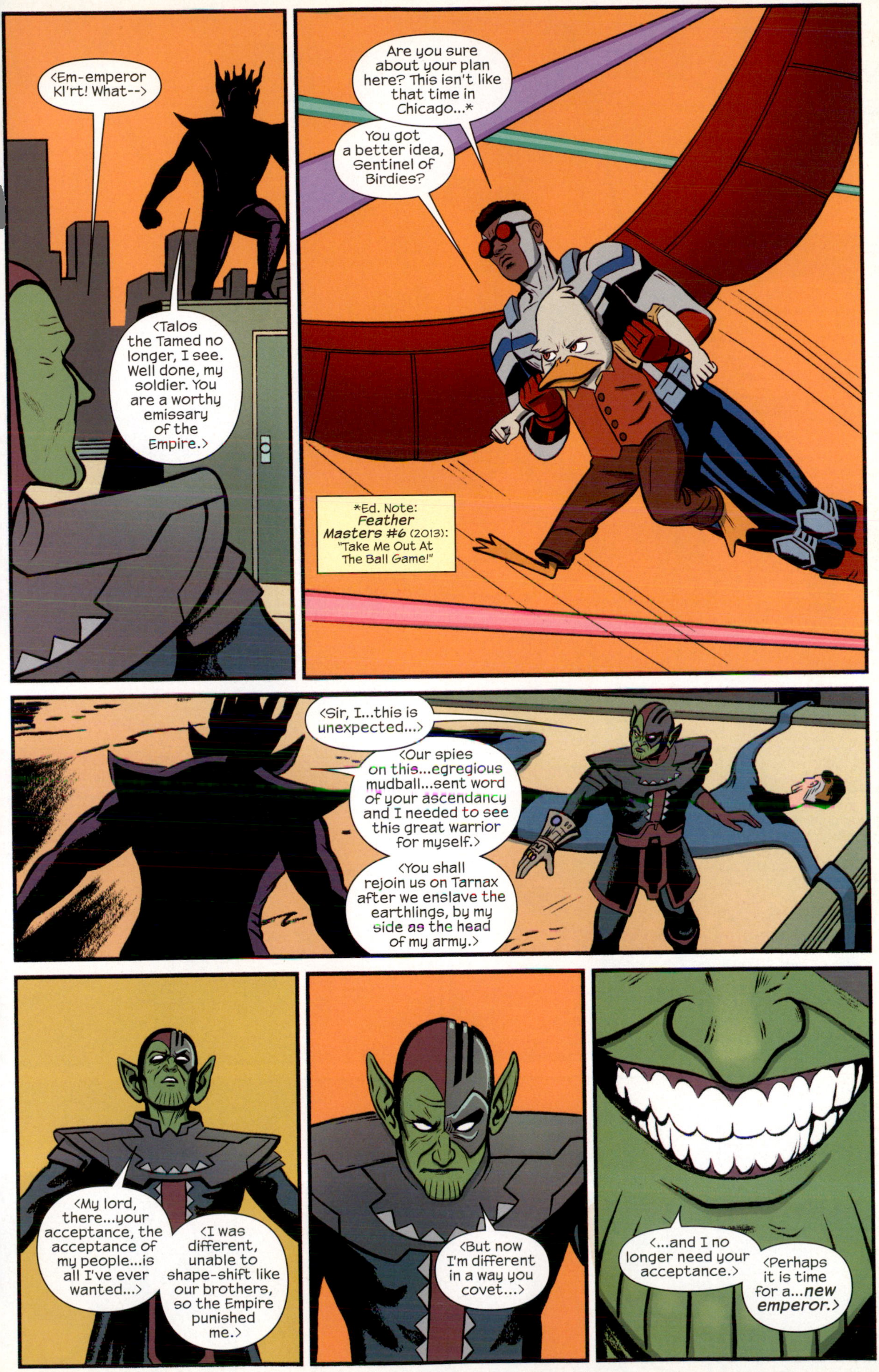

<Em-emperor Kl'rt! What-->
<Talos the Tamed no longer, I see. Well done, my soldier. You are a worthy emissary of the Empire.>
Are you sure about your plan here? This isn't like that time in Chicago...*
You got a better idea, Sentinel of Birdies?
*Ed. Note: Feather Masters #6 (2013): "Take Me Out At The Ball Game!"
<Sir, I...this is unexpected...>
<Our spies on this...egregious mudball...sent word of your ascendancy and I needed to see this great warrior for myself.>
<You shall rejoin us on Tarnax after we enslave the earthlings, by my side as the head of my army.>
<My lord, there...your acceptance, the acceptance of my people...is all I've ever wanted...>
<I was different, unable to shape-shift like our brothers, so the Empire punished me.>
<But now I'm different in a way you covet...>
<...and I no longer need your acceptance.>
<Perhaps it is time for a...new emperor.>

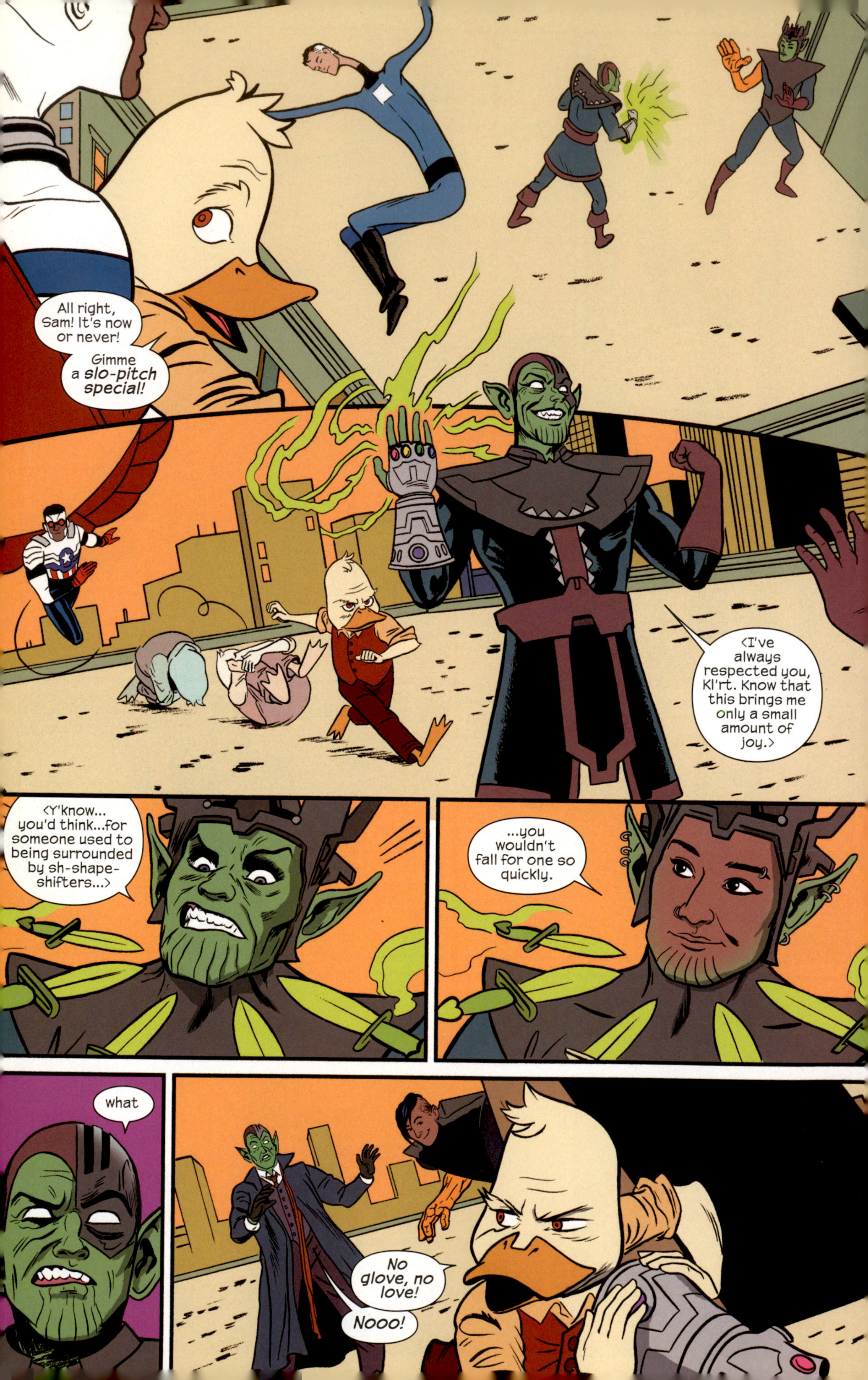

All right, Sam! It's now or never!
Gimme a slo-pitch special!
<I've always respected you, Kl'rt. Know that this brings me only a small amount of joy.>
<Y'know... you'd think...for someone used to being surrounded by sh-shape-shifters...>
...you wouldn't fall for one so quickly.
what
No glove, no love!
Nooo!

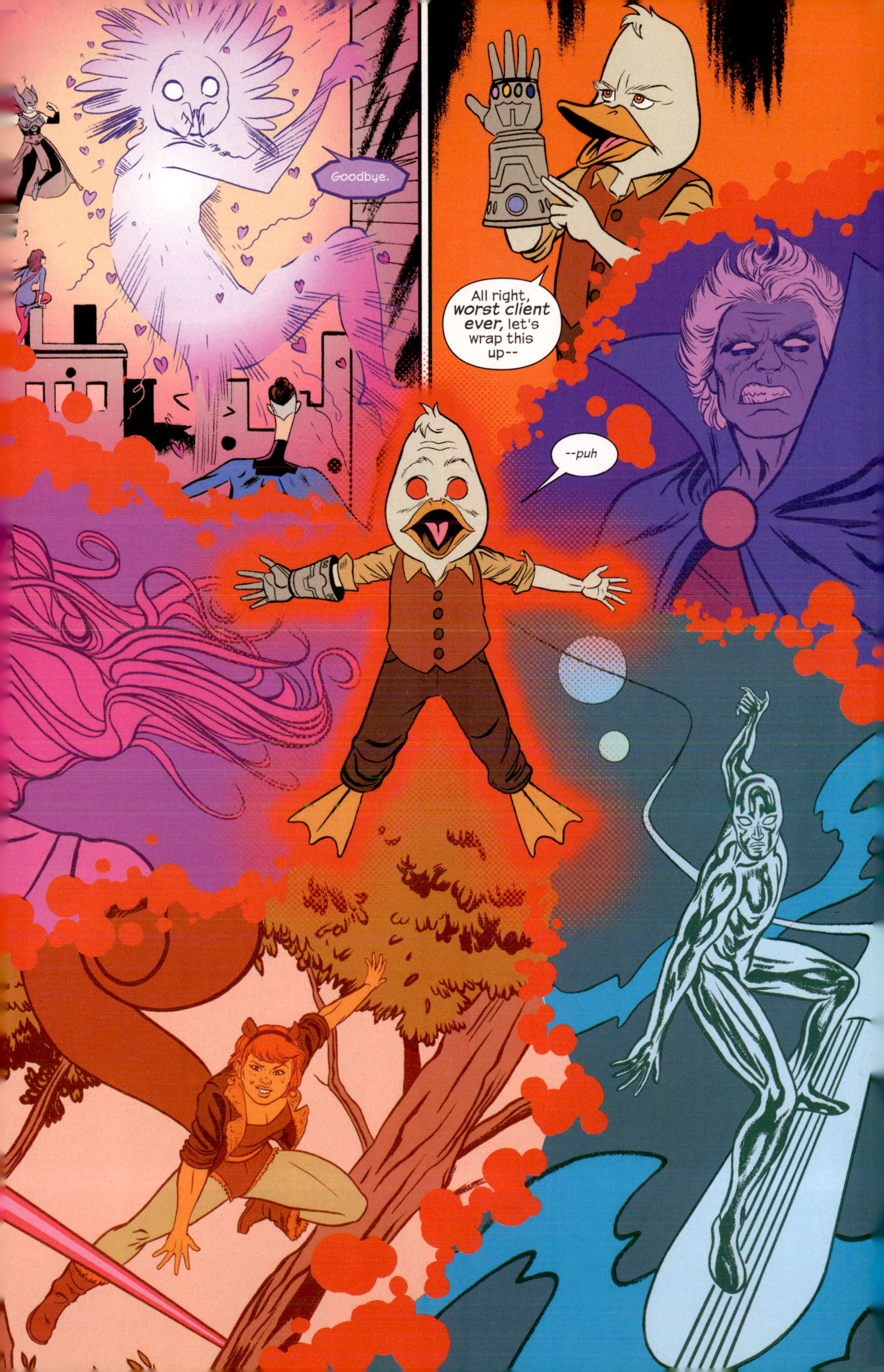
Goodbye.
All right, worst client ever, let's wrap this up--
--puh

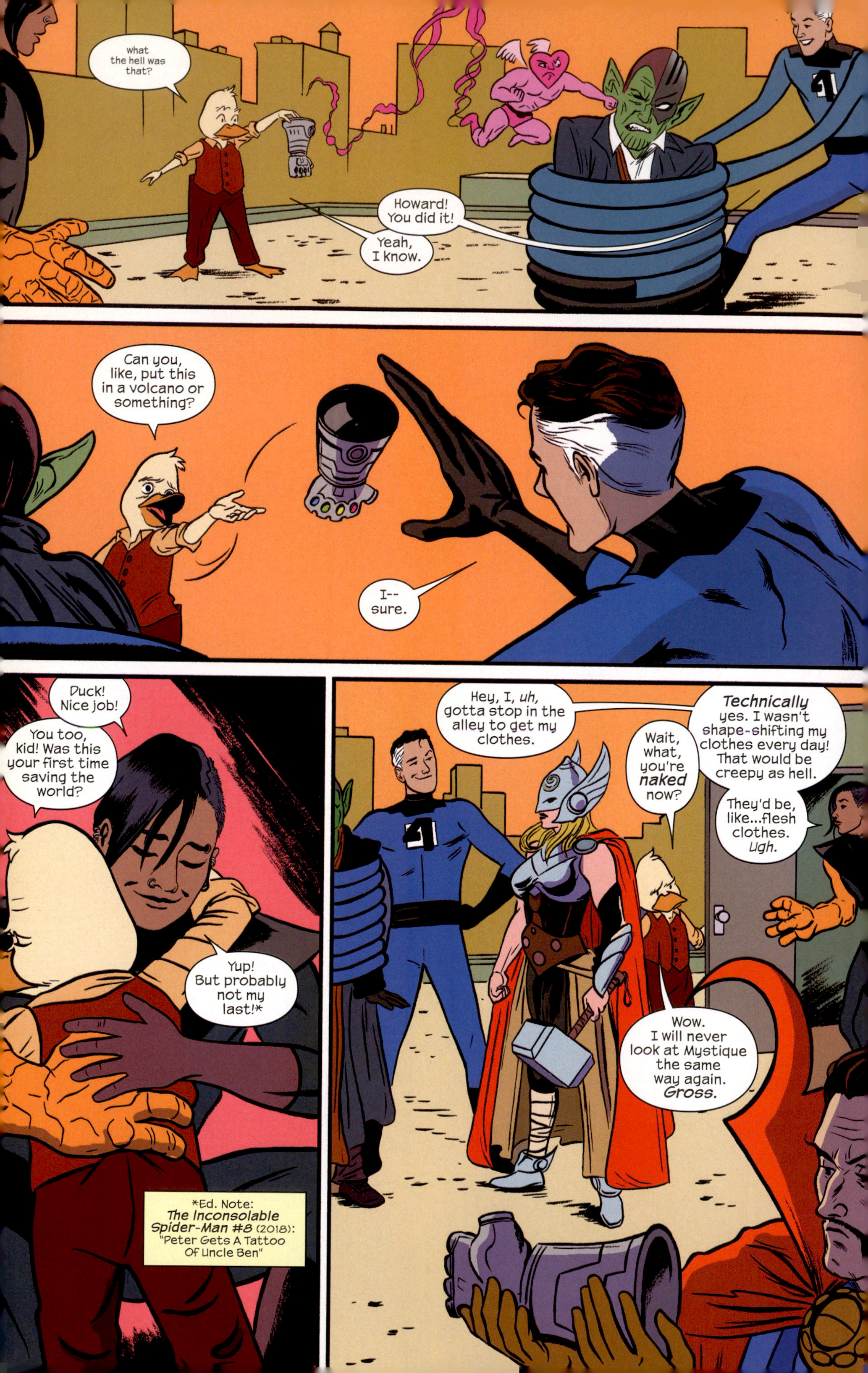
what the hell was that?
Howard! You did it!
Yeah, I know.
Can you, like, put this in a volcano or something?
I-- sure.
Duck! Nice job!
You too, kid! Was this your first time saving the world?
Yup! But probably not my last!*
*Ed. Note: The Inconsolable Spider-Man #8 (2018): "Peter Gets A Tattoo Of Uncle Ben"
Hey, I, uh, gotta stop in the alley to get my clothes.
Wait, what, you're naked now?
Technically yes. I wasn't shape-shifting my clothes every day! That would be creepy as hell.
They'd be, like...flesh clothes. Ugh.
Wow. I will never look at Mystique the same way again. Gross.

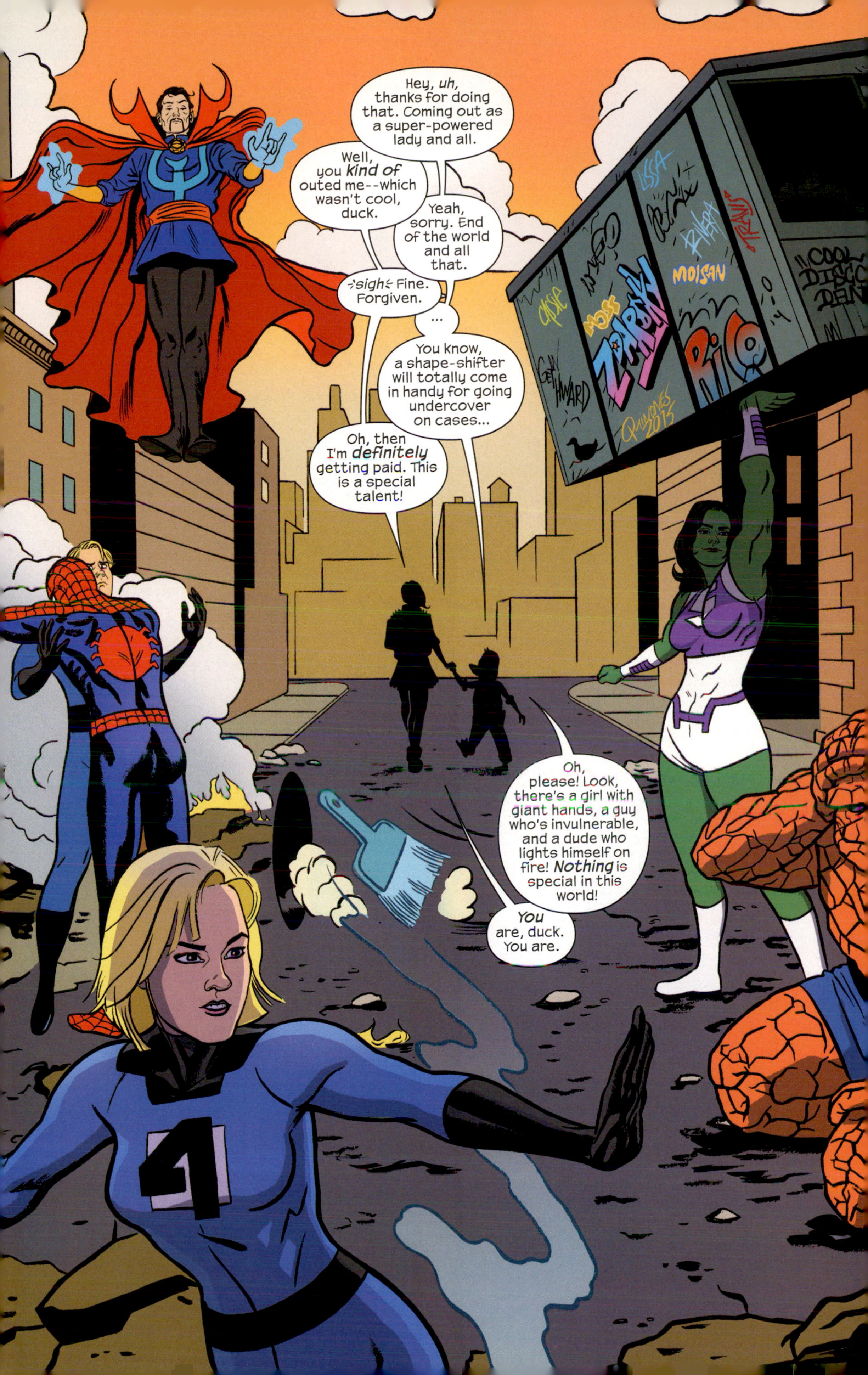
Hey, uh, thanks for doing that. Coming out as a super-powered lady and all.
Well, you kind of outed me--which wasn't cool, duck.
Yeah, sorry. End of the world and all that.
sigh Fine. Forgiven.
...
You know, a shape-shifter will totally come in handy for going undercover on cases...
Oh, then I'm definitely getting paid. This is a special talent!
Oh, please! Look, there's a girl with giant hands, a guy who's invulnerable, and a dude who lights himself on fire! Nothing is special in this world!
You are, duck. You are.

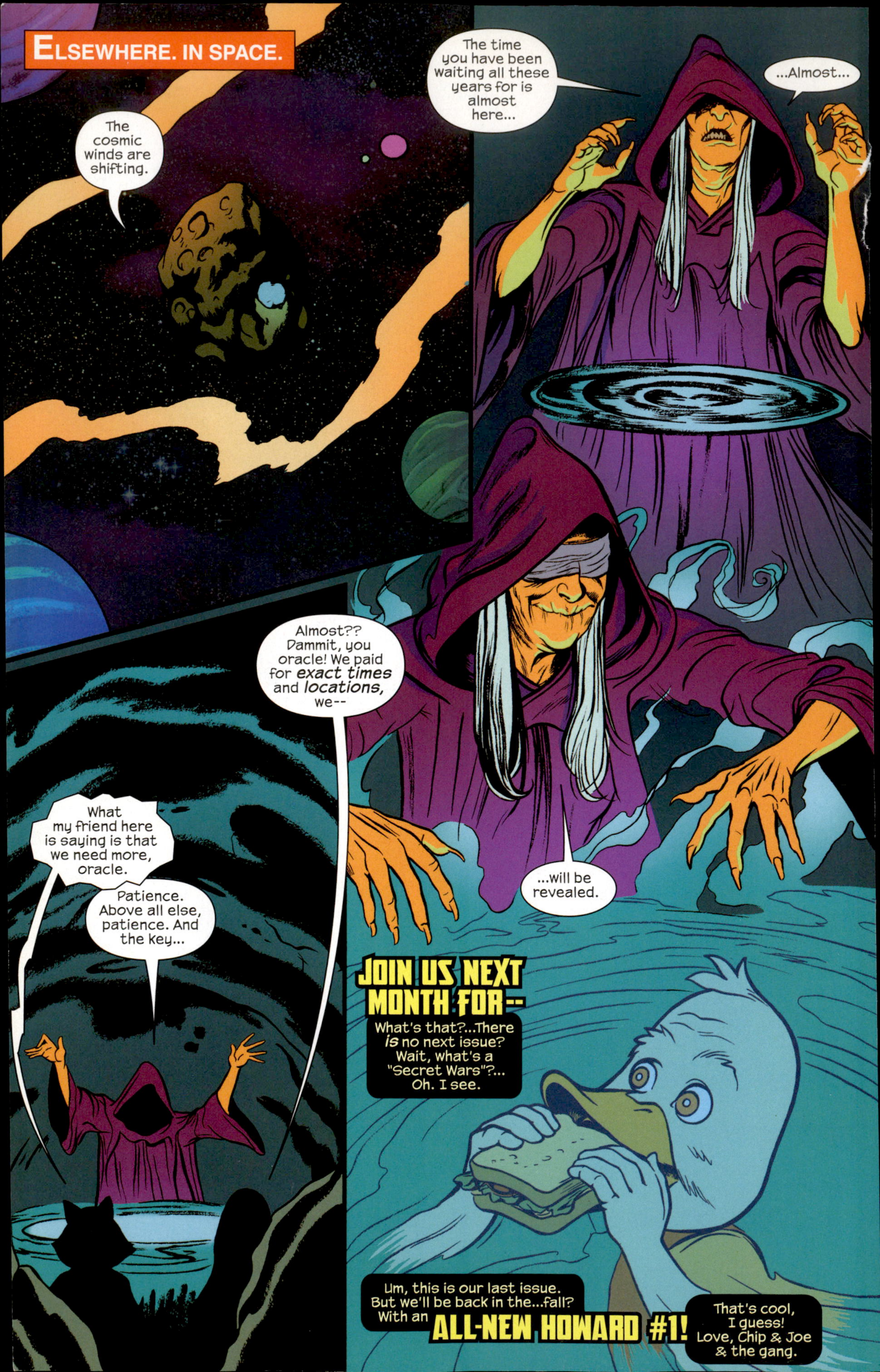
ELSEWHERE. IN SPACE.
The cosmic winds are shifting.
The time you have been waiting all these years for is almost here...
...Almost...
Almost?? Dammit, you oracle! We paid for *exact times* and *locations,* we--
...will be revealed.
What my friend here is saying is that we need more, oracle.
Patience. Above all else, patience. And the key...
JOIN US NEXT MONTH FOR--
What's that?...There *is* no next issue? Wait, what's a "Secret Wars"?... Oh. I see.
Um, this is our last issue. But we'll be back in the...fall? With an ALL-NEW HOWARD #1!
That's cool, I guess! Love, Chip & Joe & the gang.

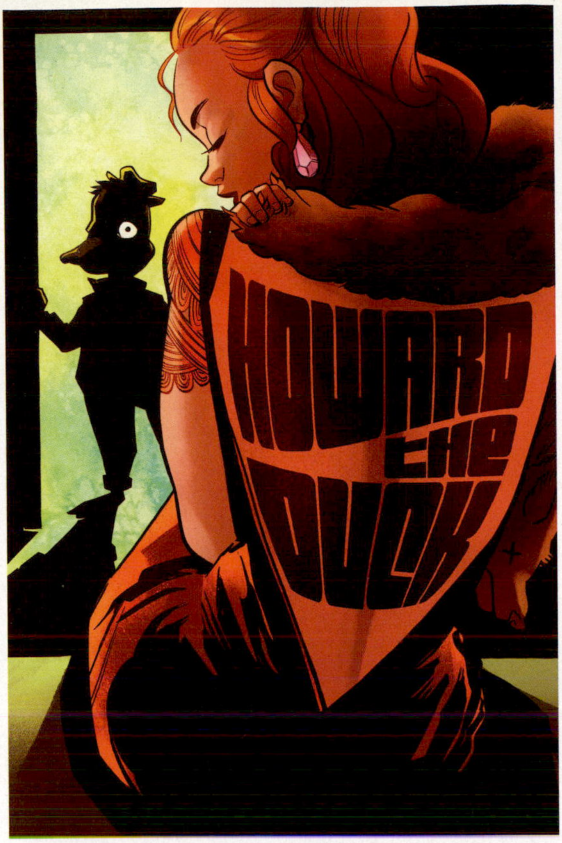
HOWARD
THE
DUCK

#1 VARIANT
BY ERICA HENDERSON

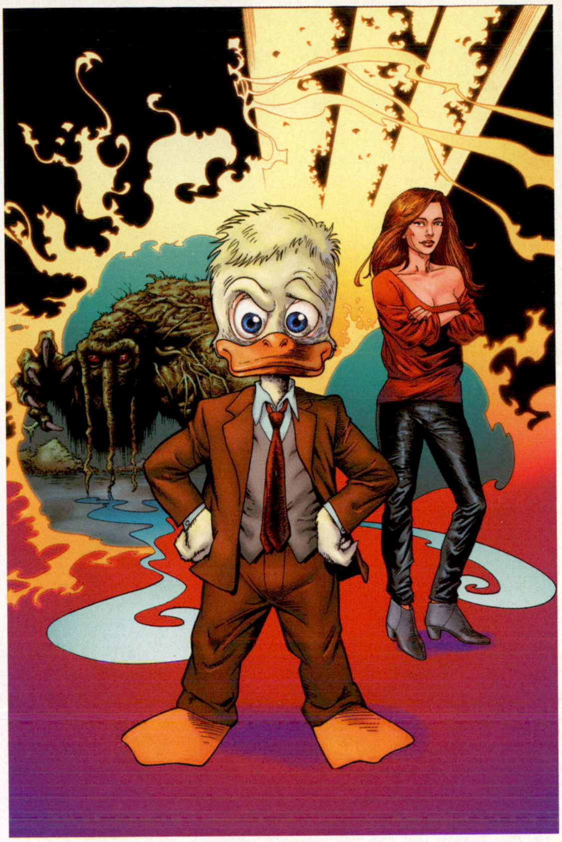

#1 VARIANT
BY VAL MAYERICK & CHRIS SOTOMAYOR

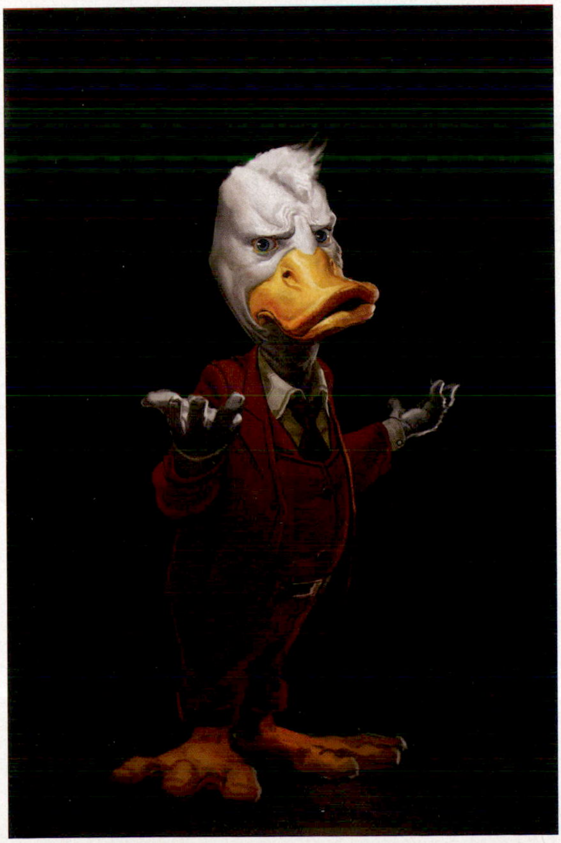

#1 MOVIE VARIANT
BY RYAN MEINERDING

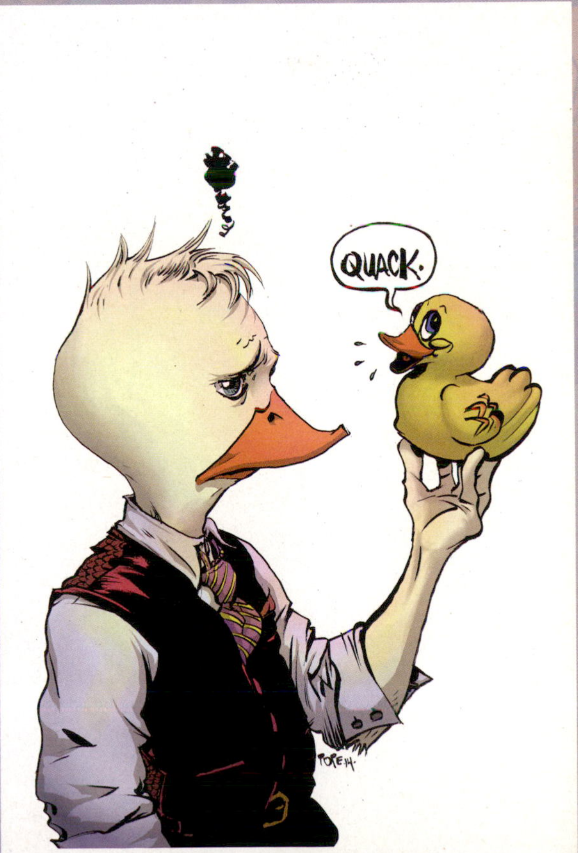
QUACK.

#1 VARIANT
BY PAUL POPE & SHAY PLUMMER

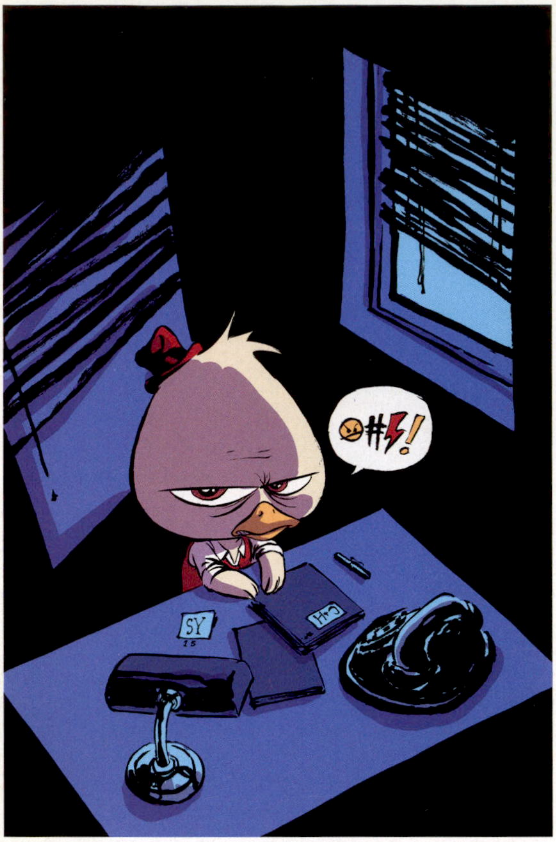

#1 VARIANT
BY SKOTTIE YOUNG

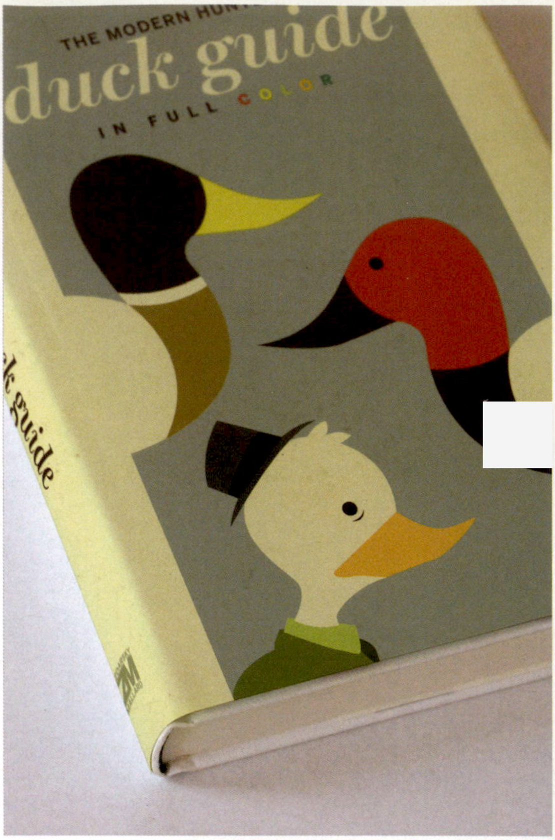
duck guide
IN FULL COLOR

#1 VARIANT
BY CHIP ZDARSKY

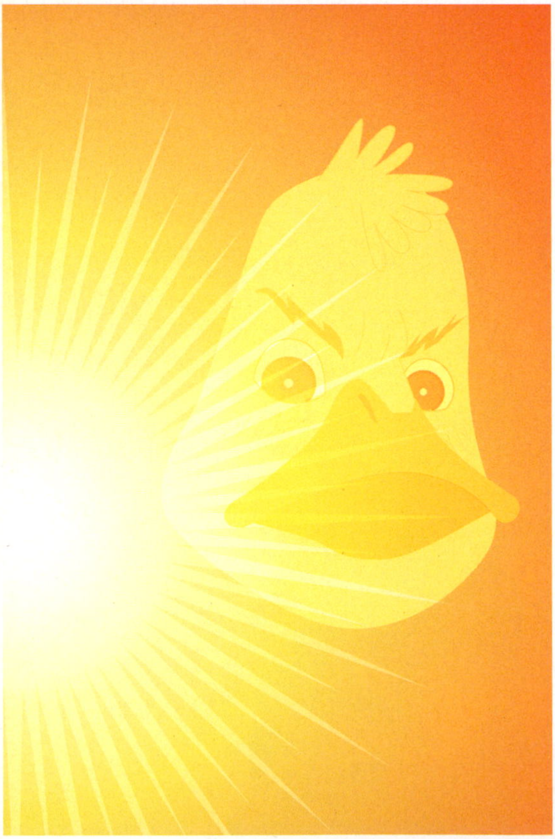

#1 EVOLUTION OF HOWARD VARIANT
BY CHIP ZDARSKY

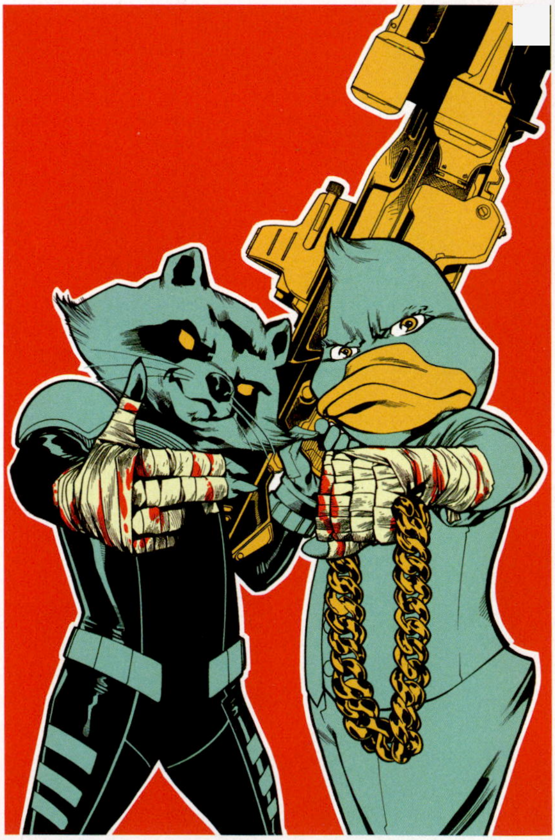

#2 VARIANT
BY MAHMUD ASRAR

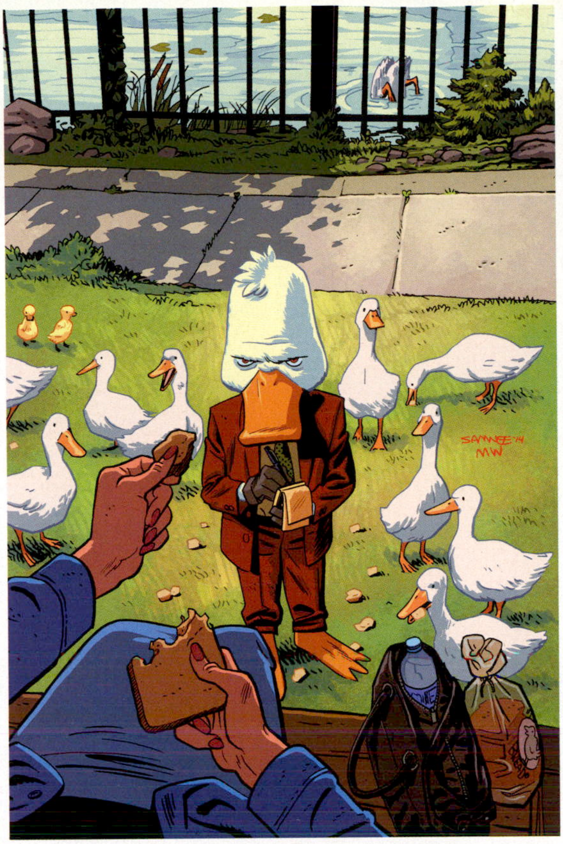
SAMNEE'14
MW

#2 VARIANT
BY CHRIS SAMNEE & MATTHEW WILSON

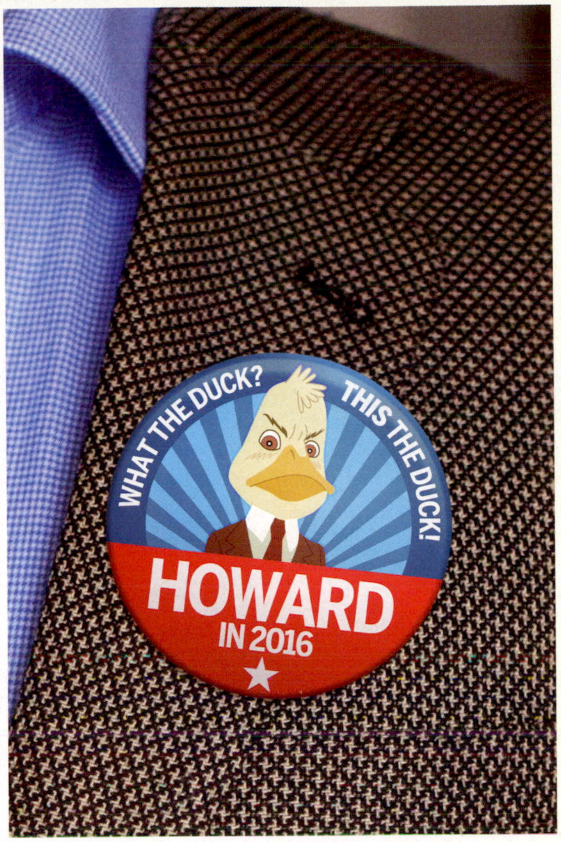
WHAT THE DUCK?
THIS THE DUCK!
HOWARD
IN 2016

#2 VOTE HOWARD VARIANT
BY CHIP ZDARSKY

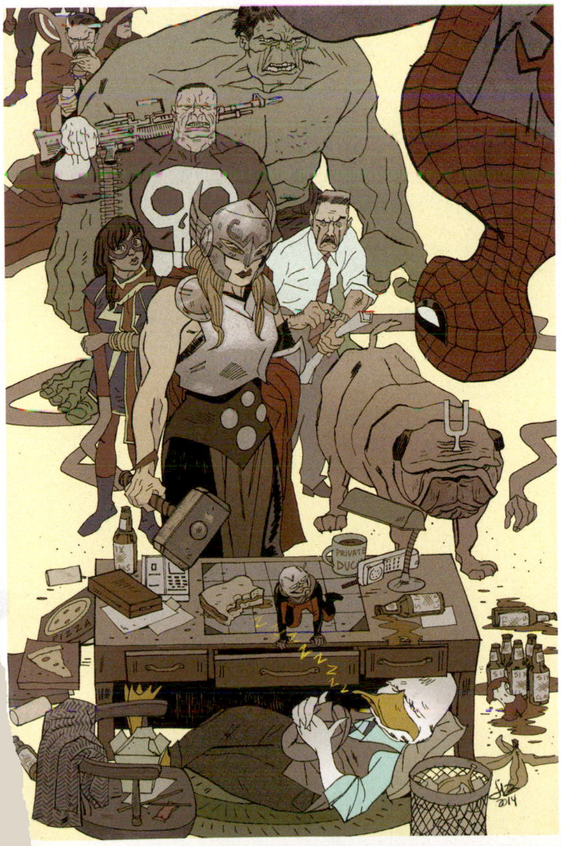

#3 VARIANT
BY JASON LATOUR

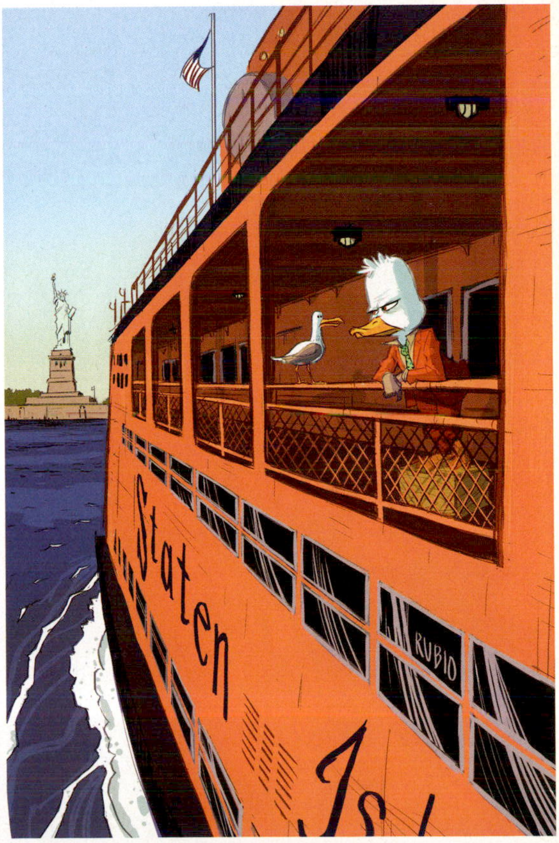
Staten
RUBIO

#3 NYC VARIANT
BY BOBBY RUBIO

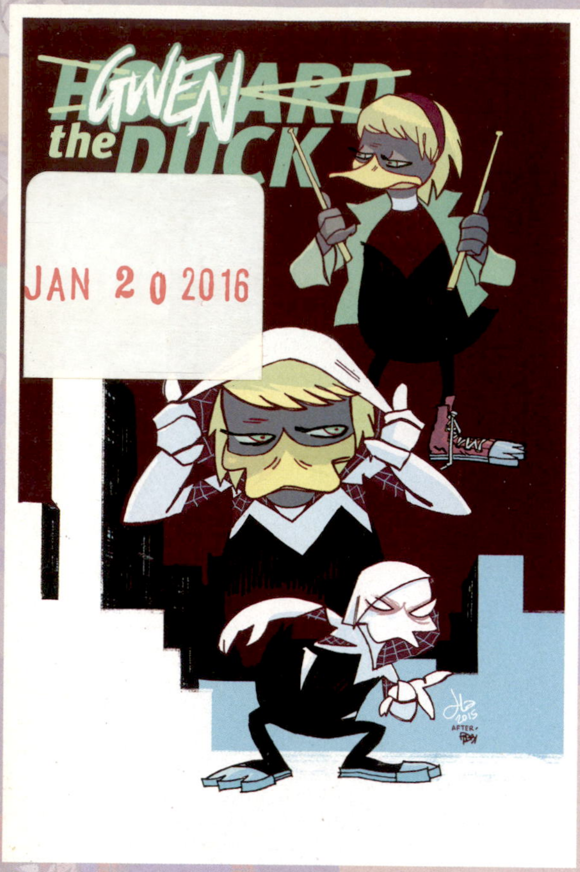
GWEN
the DUCK
JAN 20 2016

#4 GWEN THE DUCK VARIANT
BY JASON LATOUR

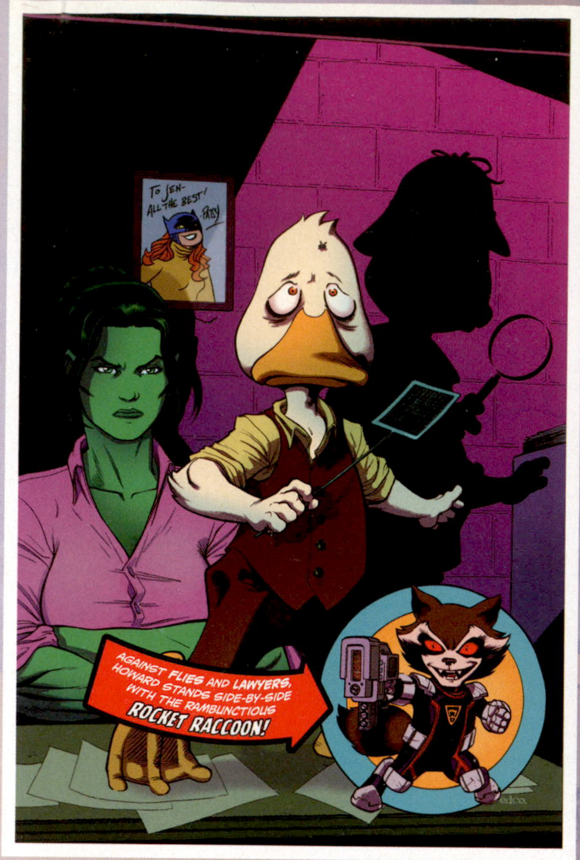
TO JEN-
ALL THE BEST!
PATSY
AGAINST FLIES AND LAWYERS, HOWARD STANDS SIDE-BY-SIDE WITH THE RAMBUNCTIOUS ROCKET RACCOON!

#4 VARIANT
BY ED MCGUINNESS & RICO RENZI

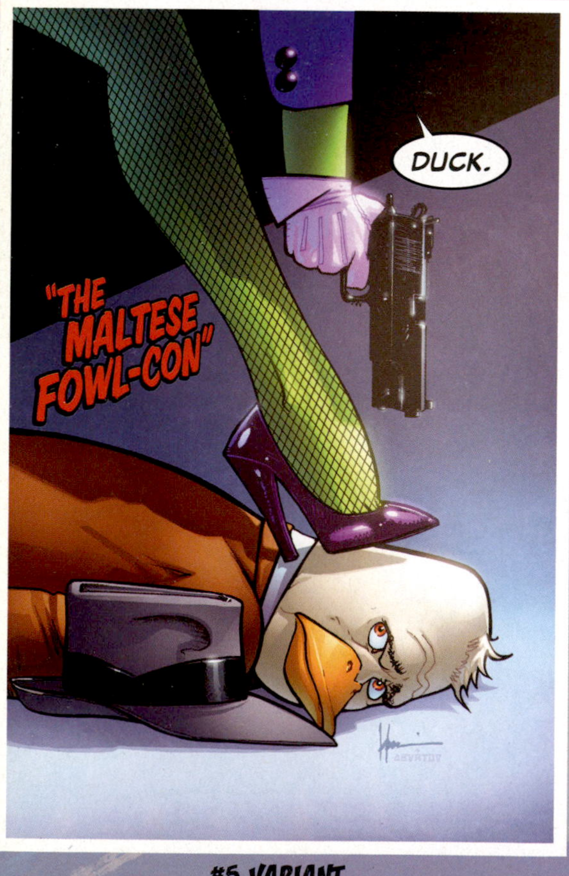
DUCK.
"THE MALTESE FOWL-CON"

#5 VARIANT
BY HOWARD CHAYKIN & JESUS ABURTOV

TO ACCESS THE FREE MARVEL AR CONTENT IN THIS BOOK*:

1. **Locate the AR logo within the comic.**
2. **Go to Marvel.com/AR in your web browser.**
3. **Search by series title to find the corresponding AR.**
4. **Enjoy Marvel AR!**

*All AR content that appears in this book has been archived and will be available only at Marvel.com/AR – no longer in the Marvel AR App. Content subject to change and availability.